THE URBAN SCENE: MYTHS AND REALITIES

THE URBAN SCENE: MYTHS AND REALITIES

edited by
JOE R. FEAGIN
University of Texas (Austin)

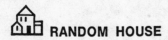 RANDOM HOUSE

First Edition
987654
Copyright © 1973 by Random House, Inc.

Library of Congress Cataloging in Publication Data

Feagin, Joe R.   comp.
  The urban scene.

    CONTENTS: An urban crisis? Banfield, E. C. From the unheavenly city: Introduction.—The Urban trek: Tilly, C. From The metropolitan enigma: Race and migration to the American city.—Urban social structure; the case of the slum: Gans, H. J. From The urban villagers. Fried, M. From The urban condition: Grieving for a lost home. [etc.]
    1. Cities and towns—United States—Addresses, essays, lectures. I. Title.
HT123.F4   301.36′3′0973   72–13286
ISBN 0–394–31647–9

Manufactured in the United States of America. Composed, printed and bound by The Kingsport Press, Kingsport, Tenn.

Preface

This reader is intentionally designed to provide those interested in studying the American city with a shorter-than-average collection of articles and excerpts that present unconventional, unique, or particularly challenging analyses of urban life and urban structure. Selections have also been chosen with an eye toward their suggestions and implications for planning and policy-making. Of course, in designing a short reader of this type, *selectivity* is necessary, and a number of important issues could not be considered here, while others could not be examined in great depth. However, my hope is that the brevity of this reader will allow it to be used in a broad variety of social science courses that would not otherwise be able to utilize a collection on urban issues and urban policy.

For those students wishing to go beyond these readings, to probe more deeply into the issues raised here, the references cited in the footnotes to the general introduction and to the chapter introductions will provide excellent starting points, together with the original sources from which I have drawn excerpts.

In most undertakings of this character an author has received aid and support from more persons than he can possibly acknowledge. But I would particularly like to thank David Bartlett, my editor, for his wise guidance in the development and completion of this project; Charles Tilly, teacher and friend, who first seduced me into the study of the urban scene; and Clairece, my wife, for extensive aid in typing and preparing this manuscript.

Contents

THE URBAN SCENE: MYTHS AND REALITIES

GENERAL INTRODUCTION

To speak of American society is to speak of urban society, for three-quarters of this country's more than 200 million residents now live in urban places, with a large proportion of these urbanites residing in metropolitan areas. But even those Americans residing in rural sections are influenced in significant ways by life in nearby or distant urban places. Much of the talk about social problems, therefore, relates almost by definition to the past, present, and future character of American cities. The urban problems that have from time to time become the focus of popular and scholarly attention have varied a great deal in their scope and significance, running from rush-hour traffic jams to large-scale, collective violence. Many of the most widely discussed issues, as Edward C. Banfield suggests in the first selection in this reader, relate primarily to questions about the comfort and convenience of white or middle-class urbanites. While some of these comfort-and-convenience issues are important, they are not the most serious issues confronting contemporary urbanites.

A major purpose of this collection of articles and excerpts is to stress research and analysis which relate directly, or in a critical contextual way, to what are in my judgment some of the more serious urban issues, such as urban disorganization, unequal distribution of wealth and power, institutional racism, the impact of urban migration, and the pluralism of urban life styles. The intent here is to provide the student of urban affairs with selected materials offering unconventional or provocative insights into the complexities of the urban scene and the dilemmas of urban planning and policy. While some selections have been available for several years now, even a cursory glance at numerous textbooks touching on urban issues will make it clear that the perspectives developed by a number of the authors herein have not as yet penetrated these influential analyses.

Basic conceptions and images of urban life and urban structure are extraordinarily important, since they often shape the ends envisioned, and the means by which these ends are implemented, by those intent on reinforcing or remaking the existing urban scene. One prominent urban sociologist, Scott Greer, has recently underlined the importance of images of the urban future in the lives of cities and their inhabitants:

It is my assumption that images of the future determine present actions. They may or may not determine the nature of the future—that depends on a much more complex set of circumstances. But willy-nilly, much of our behavior is postulated upon images of a possible and/or desirable future.[1]

One might well extend Greer's observation about images of the future city to argue that dominant conceptions or images of the *present* city also shape behavior. The impact of conceptions of city life in shaping behavior appears particularly important in the case of urban policy-makers and planners, whose interpretations of phenomena such as slums, ghettos, suburbs, or migration have had a great impact on the formulation of urban policy and the channeling of urban development. Too often, perhaps, conventional wisdom about the city—the stuff out of which images are made or the means by which images are rationalized—is not carefully examined to see if it in fact does jibe with the best available evidence on urban life. While it is never possible to be completely objective about urban issues, after careful analysis some conceptions about the city and its problems do appear more dated, restricted, or undocumented than others.

The selections included in this collection will not provide the reader with one "true" image of the city that can be used to replace other "faulty" ones. Rather, the selections will provide divergent and provocative interpretations which one may or may not be able to synthesize into a whole. The intention thus is to provoke the reader to formulate and integrate his or her own hypotheses and conclusions about the whys and wherefores of urban life.

While the diversity of perspectives on urban issues and urban policy is evident from the numerous analyses presented here, certain themes are reiterated—sometimes explicitly, sometimes implicitly—by various authors. For example, one important recurring theme that is viewed from several vantage points is the nature and extent of urban social structure or urban community. Conventional wisdom has often portrayed urbanites as somehow quite different from their counterparts in the country. One widely quoted social scientist, Louis Wirth, argued some time ago that urban social life was characterized by the "substitution of secondary for primary contacts, the weakening of bonds of kinship, and the declining social significance of the family, the disappearance of the neighborhood, and the undermining of the traditional basis of social solidarity." [2] More recently, important authors such as Herbert Marcuse, Maurice R. Stein, and Robert A. Nisbet—to name just a few—have given emphasis to the disorganizing effects of the urbanization process: eclipsed community, isolation, impersonality, and superficiality.[3] Although criticism of this view of the decline of community and family has appeared in a few urban sociology textbooks, variations on the theme still appear in the literature on cities. Particularly common has been the application of Wirth-like arguments about urbanization and urbanism in discussions of slum and ghetto areas within central cities.[4] However, several studies in this collection—including those by Herbert J. Gans, Marc Fried, Andrew M. Greeley, Charles Tilly, and Bennett M. Berger—suggest the importance and persisting structure of intimate and meaningful interpersonal relationships, primary social networks, and other aspects of community in urban areas, whether the specific focus is on poor or working-class Americans, black Americans, or suburbanites.

Images of the city that utilize the language of disorganization and pathology are not limited to those that focus on community. Scott Greer has *underlined* the extent to which general conceptions of cities have emphasized their negative dimensions: "A very common image of cities in the United States is that of disorder, regression, decadence —in short, disorganization."[5] Yet several authors in this collection indicate the need for great caution in jumping to conclusions about the disorganized nature of cities. At base there is the critical problem of definition. What some would define as disorderly, decadent, or disorganized—for example, race riots, life in a slum, poverty subcultures—others would see in terms of order, organization, and legitimacy. Collective definitions of urban phenomena become particularly problematical when, as Herbert J. Gans points out, they give legitimacy to the uprooting or manipulation of urban populations by planners and politicians—as has happened all too frequently in urban renewal programs. Thus a number of the analysts in this volume seem to be suggesting that many commonly accepted definitions and images of urban phenomena must be carefully reexamined.[6] Worth examining, too, may be the political character of the social-definition process itself.

Yet another important motif in these discussions of urban life and structure is that of heterogeneity. Some traditional images of urbanization have envisioned a homogenizing process whereby immigrants from rural areas (in the United States and elsewhere) assimilate over time to a general urban type. In American history a number of different images or models of assimilation have prevailed. Perhaps the two most influential have been what Milton M. Gordon has termed the "Anglo-conformity" and "melting pot" theories: "Both the Anglo-conformity and the melting pot theories had envisaged the disappearance of the immigrants' group as a communal identity and the absorption of the later arrivals to America and their children, as individuals, into the existing 'American' social structure."[7] Utilizing these perspectives, both popular writers and scholars have emphasized the insignificance or demise of ethnicity in modern America.[8] However, a few authors in this reader raise serious questions about premature epitaphs for ethnicity. Important in this regard is Andrew M. Greeley's provocative argument for the survival of meaningful ethnic differences in *Why Can't They Be Like Us?* He views the persistence of the "old ties of blood, faith, land and consciousness of kind" as a fundamental aspect of urban social structure. Indeed, he sees the possibility that the particularistic modes of behavior of certain ethnic groups, and the general heterogeneity of ethnic life styles, provide the stuff that in fact makes—and will make —cities livable. And the data provided by Marc Fried and Herbert J. Gans on Italian-Americans residing in a low-income area of Boston lend further credibility to the argument that ethnic diversity persists. Thus, in a chapter of Robert Coles' and Jon Erikson's *The Middle Americans* that is not reprinted here, a machinist movingly under-scores this point:

> "I'm Polish. I mean, I'm American. My family has been here for four generations; that's a lot. My great-grandfather came over here, from near Cracow. . . . It's in your blood. It's in your background. But I live *here*. My wife is the same, Polish. We're just like other people in this country, but we have memories, Polish memories. . . . How *could* I forget? My wife won't let me. She says you have to stay with your own people. We don't have only Polish people living near us, but there are a lot. Mostly we see my family and my wife's family on weekends, so there's no time to spend doing anything else." [9]

Nor are ingroup ties salient only for white ethnic Americans. While discrimination has been well documented as a major determinant in the living patterns of black Americans, the critical role of attachment to one's own kind among blacks is hinted at in the pioneering research of Lewis G. Watts and his associates in Boston, portions of which are re-produced in this book.

The role of blue-collar or working-class life styles in adding pluralism and diversity to everyday life in the urban framework is also empha-sized—life styles dominated not only by ethnic but also by class back-ground. Until recently relatively few American social scientists had studied the sometimes distinctive way of life, the types of social choices, to be found among working-class Americans. Even in Levittown, which many had come to see as the personification of middle-class suburban conformity and homogeneity, Herbert J. Gans found that life styles varied somewhat by class. Furthermore, he notes that pluralism of life styles is a reality that urbanites have difficulty grasping: "People have not recognized the diversity of American society, and they are not able to accept other life styles." Urban conflict can arise because of this very diversity of life styles. Of course, the variables of class and ethnicity are not the only determinants of pluralism or conflict between life styles within urban areas. Had we the space, we might examine other aspects of urban diversity—which are only briefly alluded to in this collection —such as counterculture developments among the younger generation or the communities of the encapsulated aged in numerous cities. [10]

Recognition of the importance of diversity leads in turn to the ques-tion of public policy. In the article reprinted in this volume, Bennett M. Berger has put the problems of planning for pluralism in relief by delineating three broad alternatives that planners can adopt: (1) they can ignore the consequences of their actions; (2) they can try in their work to bring the environments of groups with divergent life styles or values into line with planners' standards; or (3) they can foster the pluralism of values and life styles that already exist. In his emphasis on the need for planners to recognize the importance of pluralism in cities, Berger develops a theme that is touched on in one way or another by a number of authors in this collection:

> In making their assumptions, planners might first of all assume (it is the most reasonable assumption) that most groups which are displaced by planning *will take their culture with them* if they can. Planners would do well to anticipate this, and to modify their plans accordingly, to facilitate the preservation of those parts of their culture that the groups want preserved.[11]

While there are a number of other reiterated motifs that could be singled out, perhaps the most important of these is the issue of unequal distribution of wealth and power in this urban society. The existence of poverty has traditionally been viewed as problematical by Americans. Images of the poor, and of the nature and causes of economic inequality, may be among the most important images of urban life harbored by rank-and-file urbanites, as well as by urban planners and policymakers. The writings of Hyman Rodman and Charles A. Valentine, which deal with conflicting images and interpretations of poverty, are particularly thought provoking in this regard. Historically, the dominant stereotype of poor persons has emphasized character flaws and individual failures. Poverty has been blamed on the laziness or immorality of poor individuals rather than on the social and economic system.[12] Indeed, certain aspects of this popular image can be found in scholarly analyses that view the "culture of poverty" among the poor as the major determinant in perpetuating economic inequality. Valentine and Rodman, however, suggest there are serious problems in regard to prominent images of the urban poor and raise the question of stereotyping. Both authors point up alternative portraits and explanations that give greater attention to the variability of lower-class values, to the diversity of life styles among the poor, and to the role of *external structural* factors in generating inequality.

The problem of inequality encompasses the situation of black urbanites. To a great extent the lack of wealth, resources, and power among black Americans is the result of overt and covert racial discrimination. Much recent discussion of black-white problems in American cities has focused on the sociopsychological aspects of the problems—on such things as prejudice and "white racism." Remarkably little attention, however, has been given to structural analysis, to the role of existing economic and political institutions in perpetuating racial inequality. In this volume William K. Tabb, Richard E. Rubenstein, and Alan A. Altshuler touch on the issue of "institutional racism." Tabb, in his pioneering analysis, has underscored the importance of the point that "racism is perpetuated by elements of oppression within an economic and political system which must be understood *as a system*."

Racial inequality in cities, particularly the imbalance of power, is viewed in a broad political context by Rubenstein and Altshuler. The concentration of power and influence, economic and governmental, in the hands of certain individuals or groups is treated as a basic underlying cause of major urban problems. Although the stress in the excerpt from Rubenstein's book is on black Americans, in other chapters not reprinted here he elaborates the fundamental role of a variety of ethnic and nationality groups in shaping and reshaping the structure of power in America's urban places. Violent political protest did not emerge for the first time in black ghettos in the 1960s. For more than a century towns and cities have seen a lengthy procession of dissident groups using both violent and nonviolent means to carve out a niche for themselves in the American body politic.

With this procession of groups as the historical backdrop, it is not surprising that analysts such as Rubenstein, Altshuler, and Toffler view solutions to the problems of wealth and power in terms of redistribution and community control. Indeed, many other urban problems—and solutions as well—are doubtless linked, directly or indirectly, to the basic problem of inequality. Given the diversity of disenfranchised and partially enfranchised groups in this urbanized society, one should not be baffled if the suggestions and proposals of the various authors presented in this book seem at times difficult to implement. Nonetheless, Toffler may indeed be quite correct in his argument that expansion of participatory democracy may be required for the survival of this urban society, and not just for the satisfaction of those holding to egalitarian ideologies.

Another way of stating this is that, as the number of social components grows and change makes the whole system less stable, it becomes less and less possible to ignore the demands of political minorities—hippies, blacks, lower-middle-class Wallacites, school teachers, or the proverbial little old ladies in tennis shoes. In a slower-moving, industrial context, America could turn its back on the needs of its black minority; in the new, fast-paced cybernetic society, this minority can, by sabotage, strike, or a thousand other means, disrupt the entire system. As interdependency grows, smaller and smaller groups within society achieve greater and greater power for critical disruption. Moreover, as the rate of change speeds up, the length of time in which they can be ignored shrinks to near nothingness.[13]

NOTES

1. Scott Greer, *The Urbane View* (New York: Oxford University Press, 1972), p. 322.
2. Louis Wirth, "Urbanism as a Way of Life," *American Journal of Sociology*, vol. 44 (July 1938), pp. 20–21.
3. See Maurice R. Stein, *The Eclipse of Community* (New York: Harper Torchbooks, 1964); Herbert Marcuse, *One-Dimensional Man* (Boston: Beacon Press, 1964); and Robert A. Nisbet, *Community and Power* (New York: Oxford University Press, 1962).
4. See Genevieve Knupfer, "Portrait of an Underdog," in *Class, Status and Power*, R. Bendix and S. M. Lipset, eds. (Glencoe, Ill.: Free Press, 1953),

pp. 257 ff; Gunnar Myrdal, *An American Dilemma* (New York: McGraw-Hill, 1964); Kenneth B. Clark, *Dark Ghetto* (New York: Harper and Row, 1965); Office of Policy Planning and Research, U.S. Department of Labor, *The Negro Family: The Case for National Action* (Washington, D.C.: U.S. Government Printing Office, 1965).

5. Greer, *The Urbane View*, p. 322.
6. For a critical assessment of the ghetto disorganization literature, see David C. Perry and Joe R. Feagin, "Stereotyping in Black and White," in *People and Politics in Urban Society*, H. Hahn, ed. (Beverly Hills, Calif.: Sage Publications, 1972), pp. 433–463.
7. Milton M. Gordon, *Assimilation in American Life* (New York: Oxford University Press, 1964), p. 132.
8. See the discussion and authors cited in chaps. 2 and 3 of Will Herberg, *Protestant-Catholic-Jew* (Garden City, N.Y.: Anchor, 1960).
9. Robert Coles and Jon Erikson, *The Middle Americans* (Boston: Atlantic-Little, Brown, 1971), p. 43.
10. On counterculture and cities, see Theodore Roszak, *The Making of a Counter Culture* (Garden City, N.Y.: Anchor, 1969).
11. Bennett M. Berger, "Suburbia and the American Dream," *The Public Interest*, no. 2 (Winter 1966), p. 90.
12. For a discussion of contemporary American views of the poor, see Joe R. Feagin, "American Views of Poverty and Welfare," *Psychology Today*, vol. 6 (November 1972), 101–110, 129.
13. Alvin Toffler, *Future Shock* (New York: Random House, 1970), pp. 421–422.

Chapter 1

AN URBAN CRISIS?

Americans have long been critical of their cities. This has been particularly true of writers and other intellectuals, who periodically have expressed a great amount of negative feeling for urban structure and urban life. From Thomas Jefferson and Ralph Waldo Emerson, to Frank Lloyd Wright and John Dewey, to contemporary commentators, influential Americans have expressed such antipathies:

> The American city has been thought by American intellectuals to be: too big, too noisy, too dusky, too dirty, too smelly, too commercial, too crowded, too full of immigrants, too full of Jews, too full of Irishmen, Italians, Poles, too industrial, too pushing, too mobile, too fast, too artificial, destructive of conversation, destructive of communication, too greedy, too capitalistic, too full of automobiles, too full of smog, too full of dust, too heartless, too intellectual, too scientific, insufficiently poetic, too lacking in manners, too mechanical, destructive of family, tribal and patriotic feeling.[1]

As this catalog of critiques clearly indicates, negative views of the city have been varied as well as inconsistent. Sometimes, issues of comfort and convenience have been emphasized, while at other times, critical questions about ethnic, racial, or economic trends have been raised. Sometimes, the city has been viewed as too civilized, while at other times, it has been condemned as not civilized enough.

Focusing on the contemporary scene in his *controversial* analysis, *The Unheavenly City*, Edward C. Banfield contends that current conventional wisdom about the American city views it as facing a crisis of great proportions, as being well on the road to a catastrophic disaster. Yet Banfield questions this interpretation. While admitting that many aspects of urban life need significant improvement, he argues that the majority of urbanites are better off than ever before, especially in terms of housing, schools, and even transportation. Urban Americans now live more comfortably than they or their counterparts in other countries did in the recent or distant past, at least in terms of material comforts. Moreover, in Banfield's view much of the "crisis" talk about the city has really been focused on problems involving the "comfort, convenience, and business advantage of the well-off white majority."

Consequently, Banfield distinguishes between *important* urban problems and really *serious* urban problems, the former involving situations that may be inconvenient or uncomfortable but could not possibly lead to a catastrophic disaster. Among these would be such things as the urban sprawl, long journeys to work, the decline of the central business district, taxes, and general architectural ugliness. One reason why Banfield questions whether many issues can really be viewed as crisis-level dilemmas is that in numerous cases solutions are already at hand but have not been implemented because of opposition either from the business community (as in the case of rush-hour traffic) or from the general public (as in the case of the revenue problems). The fact that urbanites have not alleviated many of these problems, even when the price is not great, suggests to Banfield that the problems are not critical.

While these convenience and business-advantage problems touch the majority of urbanites, really serious urban problems—those conditions affecting the essential welfare of individuals or the society—in one sense directly involve only urban minorities. Poverty, racial injustice, and ignorance—these Banfield regards as crisis-level matters. "If there is an urban crisis in any ultimate sense, it must be constituted of these conditions."

In addition to raising provocative questions about the character of urban problems, Banfield points up other flaws in much of the talk about the urban crisis. For example, Banfield points to the issue of where urbanites actually reside. While it is true that three-quarters of the American people now live in urban areas, most do *not* live in the great metropolitan areas. In both 1960 and 1970 more than 70 percent of all Americans lived in cities with populations less than 250,000, in small towns, or in rural areas.[2] Thus, the average American does not live in a great metropolis such as New York, Chicago, Los Angeles, or Detroit, although he may sometimes be affected by what happens there. Since much of the argument over the urban crisis relates to problems of these larger cities and derives from analysts residing there, reflection on these demographic statistics again leads to questions about conventional wisdom: In what sense, where, and for whom, is there a real urban crisis?

In conclusion, we might note that in *The Unheavenly City* this excerpted chapter is followed by several chapters that provide a detailed and rather controversial analysis of what Banfield considers the serious urban problems of race and poverty; in his subsequent analysis he relies heavily on ideas about the distinctiveness of lower-class culture and the weakness of liberal remedial policies that ignore this allegedly debilitating culture. Since it is primarily these later chapters that have been systematically reviewed and attacked by critics—and the interested reader might well refer to some of these discussions [3]—it seems particularly appropriate to emphasize here important arguments made by Banfield that have been neglected by most of his critics. Moreover, in reading subsequent selections the alert reader will notice that certain arguments that Banfield makes about poverty and racial issues (some only hinted at in this excerpt) are not always consistent with data or arguments presented by other authors, such as Charles Tilly in his analysis of migration (Chapter 2) or Charles A. Valentine in his analysis of the culture of poverty (Chapter 6). Intellectual tension of this type is not only thought-provoking but also inevitable in all but the most superficial probing of urban complexities.

NOTES

1. Morton White, "Two Stages in the Critique of the American City," in *The Historian and the City,* Oscar Handlin and John Burchard, eds. (Cambridge: M.I.T. Press and Harvard University Press, 1963), pp. 86–87.
2. U.S. Bureau of the Census, *Statistical Abstract of the United States: 1971* (Washington, D.C.: U.S. Government Printing Office, 1971), p. 17.
3. See, for example, the stimulating symposium (five reviews) in the *Social Science Quarterly,* vol. 51 (March 1971), pp. 816–859.

FROM THE UNHEAVENLY CITY: INTRODUCTION

EDWARD C. BANFIELD

> . . . the clock is ticking, time is moving . . . , we must ask ourselves every night when we go home, are we doing all that we should do in our nation's capital, in all the other big cities of the country.
>
> —President Johnson, after the Watts Riot, August 1965

That we face an urban crisis of utmost seriousness has in recent years come to be part of the conventional wisdom. We are told on all sides that the cities are uninhabitable, that they must be torn down and rebuilt or new ones must be built from the ground up, that something drastic must be done—and soon—or else.

On the face of it this "crisis" view has a certain plausibility. One need not walk more than a few blocks in any city to see much that is wrong and in crying need of improvement. It is anomalous that in a society as technologically advanced and as affluent as ours there should be many square miles of slums and even more miles of dreary blight and chaotic sprawl. And when one considers that as many as 60 million more people may live in metropolitan areas in 1980 than lived there in 1960, it seems clear that unless something drastic is done things are bound to get worse.

There is, however, another side to the matter. The plain fact is that the overwhelming majority of city dwellers live more comfortably and conveniently than ever before. They have more and better housing, more and better schools, more and better transportation, and so on. By any conceivable measure of material welfare the present generation of urban Americans is, on the whole, better off than any other large group of people has ever been anywhere. What is more, there is every reason to expect that the general level of comfort and convenience will continue to rise at an even more rapid rate through the foreseeable future.

It is true that many people do not share, or do not share fully, this general prosperity, some because they are the victims of racial prejudice and others for other reasons that are equally beyond their control. If the chorus of complaint about the city arose mainly from these disadvantaged people or on behalf of them, it would be entirely understandable, especially if their numbers were increasing and their plight were getting worse. But the fact is that until very recently most of the talk about the urban crisis has had to do with the comfort, convenience, and business advantage of the well-off white majority and not with the more serious problems of the poor, the Negro, and others who stand outside the charmed circle. And the fact also is that the number of those standing outside the circle is decreasing, as is the relative disadvantage that they suffer. There is still much poverty and much racial discrimination. But there is less of both than ever before.

The question arises, therefore, not of whether we are faced with an urban crisis, but rather, *in what sense* we are faced with one. Whose interest and what interests are involved? How deeply? What should be done? Given the political and other realities of the situation, what *can* be done?

The first need is to clear away some semantic confusions. Consider the statement, so frequently used to alarm luncheon groups, that 70 percent of the population now lives in urban places and that this number may increase to 80 percent in the next two decades if present trends continue. Such figures give the impression of standing room only in the city, but what exactly do they mean?

When we are told that the population of the United States is rapidly becoming overwhelmingly urban, we probably suppose this to mean that most people are coming to live in the big cities. This is true in one sense but false in another. It is true that most people live closer physically and psychologically to a big city than ever before; rural occupations and a rural style of life are no longer widespread. On the other hand, the percentage of the population living in cities of 250,000 or more (there are only fifty-one of them) is about the same now as it was in 1920. In Census terminology an "urban place" is any settlement having a population of 2,500 or more; obviously places of 2,500 are not what we have in mind when we use words like "urban" and "city." [1] It is somewhat misleading to say that the country is becoming more urban, when what is meant is that more people are living in places like White River Junction, Vermont (pop. 2,546), and fewer in places like Boston, Massachusetts (pop. 697,197). But it is not altogether misleading, for most of the small urban places are now close to large cities and part of a metropolitan complex. White River Junction, for example, is now close enough to Boston to be very much influenced by it.

A great many so-called urban problems are really conditions that we either cannot change or do not want to incur the disadvantages of changing. Consider the "problem of congestion." The presence of a great many people in one place is a cause of inconvenience, to say the least. But the advantages of having so many people in one place far outweigh these inconveniences, and we cannot possibly have the advantages without the disadvantages. To "eliminate congestion" in the city must mean eliminating the city's reason for being. Congestion in the city is a "problem" only in the sense that congestion in Times Square on

New Year's Eve is one; in fact, of course, people come to the city, just as they do to Times Square, precisely *because* it is congested. If it were not congested, it would not be worth coming to.

Strictly speaking, a problem exists only as we should want something different from what we do want or as by better management we could get a larger total of what we want. If we think it a good thing that many people have the satisfaction of driving their cars in and out of the city, and if we see no way of arranging the situation to get them in and out more conveniently that does not entail more than offsetting disadvantages for them or others, then we ought not to speak of a "traffic congestion problem." By the same token, urban sprawl is a "problem," as opposed to an "unpleasant condition," only if (1) fewer people should have the satisfaction of living in the low-density fringe of the city; or (2) we might, by better planning, build homes in the fringe without destroying so much landscape and without incurring costs (for example, higher per-unit construction costs) or foregoing benefits (for example, a larger number of low-income families who can have the satisfaction of living in the low-density area) of greater value than the saving in landscape.

Few problems, in this strict sense, are anywhere near as big as they seem. The amount of urban sprawl that could be eliminated simply by better planning—that is, without the sacrifice of other ends that are also wanted, such as giving the satisfaction of owning a house and yard to many low-income people—is probably trivial as compared to the total urban sprawl (that is, to the "problem" defined simplemindedly as "a condition that is unpleasant").

Most so-called urban problems are more characteristic of rural and small-town places than of cities. We have been conditioned to associate "slums" with "cities," but in 1960, 74 percent of all deteriorating and 81 percent of all dilapidated housing was *outside* cities of 100,000 or more population, and about 60 percent of all families in substandard housing lived outside metropolitan areas. The situation is similar in other matters. "Low verbal ability," Sloan R. Wayland of Columbia Teachers College has written, "is described as though it could only happen in an urban slum." [2] Actually, he points out, all but a very small fraction of mankind has always been "culturally deprived," and the task of formal education has always been to attack such conditions.

Most of the "problems" that are generally supposed to constitute "the urban crisis" could not conceivably lead to disaster. They are—some of them—important in the sense that a bad cold is important, but they are not serious in the sense that a cancer is serious. They have to do with comfort, convenience, amenity, and business advantage, all of which are important, but they do not affect either the essential welfare of individuals or what may be called the good health of the society.

Consider, for example, an item that often appears near the top of the list of complaints about the city—the journey to work. It takes the average worker in a metropolitan area about half an hour to get to work, and only about 15 percent of workers spend more than three-quarters of an hour getting there.[3] It would, of course, be very nice if the journey to work were much shorter. No one can suppose, however, that the essential welfare of many people would be much affected even if it were fifteen minutes longer. Certainly its being longer or shorter would not make the difference between a good society and a bad.

Another matter causing widespread alarm is the decline of the central business district, by which is meant the loss of patronage to downtown department stores, theaters, restaurants, museums, and so on, which has resulted from the movement of many well-off people to suburbs. Clearly, the movement of good customers from one place to another involves inconvenience and business loss to many people, especially to the owners of real estate that is no longer in so great demand. These losses, however, are essentially no different from those that occur from other causes—say, a shift of consumers' tastes that suddenly renders a once-valuable patent valueless. Moreover, though some lose by the change, others gain by it: the overall gain of wealth by building in the suburbs may more than offset the loss of it caused by letting the downtown deteriorate.

There are those who claim that cultural and intellectual activity flourishes only in big cities and that therefore the decline of the downtown business districts and the replacement of cities by suburbs threatens the very survival of civilization. This claim is far-fetched, to say the very least, if it means that we cannot have good music and good theater (not to mention philosophy, literature, and science) unless customers do their shopping in the downtown districts of Oakland, St. Louis, Nashville, Boston, and so on, rather than in the suburbs around them. Public efforts to preserve the downtown districts of these and other cities may perhaps be worth what they cost; the return, however, will be in terms of comfort, convenience, and business advantage—the comfort, convenience, and business advantage of the relatively well-off —and not in terms of anyone's essential welfare.

The same can be said about efforts to "beautify" the cities. That for the most part the cities are dreary and depressing if not offensively ugly may be granted: the desirability of improving their appearance, even if only a little, cannot be questioned. It is very doubtful, however, that people are dehumanized (to use a favorite word of those who complain about the cities) by the ugliness of the city or that they would be in any sense humanized by its being made beautiful. (If they were humanized, they would doubtless build beautiful cities, but that is an entirely different matter. One has only to read Machiavelli's history of Florence to see that living in a beautiful city is not in itself enough to bring out the best in one. So far as their humanity is concerned, the people of, say, Jersey City compare very favorably to the Florentines of the era of that city's greatest glory.) At worst, the American city's ugliness—or, more, its lack of splendor or charm—occasions loss of visual pleasure. This loss is an important one (it is surely much larger than most people realize), but it cannot lead to any kind of disaster either for the individual or for the society.

Air pollution comes closer than any of these problems to threatening essential welfare, as opposed to comfort, convenience, amenity, and business advantage. Some people die early because of it and many more suffer various degrees of bad health; there is also some possibility (no one knows how much) that a meteorological coincidence (an "air inversion") over a large city might suddenly kill thousands or even tens of thousands. Important as it is, however, the air pollution problem is rather minor as compared to other threats to health and welfare not generally regarded as "crises." According to the U.S. Public Health Service, the most polluted air is nowhere near as dangerous as cigarette smoke.

Many of the "problems" that are supposed to constitute the "crisis" could be quickly and easily solved, or much alleviated, by the application of well-known measures that lie right at hand. In some instances, the money cost of these measures would be very small. For example, the rush-hour traffic problem in the central cities (which, incidentally, is almost the whole of the traffic problem in these cities) could be much reduced and in some cases eliminated entirely just by staggering working hours in the largest offices and factories. Manhattan presents the hardest case of all, but even there, an elaborate study showed, rush-hour crowding could be reduced by 25 percent, enough to make the strap-hanger reasonably comfortable.[4] Another quick and easy way of improving urban transportation in most cities would be to eliminate a mass of archaic regulations on the granting of public transit and taxi franchises. At present, the cities are in effect going out of their way to place obstacles in the paths of those who might offer the public better transportation.[5]

The "price" of solving, or alleviating, some much-talked-about urban problems is largely political. The proposal to reduce transit jams in Manhattan by staggering work hours was quickly and quietly killed by the city administration because the business community preferred the traditional nine-to-five pattern.[6]

If the rush-hour traffic problem is basically political, so is the revenue problem. A great part of the wealth of our country is in the cities. When a mayor says that his city is on the verge of bankruptcy, he really means that when the time comes to run for reelection he wants to be able to claim credit for straightening out a mess that was left him by his predecessor. What a mayor means when he says that his city *must* have state or federal aid to finance some improvements is (1) the taxpayers of the city (or some important group of them) would rather go without the improvement than pay for it themselves; or (2) although they would pay for it themselves if they had to, they would much prefer to have some other taxpayers pay for it. Rarely if ever does a mayor who makes such a statement mean (1) that for the city to pay for the improvement would necessarily force some taxpayers into poverty; or

(2) that the city could not raise the money even if it were willing to force some of its taxpayers into poverty. In short, the "revenue crisis" mainly reflects the fact that people hate to pay taxes and that they think that by crying poverty they can shift some of the bill to someone else.

To some extent, also, the revenue problem of the cities arises from the way jurisdictional boundaries are drawn or, more precisely, from what are considered to be inequities resulting from the movement of taxable wealth from one side of a boundary line to another. When many large taxpayers move to the suburbs, the central city must tax those who remain at a higher rate if it is to maintain the same level of services. The "problem" in this case is not that the taxpayers who remain are absolutely unable to pay the increased taxes; rather, it is that they do not want to pay them and that they consider it unfair that they should have to pay more simply because other people have moved away. The simple and costless solution (in all but a political sense) would be to charge nonresidents for services that they receive from the city or, failing that, to redraw the boundary lines so that everyone in the metropolitan area would be taxed on the same basis.

That we have not yet been willing to pay the price of solving, or alleviating, such "problems" even when the price is a very small one suggests that they are not really as serious as they have been made out to be. Indeed, one might say that, by definition, a serious problem is one that people are willing to pay a considerable price to have solved.

With regard to these problems for which solutions are at hand, we will know that a real crisis impends when we see the solutions actually being applied. The solution, that is, will be applied when—and only when—the inconvenience or other disadvantage of allowing the problem to continue unabated is judged to have become greater than that of taking the necessary measures to abate it. In other words, a bad-but-not-quite-critical problem is one that it would almost-but-not-quite pay us to do something about.

If some real disaster impends in the city, it is not because parking spaces are hard to find, because architecture is bad, because department store sales are declining, or even because taxes are rising. If there is a genuine crisis, it has to do with the essential welfare of individuals or with the good health of the society, not merely with comfort, convenience, amenity, and business advantage, important as these are. It is not necessary here to try to define "essential welfare" rigorously: it is enough to say that whatever may cause people to die before their time, to suffer serious impairment of their health or of their powers, to waste their lives, to be deeply unhappy or happy in a way that is less than human affects their essential welfare. It is harder to indicate in a sentence or two what is meant by the "good health" of the society. The ability of the society to maintain itself as a going concern is certainly a primary consideration; so is its free and democratic character. In the last analysis, however, the quality of a society must be judged by its tendency to produce desirable human types; the healthy society, then, is one that not only stays alive but also moves in the direction of giving greater scope and expression to what is distinctively human. In general, of course, what serves the essential welfare of individuals also promotes the good health of the society; there are occasions, however, when the two goals conflict. In such cases, the essential welfare of individuals must be sacrificed for the good health of the society. This happens on a very large scale when there is a war, but it may happen at other times as well. The conditions about which we should be most concerned, therefore, are those that affect, or may affect, the good health of the society. If there is an urban crisis in any ultimate sense, it must be constituted of these conditions.

It is a good deal easier to say what matters are not serious (that is, do not affect either the essential welfare of individuals or the good health of the society) than it is to say what ones are. It is clear, however, that poverty, ignorance, and racial (and other) injustices are among the most important of the general conditions affecting the essential welfare of individuals. It is plausible, too, to suppose that these conditions have a very direct bearing upon the good health of the society, although in this connection other factors that are much harder to guess about—for example, the nature and strength of the consensual bonds that hold the society together—may be much more important. To begin with, anyway, it seems reasonable to look in these general directions for what may be called the serious problems of the cities.

It is clear at the outset that serious problems directly affect only a rather small minority of the whole urban population. In the relatively new residential suburbs and in the better residential neighborhoods in the outlying parts of the central cities and in the older, larger suburbs, the overwhelming majority of people are safely above the poverty line, have at least a high school education, and do not suffer from racial discrimination. For something like two-thirds of all city dwellers, the urban problems that touch them directly have to do with comfort, convenience, amenity, and business advantage. In the terminology used here, these are "important" problems but not "serious" ones. In a great many cases, these problems cannot even fairly be called important; a considerable part of the urban population—those who reside in the "nicer" suburbs— lives under material conditions that will be hard to improve upon.

The serious problems are to be found in all large cities and in most small ones. But they affect only parts of these cities (and only a minority of the city populations). In the central cities and the larger, older suburbs the affected parts are usually adjacent to the central business district and spreading out from it. If these inner districts, which probably comprise somewhere between 10 and 20 percent of the total area classified as urban by the Census, were suddenly to disappear, along with the people who live in them, there would be no serious urban problems worth talking about. If what really matters is the essential welfare of individuals and the good health of the society as opposed to comfort, convenience, amenity, and business advantage, then what we have is not an "urban problem" but an "inner-central-city-and-larger-older-suburb" one.

The serious problems of these places, it should be stressed, are in most instances not caused by the conditions of urban life as such and are less characteristic of the city than of small-town and farm areas. Poverty, ignorance, and racial injustice are more widespread outside the cities than inside them.

One problem that is both serious and unique to the large cities is the existence of huge enclaves of people (many, but not all of them, Negro) of low skill, low income, and low status. In his book *Dark Ghetto*, Kenneth B. Clark presents Census data showing that eight cities—New York, Los Angeles, Baltimore, Washington, Cleveland, St. Louis, New Orleans, and Chicago—contain a total of sixteen areas, all of at least 15,000 population and five of more than 100,000, that are exclusively (more than 94 percent) Negro.[7] There are smaller Negro enclaves in many other cities, and there are large Puerto Rican and large Mexican ones in a few cities. Whether these places can properly be called ghettoes is open to some doubt, as will be explained later. However, there is no question but that they are largely cut off both physically and psychologically from the rest of the city. Whatever may be the effect of this separation on the essential welfare of the individual (and it is arguable that it is trivial), it is clear that the existence of huge enclaves of people who are in some degree alienated from it constitutes a kind of hazard not only to the present peace and safety but also to the long-run health of the society. The problems of individual welfare that these people present are no greater by virtue of the fact that they live together in huge enclaves rather than in isolation on farms, or in small neighborhoods in towns and cities (the problem of individual welfare *appears* greater when they live in huge enclaves, but that is because in this form it is too conspicuous to be ignored). The problem that they present to the good health of the society, on the other hand, is very different and vastly greater solely by virtue of the fact that they live in huge enclaves. Unlike those who live on farms and in small towns, disaffected people who live in huge enclaves may develop a collective consciousness and sense of identity. From many standpoints it is highly desirable that they do so. In the short run, however, they represent a threat to peace and order, and it must be admitted that even in the long run the accommodation that takes place may produce a politics that is less democratic, less mindful of individual rights, and less able to act effectively in the common interest than that which we have now.

This political danger in the presence of great concentrations of people who feel little attachment to the society has long been regarded by some as *the* serious problem of the cities—the one problem that might conceivably produce a disaster that would destroy the quality of the society. "The dark ghettoes," Dr. Clark has written, "now represent a nuclear stockpile which can annihilate the very foundations of America."[8] These words bring up-to-date apprehensions that were expressed by some of the Founding Fathers and that Tocqueville set forth in a famous passage of *Democracy in America:*

> The United States has no metropolis, but it already contains several very large cities. Philadelphia reckoned 161,000 inhabitants, and New York 202,-000, in the year 1830. The lower ranks which inhabit these cities constitute a rabble even more formidable than the populace of European towns. They consist of freed blacks, in the first place, who are condemned by the laws and by public opinion to a hereditary state of misery and degradation. They also contain a multitude of Europeans who have been driven to the shores of the New World by their misfortunes or their misconduct; and they bring to the United States all our greatest vices, without any of those interests which counteract their baneful influence. As inhabitants of a country where they have no civil rights, they are ready to turn all the passions which agitate the community to their own advantage; thus, within the last few months, serious riots have broken out in Philadelphia and New York. Disturbances of this kind are unknown in the rest of the country, which is not alarmed by them, because the population of the cities has hitherto exercised neither power nor influence over the rural districts.
>
> Nevertheless, I look upon the size of certain American cities, and especially on the nature of their population, as a real danger which threatens the future security of the democratic republics of the New World; and I venture to predict that they will perish from this circumstance, unless the government succeeds in creating an armed force which, while it remains under the control of the majority of the nation, will be independent of the town population and able to repress its excesses.[9]

Strange as it may seem, the mammoth government programs to aid the cities are directed mainly toward the problems of comfort, convenience, amenity, and business advantage. Insofar as they have any effect on the serious problems, it is, on the whole, to aggravate them.

Two programs account for approximately 90 percent of federal government expenditure for the improvement of the cities (as opposed to the maintenance of more or less routine functions). Neither is intended to deal with the serious problems. Both make them worse.

The improvement of transportation is one program. The urban portions of the national expressway system are expected to cost about $18 billion. Their main effect will be to enable suburbanites to move about the metropolitan area more conveniently, to open up some areas for business and residential expansion, and to bring a few more customers from the suburbs downtown to shop. These are all worthy objects when considered by themselves; in context, however, their justification is doubtful, for their principal effect will be to encourage—in effect to subsidize—further movement of industry, commerce, and relatively well-off residents (mostly white) from the inner city. This, of course, will make matters worse for the poor by reducing the number of jobs for them and by making neighborhoods, schools, and other community facilities still more segregated. These injuries will be only partially offset by allowing a certain number of the inner-city poor to commute to jobs in the suburbs.

The huge expenditure being made for improvement of mass transit facilities (it may amount to $10 billion over a decade) may be justifiable for the contribution that it will make to comfort, convenience, and business advantage. It will not, however, make any contribution to the solution of the serious problems of the city. Even if every city had a subway as fancy as Moscow's, all these problems would remain.

The second great federal urban program concerns housing and renewal. Since the creation in 1934 of the Federal Housing Authority (FHA), the government has subsidized home building on a vast scale by insuring mortgages that are written on easy terms and, in the case of the Veterans Administration (VA), by guaranteeing mortgages. Most of the mortgages have been for the purchase of *new* homes. (This was partly because FHA wanted gilt-edged collateral behind the mortgages that it insured, but it was also because it shared the American predilection for newness.) It was cheaper to build on vacant land, but there was little such land left in the central cities and in their larger, older suburbs; therefore, most of the new homes were built in new suburbs. These were almost always zoned so as to exclude the relatively few Negroes and other "undesirables" who could afford to build new houses. In effect, then, the FHA and VA programs have subsidized the movement of the white middle class out of the central cities and older suburbs while at the same time penalizing investment in the rehabilitation of the run-down neighborhoods of these older cities. The poor— especially the Negro poor—have not received any direct benefit from these programs. (They have, however, received a very substantial unintended and indirect benefit, . . . because the departure of the white middle class has made more housing available to them.) After the appointment of Robert C. Weaver as head of the Housing and Home Finance Agency, FHA changed its regulations to encourage the rehabilitation of existing houses and neighborhoods. Very few such loans have been made, however.

Urban renewal has also turned out to be mainly for the advantage of the well-off—indeed, of the rich—and to do the poor more harm than good. The purpose of the federal housing program was declared by Congress to be "the realization as soon as feasible of the goal of a decent home and a suitable living environment for every American family." In practice, however, the principal objectives of the renewal program have been to attract the middle class back into the central city (as well as to slow its exodus out of the city) and to stabilize and restore the central business districts.[10] Unfortunately, these objectives can be served only at the expense of the poor. Hundreds of thousands of low-income people have been forced out of low-cost housing, by no means all of it substandard, in order to make way for luxury apartments, office buildings, hotels, civic centers, industrial parks, and the like. Insofar as renewal has involved the "conservation" or "rehabilitation" of residential areas, its effect has been to keep the poorest of the poor out of these neighborhoods—that is, to keep them in the highest-density slums. "At a cost of more than three billion dollars," sociologist Scott Greer wrote in 1965, "the Urban Renewal Agency (URA) has succeeded in materially reducing the supply of low-cost housing in American cities." [11]

The injury to the poor inflicted by renewal has not been offset by benefits to them in the form of public housing (that is, housing owned by public bodies and rented by them to families deemed eligible on income and other grounds). With the important exception of New York and the less important ones of some Southern cities, such housing is not a significant part of the total supply. Moreover, the poorest of the poor are usually, for one reason or another, ineligible for public housing.

Obviously, these government programs work at cross-purposes, one undoing (or trying to undo) what the other does (or tries to do). The expressway program and the FHA and VA mortgage insurance and guarantee programs in effect pay the middle-class white to leave the central city for the suburbs. At the same time, the urban renewal and mass transit programs pay him to stay in the central city or to move back to it.

In at least one respect, however, these government programs are consistent: they aim at problems of comfort, convenience, amenity, and business advantage, not at ones involving the essential welfare of individuals or the good health of the society. Indeed, on the contrary, they all sacrifice these latter, more important interests for the sake of the former, less important ones. In this the urban programs are no different from a great many other government programs. Price production programs in agriculture, Theodore Schultz has remarked, take up almost all the time of the Department of Agriculture, the agricultural committees of Congress, and the farm organizations, and exhaust the influence of farm people. But these programs, he says, "do not improve the schooling of farm children, they do not reduce the inequalities in personal distribution of wealth and income, they do not remove the causes of poverty in agriculture, nor do they alleviate it. On the contrary, they worsen the personal distribution of income within agriculture." [12]

It is widely supposed that the serious problems of the cities are unprecedented both in kind and in magnitude. Between 1950 and 1960 there occurred the greatest population increase in the nation's history. At the same time, a considerable part of the white middle class moved to the newer suburbs, and its place in the central cities and older suburbs was taken by Negroes (and in New York by Puerto Ricans as well). These and other events—especially the civil rights revolution—are widely supposed to have changed completely the character of "the urban problem."

If the present situation is indeed radically different from previous ones, then we have nothing to go on in judging what is likely to happen next. At the very least, we face a crisis of uncertainty.

In a real sense, of course, *every* situation is unique. Even in making statistical probability judgments, one must decide on more or less subjective grounds whether it is reasonable to treat certain events as if they were the "same." The National Safety Council, for example, must decide whether cars, highways, and drivers this year are enough like those of past years to justify predicting future experience from past. From a logical standpoint, it is no more possible to decide this question in a purely objective way than it is to decide, for example, whether the composition of the urban population is now so different from what it was that nothing can be inferred from the past about the future. Karl and Alma Taeuber are both right and wrong when they write that we do not know enough about immigrant and Negro assimilation patterns to be able to compare the two and that "such evidence as we could compile indicates that it is more likely to be misleading than instructive to make such comparisons."[13] They are certainly right in saying that one can only guess whether the pattern of Negro assimilation will resemble that of the immigrant. But they are wrong to imply that we can avoid making guesses and still compare things that are not known to be alike in all respects except one. (What, after all, would be the point of comparing immigrant and Negro assimilation patterns if we knew that the only difference between the two was, say, skin color?) They are also wrong in suggesting that the evidence indicates anything about what is likely to be instructive. If there were enough evidence to indicate that, there would be enough to indicate what is likely to happen; indeed, a judgment as to what is likely to be instructive is inseparable from one as to what is likely to happen. Strictly speaking, the Taeubers' statement expresses *their* guess as to what the evidence indicates.

The facts by no means compel one to take the view that the serious problems of the cities are unprecedented either in kind or in magnitude. That population growth in absolute numbers was greater in the decade 1950 to 1960 than ever before need not hold much significance from the present standpoint: American cities have frequently grown at fantastic rates (consider the growth of Chicago from a prairie village of 4,470 in 1840 to a metropolis of more than a million in fifty years). In any case, the population growth of the 1950's was not in the largest cities; most of them actually lost population in that decade. So far as numbers go, the migration of rural and small-town Negroes and Puerto Ricans to the large Northern cities in the 1950's was about equal to immigration from Italy in its peak decade. (In New York, Chicago, and many other cities in 1910, two out of every three schoolchildren were the sons and daughters of immigrants.) When one takes into account the vastly greater size and wealth of the cities now as compared to half a century or more ago, it is obvious that by the only relevant measure—namely, the number of immigrants relative to the capacity of the cities to provide for them and to absorb them—the movement in the 1950's from the South and from Puerto Rico was not large but small.

In many important respects, conditions in the large cities have been getting better. There is less poverty in the cities now than there has ever been. Housing, including that of the poor, is improving rapidly: one study predicts that substandard housing will have been eliminated by 1980.[14] In the last decade alone the improvement in housing has been marked. At the turn of the century only one child in fifteen went beyond elementary school; now most children finish high school. The treatment of racial and other minority groups is conspicuously better than it was. When, in 1964, a carefully drawn sample of Negroes was asked whether, in general, things were getting better or worse for Negroes in this country, approximately eight out of ten respondents said "better." [15]

If the situation is improving, why, it may be asked, is there so much talk of an urban crisis? The answer is that the improvements in performance, great as they have been, have not kept pace with rising expectations. In other words, although things have been getting better absolutely, they have been getting worse *relative to what we think they should be*. And this is because, as a people, we seem to act on the advice of the old jingle:

> *Good, better, best,*
> *Never let it rest*
> *Until your good is better*
> *And your better best.*

Consider the poverty problem, for example. Irving Kristol has pointed out that for nearly a century all studies, in all countries, have concluded that a third, a fourth, or a fifth of the nation in question is below the poverty line.[16] "Obviously," he remarks, "if one defines the poverty line as that which places one-fifth of the nation below it, then one-fifth of the nation will always be below the poverty line." The point is that even if everyone is better off there will be as much poverty as ever, provided that the line is redefined upward. Kristol notes that whereas in the depths of the Depression, F.D.R. found only one-third of the nation "ill-housed, ill-clad, ill-nourished," Leon Keyserling, a former head of the Council of Economic Advisers, in 1962 published a book called *Poverty and Deprivation in the U.S.—the Plight of Two-Fifths of a Nation.*

Much the same thing has happened with respect to most urban problems. Police brutality, for example, would be a rather minor problem if we judged it by a fixed standard; it is a growing problem because we judge it by an ever more exacting standard. A generation ago the term meant hitting someone on the head with a nightstick. Now it often means something quite different:

> What the Negro community is presently complaining about when it cries "police brutality" is the more subtle attack on personal dignity that manifests itself in unexplainable questionings and searches, in hostile and insolent attitudes toward groups of young Negroes on the street, or in cars, and in the use of disrespectful and sometimes racist language. . . .[17]

Following Kristol, one can say that if the "police brutality line" is defined as that which places one-fifth of all police behavior below it, then one-fifth of all police behavior will always be brutal.

The school dropout problem is an even more striking example. At the turn of the century, when almost everyone was a "dropout," the term and the "problem" did not exist. It was not until the 1960's, when for the first time a majority of boys and girls were graduating from high school and practically all had at least some high school training, that the "dropout problem" became acute. Then, although the dropout rate was still declining, various cities developed at least fifty-five separate programs to deal with the problem. Hundreds of articles on it were published in professional journals, the National Education Association established a special action project to deal with it, and the Commissioner of Education, the Secretary of Labor, and the President all made public statements on it.[18] Obviously, if one defines the "inadequate amount of schooling line" as that which places one-fifth of all boys and girls below it, then one-fifth of all boys and girls will always be receiving an inadequate amount of schooling.

Whatever our educational standards are today, Wayland writes, they will be higher tomorrow. He summarizes the received doctrine in these words:

> Start the child in school earlier; keep him in school more and more months of the year; retain all who start to school for twelve to fourteen years; expect him to learn more and more during this period, in wider and wider areas of human experience, under the guidance of a teacher, who has had more and more training, and who is assisted by more and more specialists, who provide an ever-expanding range of services, with access to more and more detailed personal records, based on more and more carefully validated tests.[19]

To a large extent, then, our urban problems are like the mechanical rabbit at the racetrack, which is set to keep just ahead of the dogs no matter how fast they may run. Our performance is better and better, but because we set our standards and expectations to keep ahead of performance, the problems are never any nearer to solution. Indeed, if standards and expectations rise *faster* than performance, the problems may get (relatively) worse as they get (absolutely) better.

Some may say that since almost everything about the city can stand improvement (to put it mildly), this mechanical rabbit effect is a good thing in that it spurs us on to make constant progress. No doubt this is true to some extent. On the other hand, there is danger that we may mistake failure to progress as fast as we would like for failure to progress at all and, in panic, rush into ill-considered measures that will only make matters worse. After all, an "urban crisis" that results largely from rising standards and expectations is not the sort of crisis that, unless something drastic is done, is bound to lead to disaster. To treat it as if it were might be a very serious mistake.

This danger is greatest in matters where our standards are unreasonably high. The effect of too-high standards cannot be to spur us on to reach the prescribed level of performance sooner than we otherwise would, for that level is by definition impossible of attainment. At the same time, these standards may cause us to adopt measures that are wasteful and injurious and, in the long run, to conclude from the inevitable failure of these measures that there is something fundamentally wrong with our society. Consider the school dropout problem, for example. The dropout rate can never be cut to zero: there will always be some boys and girls who simply do not have whatever it takes to finish high school. If we continue to make a great hue and cry about the dropout problem after we have reached the point where all those who can reasonably be expected to finish high school are doing so, we shall accomplish nothing constructive. Instead, we shall, at considerable cost to ourselves, injure the boys and girls who cannot finish (the propaganda against being a dropout both hurts the morale of such a youngster and reduces his or her job opportunities) while creating in ourselves and in others the impression that our society is morally or otherwise incapable of meeting its obligations.

In a certain sense, then, the urban crisis may be real. By treating a spurious crisis as if it were real, we may unwittingly make it so.

NOTES

1. See Daniel J. Elazar, "Are We a Nation of Cities?," *The Public Interest*, no. 4 (Summer 1966), pp. 42–44.
2. Sloan R. Wayland, "Old Problems, New Faces, and New Standards," in A. Harry Passow, ed., *Education in Depressed Areas* (New York: Columbia University Teachers College, 1963), p. 66.
3. Hans Blumenfeld, "The Modern Metropolis," *Scientific American* 213 (September 1965): 67.
4. This was the finding of a six-year study directed by Lawrence B. Cohen of the Department of Industrial Engineering of Columbia University and reported in the *New York Times*, December 16, 1965.
5. J. R. Meyer, J. F. Kain, and M. Wohl, *The Urban Transportation Problem* (Cambridge, Mass.: Harvard University Press, 1965), p. 359.
6. *New York Times*, July 19, 1967, p. 33.
7. Kenneth B. Clark, *Dark Ghetto* (New York: Harper & Row, 1965), table, p. 25.
8. Kenneth B. Clark, "The Wonder Is There Have Been So Few Riots," *New York Times Magazine*, September 5, 1965, p. 10.
9. Alexis de Tocqueville, *Democracy in America*, trans. by Henry Reeve (New York: Knopf, 1945), I: 289–290.
10. Cf. Robert C. Weaver, "Class, Race and Urban Renewal," *Land Economics* 36 (August 1960): 235–251. On urban renewal in general, see James Q. Wilson, ed., *Urban Renewal: The Record and the Controversy* (Cambridge, Mass.: M.I.T. Press, 1966).
11. Scott Greer, *Urban Renewal and American Cities* (Indianapolis: Bobbs-Merrill, 1965), p. 3.
12. Theodore W. Schultz, *Economic Crises in World Agriculture* (Ann Arbor: University of Michigan Press, 1965), p. 94.
13. Karl E. and Alma F. Taeuber, "The Negro as an Immigrant Group: Recent Trends in Racial and Ethnic Segregation in Chicago," *American Journal of Sociology* 69 (January 1964): 382.
14. William G. Grigsby, *Housing Markets and Public Policy* (Philadelphia: University of Pennsylvania Press, 1963), p. 322.

15. Gary T. Marx, *Protest and Prejudice* (New York: Harper & Row, 1967), p. 6.
16. Irving Kristol, "The Lower Fifth," *The New Leader,* February 17, 1964, pp. 9–10.
17. Robert Blauner, "Whitewash Over Watts," *Trans-action* 3 (March–April 1966): 6.
18. Burton A. Weisbrod, "Preventing High-School Drop-outs," in Robert Dorfman, ed., *Measuring Benefits of Government Investments* (Washington, D.C.: The Brookings Institution, 1965), p. 118.
19. Wayland, "Old Problems," in *Education in Depressed Areas,* p. 67.

Chapter 2
THE URBAN TREK

The emergence and growth of cities have been social developments of great interest to students of human societies for centuries. Why this should be the case is not difficult to comprehend.

> Almost all social changes of any significance move people from place to place. Almost all movements of people from place to place call for changes, temporary or permanent, in their relations to other people. We do not need to know any more than that to understand why migration fascinates students of social organization.[1]

Looking at the effects of migrants on cities, and of cities on migrants, has seemed to many the best way to understand what cities are all about.

A thoroughgoing conceptualization of the process of urban migration might well encompass more than the migrating units (individuals or families) and the receiving cities, the aspects of population movement that have received the greatest attention. Also of great importance are the points of origin and the larger social structure within which migration occurs.[2] Research on points of origin, for example, can lead to new perspectives on the ongoing urban trek. While analysts have often emphasized the movement from country to city, other types of migration have also been of significance, including not only moves from city to country but also moves from one urban place to another. Thus, many readers may be surprised to learn that for the last few decades the typical migrant to a large American city has not come from a rural area but from another *urban* setting. Moreover, in recent years Americans have continued to freely exchange one place of residence for another; between March 1969 and March 1970 no less than 13.3 million persons moved from one country to another, most from one urban place to another.[3]

In the following article Charles Tilly examines common misconceptions about the character and process of migration to American cities. A number of the arguments made apply to whites and blacks alike, but the central concern is with the migration of black Americans. Historically, the great migration of black Americans to the cities began just after the turn of this century, precipitated both by the economic "pull" of industrialization at points of destination in the North and by the "push" of a declining agricultural situation in southern sending areas. For the first few decades of the twentieth century the cityward migration primarily involved rural southerners moving to the urban North. But surprisingly, in the last few decades the majority of black migrants to most large cities, North and South, have come from other urban places. "One of the great American dramas—the mass movement of Negroes from the villages and open country of the South to the metropolises of both North and South—is ending a fifty-year run." [4]

Provocative, too, is Tilly's critique of conventional wisdom about the "who" and "why" of urban migration. While many city officials seem determined to propagate the myth of the typical nonwhite migrant as a drifter or problem case seeking to misuse the city's public services or to create disorder in the central city, Tilly shows these misconceptions to be wrong headed on several counts. In the first place, research has shown that public services play a minor role in shaping the flow of migrants to particular cities; most who move to a particular city do so primarily for employment reasons. Researchers have also discovered that migrants to the cities come from the most vigorous elements at points of origin. Urban migrants rank higher in education and occupation than other persons (of their own racial group) at the point of origin, and those in the city of destination as well. Ironically, if the desires of officials who would like to reduce black migration to their areas—and spur blacks already there to leave—were to be implemented, the result would be to depress the average levels of educational and occupational qualification among the city's black residents.

One might well argue that black migrants have been widely utilized as a major explanation for critical urban problems; recent black migrants have been blamed for a variety of urban ills running from crime and juvenile delinquency to welfare problems, family disorganization, and urban rioting. However, Tilly, buttressing his contentions with data, argues that there is little evidence to show that migrant families are more unstable than those who do not migrate. As for the issues of crime and delinquency, what data there are point to the conclusion that natives are more likely to become juvenile delinquents and to have higher rates of imprisonment than are black newcomers. Likewise, Tilly notes that analysis of black rioters has shown the majority to be native-born or long-term residents rather than recent arrivals. The critical factors determining major urban problems seem to be associated with what happens to people within the urban setting, rather than with the wrenching effects of migration per se.

The concluding policy-oriented section is a welcome addition to the migration discussion. There Tilly suggests that in the future cities must provide new aid and opportunities for nonwhite migrants, perhaps by breaking down racial barriers in the areas of housing or employment, perhaps by extending public services immediately, perhaps by establishing well-run urban reception services. Migration in itself does not seem to be the underlying problem; rather, the unwillingness of white residents in cities to integrate nonwhites into urban life is one of the most serious dilemmas facing contemporary American cities.

NOTES

1. Charles Tilly, *Migration to an American City* (Newark, Del.: Division of Urban Affairs and School of Agriculture, University of Delaware, 1965), p. 1.
2. Ibid.
3. U.S. Bureau of the Census, "Mobility of the Population of the United States: March 1969 to March 1970," *Current Population Reports*, Series P-20, no. 210 (Washington, D.C.: U.S. Government Printing Office, 1970), pp. 1–2.
4. Charles Tilly, "Race and Migration to the American City," in *The Metropolitan Enigma*, James Q. Wilson, ed. (Cambridge, Mass.: Harvard University Press, 1968), p. 136.

FROM **THE METROPOLITAN ENIGMA:** RACE AND MIGRATION TO THE AMERICAN CITY

CHARLES TILLY

Not long ago, the movement of Negroes from rural to urban areas in the United States reached a crucial marker: a higher proportion of Negroes than of whites is now living in cities, especially big cities. For a long time, a majority of the nation's Negro population has lived outside the rural South. Most other "nonwhite" groups in the United States have spent most of their time in big cities; American Indians are the major exception. Anyone who keeps echoing the old idea of nonwhite migration to cities as simply an invasion of bewildered country folk is now, at best, behind the times.

Not that migration, or even migration from rural areas, has stopped. Americans are still very much on the move, and the countryside is still sending millions of people to the city each decade. But with increasing exchanges of inhabitants among cities and a shrinking share of the total population in rural areas, *the majority of migrants to most American cities, whatever their color, are now coming from other urban areas.*

One of the great American dramas—the mass movement of Negroes from the villages and open country of the South to the metropolises of both North and South—is ending a fifty-year run. It has left a mark; the very title of Claude Brown's *Manchild in the Promised Land* recalls the hopeful exodus to the North. A thousand theories about the peculiarities of Negro life in the United States rest on beliefs about the wrenching effects of that migration.

Migration could plausibly explain such serious matters as the pattern of racial segregation in large cities, the bad housing and inferior services in urban areas inhabited by racial minorities, the violent outbursts of the nation's ghettos during the last few summers, and the white flight from the central cities of major northern metropolitan areas. Plausibly, but not certainly. This analysis will review some of the plausible relationships between migration and the living conditions of Negroes in

I am grateful to S. D. Clark, Roger Davidson, William Michelson, Morton Rubin, Louise Tilly, Ian Weinberg, and James Q. Wilson for advice and criticism, not all of which I had the wit or knowledge to act on.

Reprinted by permission of the publishers from James Q. Wilson, ed., *The Metropolitan Enigma: Inquiries into the Nature and Dimensions of America's Urban Crisis.* Cambridge, Mass.: Harvard University Press, Copyright, 1968, by the President and Fellows of Harvard College; 1967 by the Chamber of Commerce of the U.S.A., pp. 136–157.

cities, consider which of those relationships are solidly established, and offer some thoughts on what might be done to change them.

HOW MANY MIGRANTS, WHERE, AND WHEN?

Although they have probably moved around locally more often, America's racial minorities have generally done less long-distance migrating than have whites. We know surprising little about the volume and direction of their migration before the last few censuses. As a rough-and-ready approximation, we might say that in an average recent year five million of the twenty-odd million nonwhite Americans moved from one dwelling to another. Of them, some four million stayed in the same county, and the remaining million divided more or less equally between people moving elsewhere in the same state and people moving from one state to another.[1] Even more so than in the case of whites, the long-distance migrants were only a small minority of all the nonwhite movers.

Where did the interstate migrants go? If you took a map of the United States and drew a broad straight line from Tallahassee to Boston, another heavy line from New Orleans to Chicago, and a spindly one from Houston to Los Angeles, then sketched branching lines leading to the cities along the way—thicker for the bigger cities and the ones farther south—the three trees on your map would represent quite well the main established paths of nonwhite migration. The 1960 Census showed the importance of those paths.[2] In most states outside the South, about half the nonwhite population consisted of persons born in other states. Migration, that is, has added enormously to the nonwhite populations of northern and western states.

The states of origin and destination are most commonly on the same tree. For example, the South Atlantic states (from Delaware down to Florida and Georgia) were by far the most frequent places of birth reported for nonwhite persons; such northern states as New York, New Jersey, and Pennsylvania drew very heavily on them for their nonwhite migrants. But the state contributing the most to Illinois' population was outside the South Atlantic area. It was Mississippi, with Tennessee, Alabama, and Arkansas next but far behind. The chief feeder to California was Texas, followed by Louisiana. The "migration trees" are still very much alive.

But their shapes are changing. A growing number of Negro migrants are moving from one northern or western metropolitan area to another,

[1] For an excellent review of national and regional data concerning American internal migration, see Henry S. Shryock, Jr., *Population Mobility within the United States* (Chicago: Community and Family Study Center, University of Chicago, 1964).

[2] See especially *U.S. Census of Population: 1960. Subject Reports: State of Birth,* Final Report PC(2)–2A, and *Lifetime and Recent Migration,* Final Report PC(2)–2D.

and the number going directly from the rural South to big cities of the North and West has shrunk. Although during the late 1950's most of the nonwhite migrants to big southern cities like Atlanta and Memphis were still coming from small towns and the country, the majority of nonwhite migrants to big northern metropolitan centers like Detroit and Philadelphia were coming from *other* metropolitan areas. In the previous forty years so many Negroes had made the move from farm to village, village to town, and town to city that in 1960 the Negro population still contained much more than its share of people who at some time in their lives had made a major change in the *kind* of community they lived in. Nevertheless, only a fifth of the 1960 nonwhite population of American metropolitan areas (as compared with a tenth of the white population) consisted of persons born on farms. And the people then on the move were more urban than that.

Even in Wilmington, Delaware—a city of 100,000 located in a largely southern state with many Negroes in rural communities—well over half the nonwhite migrants by 1960 were coming to the city from other metropolitan centers.[3] In fact, by that time, once occupational differences were taken into account, there was little difference in urban experience between white and nonwhite migrants to Wilmington. Many Negroes were coming from Philadelphia, or Baltimore, or Detroit. The branches of the migration trees are crossing increasingly, and are growing to be more substantial than the trunks that used to support them.

THE IMPACT OF BIG CITIES

Most urban Americans have noticed at least one part of this complex process: the swelling of the nonwhite population of the central section of major metropolitan areas. They have noticed the changes in New York's Bedford-Stuyvesant, Chicago's West Side, Cleveland's Hough, Boston's Roxbury. In all these cities and many more, the white population has dwindled since 1940 or so, as the net effect of many moves into central cities and many more moves out of them. At the same time, Negroes in cities have more than reproduced themselves and migration has added mightily to their numbers. One result has been the familiar but still impressive rise in the proportion of Negroes in central cities. Over the decade 1950–1960 the percentage nonwhite in Washington went from 35 to 55, in New York from 10 to 15, in Cleveland from 16 to 29, in Boston from 5 to 10, in Chicago from 14 to 24; in all these cities the nonwhite population was over nine-tenths Negro. If we play the risky game of projecting these increases in a straight line, for the year 1980 we arrive at the following percentages nonwhite:

Washington	95
Cleveland	55

[3] Charles Tilly, *Migration to an American City* (Newark, Delaware: Division of Urban Affairs and School of Agriculture, University of Delaware, 1965).

Chicago	44
New York	25
Boston	20

As predictions, these numbers are worthless. As signs of what has been going on, they are very telling.

The less obvious part of this process was the bleaching of the suburbs through the addition of huge numbers of whites and almost no Negroes. Some of the bleaching occurred because of the flight of whites from the problems and people of the central city, some of it because jobs and housing attracted new white migrants directly to the suburbs rather than to central cities, more of it because, in the normal process of moving around and out toward the sites of new housing, low incomes and organized discrimination barred Negroes from taking part. A second result, then, has been the emergence of increasingly black central cities surrounded by increasingly white suburbs. This is the situation that gave one of the last decade's most intelligent essays on big cities the title *The Metropolitan Area as a Racial Problem.*[4]

At least the flight of the whites left some small benefits for Negroes. Though the piling up of families in the constricted central city housing market of the 1940's had actually increased crowding and decreased the average quality of dwellings available to Negroes in many cities, the loosening of the 1950's and 1960's gave them more choice, more room, and better quality. Many whites moved out of housing in good condition, public action like highway construction or urban renewal flattened many of the worst dwellings, a smaller number of new dwellings open to Negroes went up, and some landlords, faced with less of a seller's market than before, renovated their properties.[5]

Of course, these changes meant that Negroes ended up paying much higher rents; the regularity with which urban renewal programs subtract low-rent housing from the stock and replace it with fewer units of high-priced housing is only one example. These changes also look much less impressive when compared with the even greater gains in space, choice, and housing quality whites made throughout American metropolitan areas. The multiple shifts of population and housing stock, taken all together, left big-city Negroes with an absolute improvement and a relative loss.

These streams of migration, local moves, and housing changes depend on each other so intricately that it is hard to say what difference migration in itself makes. In a strict sense, migration—in the form of net movements of Negroes into big cities and net movements of whites away from central cities and from areas of expanding Negro popula-

[4] Morton Grodzins, *The Metropolitan Area as a Racial Problem* (Pittsburgh: University of Pittsburgh Press, 1959).

[5] Karl E. Taeuber and Alma F. Taeuber, *Negroes in Cities* (Chicago: Aldine, 1965); Bernard Frieden, *The Future of Old Neighborhoods* (Cambridge: M.I.T. Press, 1964); Charles Tilly, Wagner D. Jackson, and Barry Kay, *Race and Residence in Wilmington, Delaware* (New York: Bureau of Publications, Teachers College, 1965).

tion—accounts directly for the pattern of segregation. Furthermore, the tendency of those migrants who come to the city through contacts with friends or kinsmen to settle first with them or near them, as well as the tendency of other Negro families to seek protection and familiar surroundings near the ghetto, add a measure of self-segregation to the city. Yet these tendencies toward a voluntary clustering of the Negro population are surely far less important than the extraordinarily limited range of dwellings open to the newcomer; besides the deliberate discrimination of owners and agents, the range is limited by the insufficient information concerning the market which new arrivals have at their disposal, their low incomes, and the problem of traveling to work in those central city enterprises which employ Negroes in any number.

These factors affect not only the location but the *quality* of housing available to racial minorities. A highly segregated market gives the minority group less room to compare or bargain, and in that sense any regional and local moves that raise the level of racial concentration also aggravate the housing situation. Still, it is not so simple. Despite the common-sense presumption that in a restricted market there would be more for everyone if fewer new people came to town, and despite the near certainty that the piling up of new arrivals during the 1940's worsened the housing of Negroes, it looks as though over the long run the vitality of new construction in a metropolitan area—which depends on the area's general prosperity and is therefore related to its attractiveness to new migrants—matters a great deal more than the number of Negro newcomers.[6] Where plenty of new suburban housing is going up, vacancies appear in the older sections of the central city, and Negroes are in a better competitive position. Under these conditions, to be sure, the whites are usually improving their housing at an even faster rate, so the gap between the races is remaining or increasing. The "trickling down" of used housing to Negro families does improve their lot; it falls far short of equalizing their opportunity.

WHO MIGRATES? WHY?

We often encounter the argument that if a town improves its living conditions and public services too energetically, it will simply see its resources consumed by a rush of new, poor, dependent migrants—drifters, welfare chiselers, and problem families. There are two things wrong with this idea. First, living conditions and public services play only a small part in determining the number of migrants to any particular city. Second, migrants to cities are drawn especially from favored and vigorous elements of the general population.

When interviewers ask American migrants why they have moved, the migrants give answers relating to jobs far more than any other answers; the largest number usually report a specific job brought them

[6] See especially Taeuber and Taeuber, *Negroes in Cities*, chap. 7.

to the city, but another sizable number say they came looking for work.[7] This is about as true for Negroes as it is for whites. However, since workers in relatively unskilled occupations more often migrate without having a job already nailed down, and since Negroes include a higher proportion of workers in relatively unskilled occupations, Negroes who migrate are more often looking for work than migrating whites.

Our information on why migrants choose one destination rather than another is less abundant.[8] For people who have received specific offers of jobs, the climate, amenities, and services of a given city normally enter in a secondary way into their evaluation of the offer. For people retiring or in bad health they often determine the choice. But for people moving without a guarantee of a job the presence of friends and relatives matters a great deal more than such things as the housing supply or the availability of public assistance. If these conditions do make some marginal difference in the volume of a city's migration, most likely it is through the encouragement or discouragement friends and relatives already there give to potential migrants, rather than through a general spreading of the word among the would-be freeloaders.

If we move away from what people *say* about their own motives for moving and toward the *objective conditions* differentiating cities receiving many migrants from cities receiving few, we find jobs looming even more important than before. In the United States, the net migration to an area corresponds very closely to its income level and its production of new jobs as compared with other potential destinations for migrants. An exhaustive analysis of net migration from 1870 to 1950 conducted by the demographers and economists of the University of Pennsylvania shows that during this period Negroes as a group, even though they had less to hope for, responded more sharply to changes and regional variations in economic opportunity than did whites.[9] We have no good reason to think the situation has changed. Though booming cities often have both good public services and numerous migrants, there is no sign that public services themselves affect the volume of migration, and there is every sign that new employment does.

Anyway, who comes? [10] The "Grapes of Wrath" picture of migrants as

[7] Ralph H. Turner, "Migration to a Medium-Sized American City," *Journal of Social Psychology*, 80 (1949), 229–249; Shryock, *Population Mobility*, chap. 12.

[8] See Leonard Blumberg and Robert Bell, "Urban Migration and Kinship Ties," *Social Problems*, 6 (1959), 328–333; John S. MacDonald and Leatrice MacDonald, "Chain Migration, Ethnic Neighborhood Formation, and Social Networks," *Milbank Memorial Fund Quarterly*, 42 (1964), 82–97; Morton Rubin, "Migration Patterns of Negroes from a Rural Northeastern Mississippi Community," *Social Forces*, 39 (1960), 59–66; Harry Schwarzweller, *Family Ties, Migration, and Transitional Adjustment of Young Men from Eastern Kentucky* (Lexington: University of Kentucky Agricultural Experiment Station, 1964).

[9] Hope T. Eldridge and Dorothy Swaine Thomas, *Demographic Analyses and Interrelations* (Philadelphia: American Philosophical Society, 1964), vol. III of *Population Redistribution and Economic Growth, United States, 1870–1950*. Memoirs of the American Philosophical Society, no. 61.

[10] In addition to Shryock, Taeuber and Taeuber, Rubin, Schwarzweller, and

the dispossessed has such a grip on American imaginations that one of the most popular explanations of the big-city riots of 1964, 1965, and 1966 has been the arrival of unhappy wanderers from the South. In reality, cityward migrants tend to be *above* the average in education and occupational skill at their points of origin. They come heavily concentrated in the most energetic age groups—the late teens and early twenties. *And they even tend to rank higher in education and occupation than the population already in the city.* (Of course, those who leave any particular city also average high in occupation and education, so the net effect of migration in and out is often to depress the level of skill in a city's population.)

People moving off farms are a little different. They are not consistently better off than the people they leave behind: both the least and the most educated predominating in the younger ages, the least educated in the older ones. They tend to be even younger than other migrants, and they are on the whole below the standard levels of education and occupational skill for the city's population. But migrants from farms are only a small part of all people coming to any particular city, and so their arrival does not significantly depress the population's level of qualifications.

We already know that nonwhite migrants to cities have more often come from farms and from regions with generally low educational standards than have white migrants. We also know that nonwhite persons, whether migrants or not, generally get less education and hold poorer jobs than white persons. No one should be surprised to learn that the average nonwhite migrant comes to the city with less education and occupational skill than either the white migrant or the bulk of the urban population. *But compared to the nonwhite population already in the city,* the average nonwhite migrant has a distinct *advantage* in age, occupation, and education.

These complicated comparisons hold an ironic implication for those city fathers who wish they could speed the departure of Negroes from their towns and keep new Negro migrants from coming in. Such a strategy would be a very good way to depress the average level of qualification of the city's Negro population. It would probably increase the proportion, if not the absolute number, of the Negro population heavily dependent on public services. The way to insure a young and skilled Negro population would be to attract new migrants and make sure that

Eldridge and Thomas, cited above, see C. Harold Brown and Roy C. Buck, *Factors Associated with the Migrant Status of Young Adult Males from Rural Pennsylvania* (University Park: Pennsylvania State University Agricultural Experiment Station, 1961); Ronald Freedman, "Cityward Migration, Urban Ecology and Social Theory," in Ernest W. Burgess and Donald J. Bogue, eds., *Contribution to Urban Sociology* (Chicago: University of Chicago Press, 1964); C. Horace Hamilton, "Educational Selection of the Net Migration from the South," *Social Forces*, 38 (1959), 33–42; Arnold M. Rose, "Distance of Migration and Socio-economic Status of Migrants," *American Sociological Review*, 23 (1958), 420–423.

the mobile people already in the city were too satisfied to depart. Of course, stimulating job opportunities and providing a decent education for Negroes already in the city would complement such a policy.

One part of this prescription is already in effect without much help from the city fathers. More and more of the recent Negro migrants to big cities are people with relatively good job skills and educational backgrounds moving in from other metropolitan areas. If these new migrants have not attracted as much attention as the displaced croppers from depressed farming areas of the South, maybe it is because they do not fit everyday prejudices so well.

DOES MIGRATION DISORGANIZE?

If we come to realize that most Negro migrants are neither drifters nor dregs, we may have to abandon other commonplace prejudices concerning the disorganizing effects of migration. No doubt it is true—as a long line of acute observers from W. E. B. DuBois to Gilbert Osofsky have noted—that migration from the South to an urban North in which Negro women had a niche (if not a very pleasant one), while Negro men often had no place at all, wrenched and reshaped the family lives of Negroes.[11] No doubt this wrenching even affected the later genera-

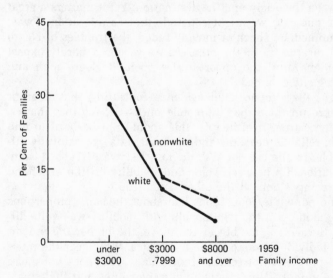

Percent of families headed by women, by income class: U.S. central cities, 1960

[11] W. E. B. DuBois, *The Philadelphia Negro* (Philadelphia: University of Pennsylvania, 1899); Gilbert Osofsky, *Harlem: The Making of a Ghetto* (New York: Harper and Row, 1966).

tions born in the city. Although the difference in family stability between whites and Negroes of the same income or occupations is less than many people think, Negro households do break up and regroup more often than do white ones. Rates of divorce and separation are generally higher for Negroes.[12] The greater frequency of divorce and separation in turn helps make families headed by women more common among Negroes. The figure above shows, for 1960, the proportion of female-headed families in various income and color groups, within central cities.[13] This comparison suggests (but certainly does not prove) that income is the big factor and racial difference in family life a somewhat smaller one. A finer comparison by income, indeed, would show less difference between the racial categories, since within each of these broad income classes the nonwhites are concentrated toward the bottom. If so, Negroes still come out disadvantaged because their incomes are on the whole much lower and less reliable than those of whites. Though the majority of Negro families are unbroken, a substantially higher proportion of Negro children than of white children grow up without a father continuously at hand, and suffer both economically and psychologically from the absence of that father.

All this amounts to saying that the situation in the city, rather than the fact of moving, shook Negro family life in the time of the great northward migration. The distinction may seem academic: the impact of any move on the individual always includes the differences in living conditions between the origin and the destination. Yet it matters a great deal. For in the one case we might conclude that as migration slowed down and the immediate shock of moving faded, the troubles of Negro families would disappear. In the other case, we could hardly expect much improvement until the opportunities open to Negro men and women in the big city changed.

Oddly enough, there is no solid evidence indicating that migrant families are more unstable than immobile ones—or, for that matter, that the opposite is true. In principle, this should not be hard to find out; in practice, reliable measures and adequate data are painfully difficult to assemble. In the case of Wilmington, Delaware, Table 1 summarizes the relationship between color and mobility on the one hand and household composition on the other, as of 1960.

The white and nonwhite populations had about the same proportions of people living alone. But the relationship with mobility was quite different: among the whites, the bigger the move, the higher the proportion of solitary individuals; among the nonwhites, the bigger the move the smaller the proportion of solitary individuals. This does not mean there were more *unmarried* migrants among the whites, but that single nonwhite migrants were much more likely to lodge with friends or rela-

[12] See, for example, *Divorce Statistics Analysis* (Washington: U.S. Department of Health, Education and Welfare, Public Health Service, 1965; National Center for Health Statistics, Series 21, No. 7).

[13] Data from *The Negroes in the United States* (Washington: United States Department of Labor, Bureau of Labor Statistics, 1966; Bulletin No. 1511), table IVA-5.

Table 1. Household types of whites and nonwhites migrating to Wilmington between 1955 and 1960.

| | Percent of all households consisting of | | | | | |
| | An individual living alone | | A married couple with or without dependents | | A head with no spouse present, plus others | |
Moves made from 1955 to 1960	White	Non-white	White	Non-white	White	Non-white
Stayed in same house	20	28	62	47	18	25
Moved within the city of Wilmington	24	20	61	52	15	28
Moved into the city from the suburbs	23	18	62	56	15	26
Moved in from another metropolitan area	30	14	64	61	6	25
Moved in from a nonmetropolitan area	36	7	54	91	10	2
Total	22	22	61	51	17	27

Source: Unpublished tabulation of the 1960 Census of Population.

tives instead of taking rented rooms. In fact, both single and married Negro migrants to Wilmington often come alone, and stay for at least a short time with friends or relatives. After finding jobs and getting used to the city, the married men ordinarily secure separate lodgings and then send for their families. The single men often continue to lodge with their friends or relatives for quite some time. The common picture of recent migrants as footloose, solitary individuals applies to the whites of Wilmington much more accurately than to the nonwhites.

The rest of the table contains an even more interesting message. Here we find the proportions of households headed by intact married couples contrasted with the proportions we might call "broken." The general comparison follows the national pattern: the whites have significantly more intact families. The comparisons in terms of mobility, however, look quite different for the two groups. The various categories of whites do not differ very much, except that the migrants from nonmetropolitan areas (which means essentially small towns and open country) include fewer married couples than the rest. Among the nonwhites, the bigger the move, the higher the proportion of married couples. The range goes from less than half for people staying in the same house between 1955 and 1960, up to more than nine-tenths for people moving in from nonmetropolitan areas. The statistics directly contradict everyday ideas on the subject.

Among both whites and nonwhites, the long-distance migrants include *fewer* broken families (compare the last two columns of the table). There are two significant differences between the white and nonwhite patterns. The white migrants from other metropolitan areas do not look much different from the local population. The comparison between white and nonwhite migrants from nonmetropolitan areas goes the other way, with almost no broken families among the nonwhites coming from the countryside. If migration is disrupting family life in Wilmington, it must be doing so over a longer time span than the five years our table covers. Whatever the explanation of the greater instability of nonwhite households, it can hardly be the disruptive effects of migration.

While the great differences in size and in sources of migrants between the two cities produce some interesting variations in the pattern, both Wilmington and New York display the same general tendencies. Table 2 is a parallel tabulation for New York City. A higher proportion of New

Table 2. Percentage of whites and nonwhites migrating to New York City between 1955 and 1960 (according to household composition).

	Percent of all households consisting of					
	An individual living alone		A married couple, with or without dependents		A head with no spouse present, plus others	
Moves made from 1955 to 1960	White	Non-white	White	Non-white	White	Non-white
Stayed in same house	21	27	65	49	14	24
Moved within the central city	19	24	71	54	9	22
Moved into the city from the suburbs	28	23	63	64	9	12
Moved in from another metropolitan area	44	34	50	49	6	18
Moved in from a non-metropolitan area	38	23	50	63	12	14
Total	21	26	66	51	12	23

Source: U.S. Census of Population, 1960, Subject Report PC(2)–2C, Mobility for Metropolitan Areas, calculated from table 4.

York's recent migrants are living alone, and a few more of the migrants from nonmetropolitan areas are in broken families. Yet the main conclusion holds: if anything, the recent migrants are less likely than the rest to have broken families, and this is especially true within the nonwhite population.

When it comes to the related matter of emotional adjustment, it now looks as though major mental disorders are more common among long-distance migrants than in the general population (although even that fact could not in itself establish that mobility *causes* mental disorder), but comparisons for other types of personal disorganization remain inconclusive.[14]

[14] H. B. M. Murphy, "Migration and the Major Mental Disorders: A Reappraisal," in Mildred Kantor, ed., Mobility and Mental Health (Springfield, Ill.: Charles C. Thomas, 1965), plus other articles in the same volume.

As for the crime and delinquency so regularly attributed to the new-comers, what evidence there is points the other way: it takes some time in the city for the migrant to catch up with the old residents. A long series of studies first stimulated by arguments offered for the restriction of immigration after World War I showed lower rates of criminal ac-tivity for immigrants than for the native population. In a careful recent study of about 900 Negro boys from a high-delinquency section of Phil-adelphia, Leonard Savitz found the boys born and brought up in the city to have delinquency rates about 50 percent *higher* than the migrants from elsewhere, even after making allowance for the greater number of years the natives had been around to be caught. As Savitz summed up: "There was no confirmation of internal migration as a disorganiz-ing process in modern life. The migrants not only tended to be lower than the natives in the frequency and seriousness of delinquencies, but also were less likely to come from broken homes, have illegitimate sib-lings or engage in considerable intracity mobility." [15] Most of the studies seeming to show otherwise, it turns out, establish that crime, delin-quency, illegitimacy, and family instability concentrate in *areas* of high mobility, but fail to show that the mobile *persons* in those areas create disorder.

A detailed analysis of commitments to Pennsylvania prisons by Judith Kinman and Everett Lee brought out an even more interesting conclu-sion than that of Savitz.[16] As was already well established, they found the rates of imprisonment to be much higher for Negroes than for whites. Like Savitz, they also found that among Negroes the rates were higher for natives than for migrants. But among whites, it was the other way around: the migrants went to prison more often. Further-more, the really big differences showed up among migrants from the South, with the whites, compared with the natives and the whites from other regions, having exceptionally *high* rates of commitment, and the Negroes (likewise compared to the natives and the Negroes from other regions) having exceptionally *low* rates. So the most convenient explana-tion for the greater frequency with which Negroes are convicted of crimes—the disorientation of the new arrivals from the South—appears to be wrong on every count. Perhaps one part of the correct explanation is that the white criminal has an easier time escaping detection, convic-tion, and imprisonment than the Negro criminal. Perhaps another is that the Negro migrant from the South is more often drawn temporarily into a protective web of kinsmen and fellow migrants, whereas the white Southerner is more often cast into miserable circumstances on his own. Whatever the ultimate explanation, it must have more to do with what happens to migrants *after* they are in the city than with the shock of moving itself.

[15] Leonard Savitz, *Delinquency and Migration* (Philadelphia: Commission on Human Relations, 1960), p. 16.

[16] Judith L. Kinman and Everett S. Lee, "Migration and Crime," *International Migration Digest*, 3 (1966), 7–14.

THE ASSIMILATION OF THE NEWCOMER

Sociologists and politicians alike have often tried to analyze what has been happening to racial minorities as a process of assimilation "into the mainstream of American life." They have relied on analogies with the fairly regular ways in which Italians or Poles went from isolation, deprivation, and cultural distinctness toward the normal rewards and involvements of American life.

The basic argument stands out in both the title and the text of Irving Kristol's stimulating *New York Times Magazine* article: "The Negro Today Is Like the Immigrant Yesterday." [17] The article rightly reminds us how much of the ugly language and uglier fact of current accounts of Negro urban life applied to the Irish of our cities only a few generations ago and holds out assurances that this crisis, too, will pass away. A number of historians of American immigration and assimilation, like Oscar Handlin, have urged the same thesis.[18]

The idea is attractive because of its simplicity and its optimism. Even if they didn't come from overseas, many Negroes have recently made the big move from region to region and from country to city. Over the last century Negroes and Orientals have won access to significantly better jobs, incomes, and education. These changes make the assimilationist idea plausible. The argument also makes it easier for the descendants of nineteenth- or twentieth-century immigrants to reply to Negro demands with: "We made it on our own . . . Why can't you?"

The idea of an inevitable movement toward assimilation faces some difficult facts, however. The ancestors of most of America's Negro population were here well before most of the Europeans on whose assimilation the scheme is based. Some forms of racial discrimination and segregation (the World War II roundup of Japanese, the rising residential segregation of big cities in the 1940's, the earlier elaboration of Jim Crow legislation are examples) have worsened several times in the memory of living men. And Negroes (if not Orientals or American Indians) have publicly expressed a greater sense of alienation from the rewards and involvements of American life in recent years than before.

In some broad ways, to be sure, assimilation has been moving on. Over the last few decades Negroes have been gaining better jobs, more education, higher incomes, sounder housing, fuller medical care, even greater life expectancy. But so have whites. In all these respects, the gap between whites and Negroes has closed little (if at all) over the last twenty years. Negro unemployment rates remain consistently higher, especially in bad times. Broken families remain common, illegitimacy

[17] *New York Times Magazine*, Sept. 11, 1966.

[18] Oscar Handlin, *The Newcomers* (Cambridge: Harvard University Press, 1959). See also Marc Fried, "The Transitional Functions of Working-Class Communities," in Kantor, *Mobility and Mental Health*.

rates rise, the need of Negro households for public assistance persists. The essence of assimilation is not just material improvement in absolute terms, but a closing of the gap between a group of newcomers and the rest of the nation. For a process often billed as steady and irreversible, the assimilation of Negroes does not seem to be working right.

At the beginning of their discussion of the position of Negroes in New York City, Nathan Glazer and Daniel Patrick Moynihan seem to accept the standard argument: "The Negro population is still in large part new to the city. In 1960 half of the entire nonwhite population of the city above the age of 20 had come from the South. These Americans of two centuries are as much immigrant as any European immigrant group, for the shift from the South to New York is as radical a change for the Negro as that faced by earlier immigrants." [19] Then the qualifications begin. As their analysis unfolds, Glazer and Moynihan slowly come to the conclusion that the conditions for getting ahead have changed too much, that the Negro family has suffered too much damage, that the internal cohesion of the Negro population is too low, for anyone to expect an updated repetition of the classic American success story. Now, this is not exactly the argument of civil rights leaders or of radical critics of American society, but it differs greatly from the more optimistic assimilationist account of what is going on.

At first glance, these disagreements may look like tedious professorial wrangling over definitions and historical analogies. In fact, they set the terms of one of the great questions for research and action in urban life over the next decade. Has there been a standard process of assimilation into an American mainstream via the big city, one that is still working today for Negroes and other racial minorities? Or have the mechanisms broken down, has the economic situation changed too much, has the system of exclusion become too efficient, are the groups now seeking inclusion too different in character? Or is the notion of assimilation into the mainstream itself based on a misunderstanding of how American life works?

If the standard process of assimilation is still working, then designers of American public policy could reasonably seek ways to speed up an established pattern of change. If the process is not working, then they would have to envisage changes in the very structure of American society. For once, a problem with extensive theoretical implications and a question of great significance for public policy come together. Although I cannot guarantee that the social scientists, the policy makers, or the critics will come up with satisfactory answers, I am sure that they will all soon be pouring an extraordinary effort into the analysis of assimilation.

That prediction is all the safer because when forced to account for racial protests or ghetto riots, Americans so readily turn to migration and its aftermath as the explanations. The Governor's Commission on

[19] Nathan Glazer and Daniel Patrick Moynihan, *Beyond the Melting Pot* (Cambridge: M.I.T. Press, 1963), p. 26.

the Los Angeles Riots (the McCone Commission), after pointing out the hardships suffered by Negroes everywhere in the United States, had to ask, "Why Los Angeles?" Here is what they said:

> Yet the riot did happen here, and there are special circumstances here which explain in part why it did. Perhaps the people of Los Angeles should have seen trouble gathering under the surface calm. In the last quarter century, the Negro population here has exploded. While the County's population has trebled, the Negro population has increased almost tenfold, from 75,000 in 1940 to 650,000 in 1965. Much of the increase came through migration from Southern States and many arrived with the anticipation that this dynamic city would somehow spell the end of life's endless problems. To those who have come with high hopes and great expectations and see the success of others so close at hand, failure brings a special measure of frustration and disillusionment. Moreover, the fundamental problems, which are the same here as in the cities which were racked by the 1964 riots, are intensified by what may well be the least adequate network of public transportation in any major city in America.[20]

Migration bears the blame.

That migration is to blame seems at first glance to be confirmed by the special census of South Los Angeles conducted after the Watts riots. From 1960 to 1965, unemployment stayed almost constant (in the face of dramatic increases in employment elsewhere), incomes had dropped, housing had deteriorated, and broken families had become more common.[21] When unveiling the census report, Andrew Brimmer, Assistant Secretary of Commerce for Economic Affairs, interpreted it to mean that "the most successful families had moved to more desirable neighborhoods and had been replaced by lower income groups moving in from other parts of the state and nation." [22] The new findings seemed to corroborate the Commission's explanation of the riots.

But the facts are more complicated. If migration is such a powerful factor, we should find that cities receiving many underprivileged migrants are more violent than the rest, we should expect violence in those sections of cities where populations are swelling with new migrants, and we should discover that recent migrants are peculiarly prone to violence. What is the evidence?

The efforts of sociologists to get at the origins of collective violence have not revealed any reliable tendency for high-migration cities to produce more interracial mayhem or more frequent ghetto explosions than the rest. An analysis of 76 urban riots during the years 1913–1963 done by Stanley Lieberson and Arnold Silverman of the University of Wisconsin identified some revealing tendencies for riots to break out

[20] *Violence in the City—An End or a Beginning?* (Los Angeles: Governor's Commission on the Los Angeles Riots, 1965), pp. 3–4.

[21] U.S. Bureau of the Census, *Special Census Survey of the South and East Los Angeles Area, November, 1965* (Series P-23, no. 17, 1966).

[22] According to a report in the *New York Times*, March 9, 1966.

in cities where Negroes were underrepresented in the police force or in the city council, but detected no difference attributable to migration.[23] In any case, the Watts of just before the 1965 riots was actually a *declining* community in population as well as in standard of living, not a staging area for new arrivals. And the Los Angeles County Probation Department found:

1. Over half the juveniles picked up for participation in the riots were California born.
2. More than three-quarters had lived in the country at least five years.
3. Only one in twenty had been there less than a year.
4. The proportions of natives and long-term residents were even higher among those juveniles whose cases the courts considered worth prosecuting.[24]

The findings sound something like the studies of crime and delinquency we reviewed earlier. It apparently takes time to learn to riot. Again we discover that the way assimilation to the city works is more important than how much stress and strain moving around creates.

MIGRATION AS A PROBLEM FOR PUBLIC POLICY

The most acute problems we have encountered in this survey of race and migration are not really problems created by migration at all. Some are difficulties faced by members of racial minorities wherever they are in America, difficulties that migration simply transplants and concentrates in cities. Job discrimination is one important example. In these cases, a change in the conditions of migration might affect which communities had to take the largest direct responsibility for meeting the problem, but it would not make much difference in the gravity of the problem as a whole.

Other problems are forms of discrimination more prominent in cities than elsewhere and therefore aggravated by the movement to the cities of more of the people they hurt. Big-city residential segregation is like that. In these cases, a slowdown of migration might ease the problem, but it certainly would not eliminate it.

As for problems directly produced by migration, my main message has been that they have been seriously misunderstood and exaggerated. Migrants as a group do not notably disturb public order, their arrival

[23] Stanley Lieberson and Arnold R. Silverman, "The Precipitants and Underlying Conditions of Race Riots," *American Sociological Review*, 30 (1965), 887–898.

[24] *Riot Participant Study, Juvenile Offenders* (Los Angeles County Probation Department, 1965). According to a *New York Times* article of September 4, 1966, a similar study of adult offenders done by the state's Bureau of Criminal Identification and Investigation yielded the same conclusions. After I wrote this paper, in 1966, much more evidence pointing in the same direction came in. See especially Louis H. Masotti, ed., "Urban Violence and Disorder," *American Behavioral Scientist*, 2 (March–April 1968), entire issue.

does not lower the quality of the city's population, they place no extraordinary demands on public services, and they do not arrive exceptionally burdened with personal problems. These things happen to them later. The difficulties faced by inhabitants of ghettos and by cities containing them are not to any large degree products merely of migration.

Yet in two ways the migrant *does* present a challenge to public policy. First, moving over long distances often imposes hardships and confusion on families at the same time as it cuts them off from the agencies that might be able to help them; instead of recognizing the special problems of people on the move, American public services tend to discriminate against them. Second, the newcomer—already by definition an innovator, having an advantage in age, education, and skill, bound to the old ways of his new city by fewer commitments and routines—is in an extraordinarily good position to take advantage of programs breaking down racial barriers, if only they are open to him. The challenge is to make maximum use of the migrant's talents, give him the greatest possible access to the rewards the city has to offer, make sure he can get past the personal crises almost all big moves involve without breaking down, and assure that he has attractive alternatives to the social and geographic isolation of the ghetto.

Open-housing arrangements directed to the newcomers would make sense. Some of the recent migrants might be too dependent on friends and relatives already in the city to consider living far from them. But we have seen that the more detached and highly skilled migrants from other big cities are increasing in number. They might well be more interested in integrated housing than the long-time ghetto residents who are the prime concern of most current open-housing programs. Since the creation of new jobs so regularly stimulates migration, why not encourage or require expanding firms to assure the availability of unsegregated housing?

Because migrants normally face their grimmest moments shortly after arrival, the usual residence requirements for public services have an unpleasant illogic to them. So long as cities think of themselves as involved in a curious sort of market in which generous public services infallibly attract more of the dispossessed, it is not hard to understand the occasional temptation to erect high walls and long waiting periods. But in fact, as we have seen, the quality of public services does not seem to make much difference to the flow of migrants, and the migrants who do come place no exceptional demand on services. In any case, equalizing the assistance available to newcomers in one city or another (possibly through federal programs concentrated in the first year of residence) would eliminate the competition among cities to keep migrants away. It would also mean the responsibility of paying for such assistance would be equally shared. Facilities like public housing are mostly paid for with funds coming from outside the city anyway. They ought to be available to those new arrivals who need them.

There are other services that need to be specially designed for migrants. Since the Welcome Wagon rarely calls in the ghetto, and social agencies do not usually make contact with a family until its serious troubles have begun, something as simple as a reception service could be very effective. Many migrants do not know where they can get medical attention, job information, help in finding housing, or legal assistance; they can only get unreliable, fragmentary information from their friends and neighbors. They are at a point where established routines and obligations are less likely to keep them from taking opportunities—for jobs, for housing, for training—outside the cramped circle of minority group life.

A well-run urban reception service would produce an important extra benefit: a good pool of information about current migration and migrants. For a country that has done so famously in the collection and storage of other kinds of data, the United States has pitifully little reliable information on migration. The Census does provide sound, voluminous data on long-term trends and new movements of population. Some scholars have learned to squeeze sources like city directories long and ingeniously enough to produce finer detail on who migrates and fuller descriptions of short-run fluctuations. Their procedures are still no substitute for the rich, accurate, up-to-date quantitative picture of migration to be gained from an intelligent combination of data already in the records of utilities installations, real-estate transactions, truck movements, new employment, school enrollments, and voting registrations, or for the full qualitative picture to be gained from the household interviews a reception service might conduct. At present the feedback of information on migrants to and from American cities is far too slow and fragmentary to permit effective action in meeting the pains they face or the problems they pose.

CONCLUSION

Migration, as such, is not a major public problem. But it points up grave problems. In the long run, the assimilation of racial minorities into the social life and opportunities of the city is the fundamental problem of American civil rights. Negroes, Orientals, and members of other racial minorities are increasingly concentrating in the great metropolitan centers. That is where the new opportunities and the possibilities of massive change are opening up. How cities meet the needs and aspirations of their nonwhite citizens will determine how America as a whole meets those needs and aspirations. If Negro separatism of any kind works effectively, it will have to work in the city. That is why the simple question, "Is the Negro today like the immigrant yesterday?" matters so much, and is so likely to obsess scholars and policy makers over the next decade.

Chapter 3

URBAN SOCIAL STRUCTURE: THE CASE OF A SLUM

The typical American city has been depicted by some urban sociologists as a series of concentric geographical and socioeconomic zones rippling out from a downtown business area. Termed the *concentric zone theory,* one such model of urban growth and structure was developed by Ernest W. Burgess several decades ago;[1] since then, many have viewed contemporary cities as a set of progressively larger circles, each zone with its own distinctive characteristics. The bull's-eye of this targetlike pattern has been termed the *central business district,* with its skyscrapers and commercial enterprises. This area is in turn surrounded by a *zone in transition,* a zone predominantly inhabited by poor individuals enmeshed in the decaying and disorderly environment abandoned by earlier groups now dispersing to outlying areas. In everyday language this is an area of slums and ghettos. Beyond this zone are, successively, the *zone of workingmen's homes,* the *middle-class residential zone,* and the *commuters' zone.* In everyday language these outer rings might be called suburbs.[2]

Slums and suburbs—these ecological areas have been of great interest not only to social scientists but also to the general public. Controversies have raged, and are raging, over the meaning of these terms, as well as over the character of life in the areas they denote. Take the definition of "slum," for example: "A highly congested usually urban residential area characterized by deteriorated unsanitary buildings, poverty, and social disorganization."[3] Stressed in this representative definition are certain social aspects, the disorganization and poverty, and certain physical aspects, the congestion and unsanitary buildings. Moreover, conventional wisdom often stresses that slums are little more than decaying areas of crime, delinquency, broken families, and immorality.

The Urban Villagers deals directly with the definition and character of urban slums. This study of Italian-Americans residing in a low-rent area of downtown Boston, an area that came to be defined negatively by city officials as a "slum," raises some very serious questions about the social-definition process, for once an area has been defined publicly as a "slum" it has been an easy next step for officials to bulldoze the area and rebuild it according to their values. Here Herbert J. Gans has argued that the term "slum," particularly as used by those who have dominated the urban redevelopment process, has been an evaluative concept, not an analytical one. Evaluation of certain conditions or behavior in a given area as pathological has more often than not reflected a class bias rather than an objective appraisal. Only certain housing characteristics and antisocial behavior are singled out by officials and planners according to their own values, without careful studies of the actual harmfulness of the physical and social environment for a majority of the local residents (perhaps most important) or for the city as a whole.

> Consequently, unless urban renewal is drastically altered, other definitions of the slum should be developed. Existing physical standards so far have failed to make a distinction between *low-rent* and *slum* housing, or low-rent and slum districts, community facilities, street patterns, and the like. This distinction, however, is an important one. Residential structures —and districts—should be defined as slums only if they have proven to be physically, socially, or emotionally *harmful* to their residents or to the larger community. Low-rent structures and districts may be distinguished from slums by the fact they provide shelter that may be *inconvenient* but that is not harmful. . . . A set of parallel social standards is even more difficult to define, because most of the social problems found in slums cannot be traced to the area itself. Undoubtedly, some people live in slums because they have problems or unacceptable behavior patterns. But economic and social conditions, rather than the slum itself, have caused these.[4]

One might even press this argument a bit further and raise the fundamental question of self-determination; that is, should officials have the right to disrupt or destroy a community without seriously considering the desires and needs of the local residents?

Carefully researching the social structure and living patterns of a large Italian-American community in Boston's West End using the criteria above, Gans concludes the area was not a "slum." Rather, the Italian section of the West End could best be described as a low-rent area of solidary kinship networks and stable working-class families; the suggestion is that the district could not be (and had not been) proved to be harmful to most of the local residents or to the larger community. In the selection reprinted here Gans discusses some of his findings, based on a variety of research techniques including living in the West End area as a participant observer. The existence of the "peer-group society" is demonstrated, a social framework contradicting the common image of the anonymity, disorganization, and lack of community among slum residents. A distinctive urban life style is documented.

The second excerpt included in this chapter examines the grief reactions of rank-and-file urbanites who were *forced* by the urban renewal process to leave the West End area of Boston, the same area that
Gans had studied just prior to the bulldozing process. The urban renewal plan had been approved in 1956; by 1960 only debris existed
where thousands had once lived; by 1962 new residents had begun to
move into the luxury housing that replaced the homes of the West
Enders. The despair, the grieving for a lost home, that Marc Fried found
among those relocated is not surprising in light of Gans' data on the
vital social ties that existed there prior to urban renewal. These data
clearly indicate the importance of urban social structure, including
peer-group societies, in integrating individuals and providing a sense of
belonging—*spatial* and *social*—within the urban context. Given the findings of Gans and Fried, critical policy questions about the traditional
process of remaking American cities arise; Fried's answers to these
questions seem both sensible and challenging.

NOTES

1. See Ernest W. Burgess, "The Growth of the City: An Introduction to a
   Research Project," in *Studies in Human Ecology*, George A. Theodorson,
   ed. (New York: Harper and Row, 1961), pp. 37–44.
2. Alternative and competing models of urban growth and structure have also
   been developed, most notably the *sector* and *multiple nuclei* theories.
   For a lucid discussion of models of urban ecology, see Noel P. Gist and
   Sylvia F. Fava, *Urban Society*, 5th ed. (New York: Thomas Y. Crowell,
   1964), pp. 95 ff.
3. *Webster's Third New International Dictionary* (Springfield, Mass.: G. & C.
   Merriam Co., 1961), p. 2147.
4. Herbert J. Gans, *The Urban Villagers* (New York: Free Press, 1962), pp.
   309–310.

FROM **THE URBAN VILLAGERS**

HERBERT J. GANS

. . . The life of the West Ender takes place within three interrelated sectors: the primary group, the secondary group, and the outgroup. The primary group refers to that combination of family and peer relationships which I shall call the *peer group society*. The secondary group refers to the small array of Italian institutions, voluntary organizations, and other social bodies which function to support the workings of the peer group society. This I shall call the *community*. I use this term because *it*, rather than the West End or Boston, is the West Ender's community. The outgroup, which I shall describe as the *outside world*, covers a variety of non-Italian institutions in the West End, in Boston, and in America that impinge on his life—often unhappily to the West Ender's way of thinking.

Although social and economic systems in the outside world are significant in shaping the life of the West Ender, the most important part of that life is lived within the primary group. National and local economic, social, and political institutions may determine the West Ender's opportunities for income, work, and standard of living, but it is the primary group that refracts these outside events and thus shapes his personality and culture. Because the peer group society dominates his entire life, and structures his relationship with the community and the outside world, I shall sometimes use the term to describe not only the primary relationships, but the West Enders' entire social structure as well.

The primary group is a peer group society because most of the West Enders' relationships are with peers, that is, among people of the same sex, age, and life-cycle status. While this society includes the friendships, cliques, informal clubs, and gangs usually associated with peer groups, it also takes in family life. In fact, during adulthood, the family is its most important component. Adult West Enders spend almost as much time with siblings, inlaws, and cousins—that is, with relatives of the same sex and age—as with their spouses, and more time than with parents, aunts, and uncles. The peer group society thus continues long past adolescence, and, indeed, dominates the life of the West Ender from birth to death. For this reason I have coined the term "peer group society."

In order to best describe the dominance of the peer group principle in the life of the West Ender, it is necessary to examine it over a typical life cycle. The child is born into a nuclear family; at an early age, however, he or she—although girls are slower to do this than boys—transfers increasing amounts of his time and allegiance to the peers he meets in the street and in school. This transfer may even begin long before the child enters school. Thus, one West Ender told me that when he wanted his two-year-old son to attend an activity at a local settlement house, bribery and threats were useless, but that the promise that he could go with two other young children on the block produced immediate assent.

From this time on, then, the West Ender spends the rest of his life in one or another peer group. Before or soon after they start going to school, boys and girls form cliques or gangs. In these cliques, which are sexually segregated, they play together and learn the lore of childhood. The clique influence is so strong, in fact, that both parents and school officials complain that their values have difficulty competing with those being taught in the peer group. The sexually segregated clique maintains its hold on the individual until late adolescence or early adulthood.

Dating, the heterosexual relationship between two individuals that the middle-class child enters into after puberty—or even earlier—is much rarer among West Enders. Boys and girls may come together in peer groups to a settlement house dance or a clubroom. Even so, they dance with each other only infrequently. Indeed, at the teenage dances I observed, the girls danced mostly with each other and the boys stood in the corner—a peer group pattern that may continue even among young adults. A West End girl in her twenties described her dates as groups of men and women going out together, with little social contact between individual men and women during the evening. Individual dating takes place not as part of the group activity, as in the middle class, but only after the group has dispersed. Judging from the descriptions given by young West End men, the relationship then is purely sexual—at least for them.

The hold of the peer group is broken briefly at marriage. During courtship, the man commutes between it and his girl. Female peer groups—always less cohesive than male—break up even more easily then, because the girl who wants to get married must compete with her peers for male friends and must be at their beck and call. At marriage, the couple leaves its peer groups, but after a short time, often following the arrival of the first child, they both re-enter peer group life.

• • •

The basis of adult West End life is peer group sociability. By sociability I do not mean the entertaining and party-giving of the middle class. Nor do I mean the informal conversational activity that the middle class ranks well below occupational, familial, and self-improvement activities in importance. For the West Ender, sociability is a routinized gathering of a relatively unchanging peer group of family members and friends that takes place several times a week. One could almost say that the meetings of the group are at the vital center of West End life, that they are the end for which other everyday activities are a means.

Membership in the group is based primarily on kinship. As already noted, brothers, sisters, and cousins of the husband and wife—and their spouses—are at the core. The group also includes godparents and friends who may come less regularly. Godparents are friends who, because of their closeness, are given quasi-familial status. Godparentage is awarded to best men at a wedding or to the children of one's godparents, as well as to true godparents; in short, to people who become "friends of the family" in middle-class American kinship terminology.[1] It is also used as a way of cementing relationships. For example, one West Ender asked his neighbors, with whom he had long been friendly, to be godparents for his newborn child, in order to maintain contact between the two families after redevelopment. In adult life, West Enders have little contact with their actual godparents, since the older generation is not part of the peer group social life.

Included among other unrelated individuals are friends of long duration, as well as more recent friends. Though the latter may be newcomers to the group, they are likely to have been known to the group before, because, as already noted, everyone knows of everyone else. Consequently, nearly everyone is a potential friend who can join a peer group at any time. This happens most often after people have extended help to each other, met at ceremonial occasions, or have had prolonged contact, for example, as hospital patients. Recruitment is not deliberate, however, and self-conscious "mixing with people" is explicitly rejected. A mobile woman who had left the West End suggested to West End relatives one night that women should get out of the house and mix with people. But her relatives, discussing it afterwards, thought that this belief was a result of her being childless, for which they pitied her. Similarly, when a relocation official spoke to a West Ender about the new social experiences he would encounter in a new neighborhood, the West Ender replied angrily: "I don't want to meet any new people. I get out quite a bit all over Boston to see my brothers and sisters, and, when they come over, we have others in, like neighbors. You can't do that in the suburbs."

Neighbors also may be included in the group if they are friends, but they are not eligible merely because they live next door. As neighbors, they may have frequent physical contact that might facilitate the social contact prerequisite to a friendship.[2] But it also might reveal differences

---

[1] This is one of the few instances in which West Enders still use an Italian term to describe a phenomenon. They refer to their "compares" (male) and "commares" (female), perhaps because the term godparent is not quite the same, and because there is no other English word that quite describes the relationship.

[2] In most of the tenements, neighbors were residents of adjacent buildings who faced on a common fire-escape or airshaft. In the building in which I lived, kitchens faced each other, thus giving housewives frequent opportunity for visual contact. There was less contact with people on other floors of one's own building, since they were seen only fleetingly when using the stairs.

[3] The role of physical propinquity and background homogeneity in friendship is discussed further in Herbert J. Gans, "Planning and Social Life," *Journal of the American Institute of Planners*, vol. 27 (1961), pp. 134–140, at pp. 134–136.

in background and behavior that could preclude friendship.[3] In the West End, neighbors quite often were also socially close because of the previously noted tendency of landlords to rent apartments to relatives or friends.

Potential peer group members are many, but their number is effectively reduced by the requirement that people must be relatively compatible in terms of background, interests, and attitudes: what they have to say and what they want to listen to must be of common interest. They also must hold somewhat similar attitudes toward marriage, child-rearing, religion, politics, taste, and other important issues, because West Enders cannot cope effectively with disagreements.[4] As a result, the group is limited to people of similar ethnic background and class. There is no formal exclusion, but since the conversation may be unkind to other ethnic groups, they do run the risk of being antagonized. Even within the Italian group itself, those who are more or less acculturated than the rest stay away. The former are uncomfortable because they are "too American"; the latter, because they become embarrassed when the group makes fun of old-fashioned people. A woman with old-fashioned ideas is more acceptable than a man, since she is likely to keep quiet and not upset the group. Also, being old-fashioned is more of a virtue for women. The people who are mobile are kidded so much about their wealth that they come only rarely. Very mobile women are likely to be antagonized by references to wild or unwomanly ways, or by scornful stories about "society ladies." Those of lower status than the rest of the group are not rejected unless they are "bums," but remain away because they may be weighed down by problems that do not concern the others.

Single individuals often are part of the group even if they do not meet the standards of compatibility. Included because they are alone—a dread scourge in Italian culture—they nevertheless remain on the fringes of the group's conversational and other activities even though they are likely to be present more often than people with familial responsibilities. Our own participation in one of the peer groups was due in part to the fact that we were new to Boston and, having few friends in the city, were thought to be isolated somewhat like the single people in the group. The initial invitation was extended, however, because we were neighbors, and because the wives, who had met across the fire-escape, took a liking to each other.

The peer group meets regularly in the kitchens and living rooms of innumerable West End apartments. There are no formal invitations or advance notifications; people arrive regularly one or more evenings a week. Generally speaking, the same people come the same days of the week. Certain evenings are thus reserved for being with the peer group, and the gathering is called off only for unusual events.

While a few people may come for dinner, the gatherings usually begin shortly afterwards and others may drop in all through the evening. The talk goes on for hours—often past midnight—even though the men

[4] The reasons are discussed on [p. 61].

have to be at work early the next morning. As noted earlier, the sexes remain separate most of the evening, and, even when they gather around the kitchen table for coffee and cake, the men often sit at one end, the women at the other. Some people bring their children, especially if they do not have older ones who can stay home with the younger ones. The children sit and listen until they become sleepy, and then are sent off to the bedrooms until their parents leave.

The peer group conversation covers a relatively small number of topics: accounts of the participants' activities since the last gathering; news of people they all know; plans for special events such as weddings, showers, and other celebrations; current topics of interest; stories and anecdotes; and memories of younger days or highlights of the more recent past. Quite often, a current happening will set off talk about the past, and people contribute stories of parallel events that took place earlier. From there, it is easy to drift into talk about the good old days. The conversation also may turn to reports—and judgments—of deviant behavior. In addition, advice is exchanged, but there is little systematic attempt at problem-solving. Usually, people discuss problems encountered by others, especially those who are not present at the gathering. Problems common to the group as a whole also enter the conversation. I was always surprised, however, that what I thought to be the most pressing problem—redevelopment and relocation—received relatively little attention. Most West Enders felt that as there was not much they could do about this, there was little sense in discussing an unpleasant reality. This principle also covers the discussion of problems in general. The men talk about current happenings at work, in sports, in the area, and occasionally in the city and the country. But there is little concern with politics, except when events have occurred that illustrate once again the West Enders' belief that politics is corrupt. The women talk about housekeeping, child-rearing, and other subjects relevant to their occupational role.

Much of the conversation is devoted to the exchange of reportage— and gossip—about people known to the group. As noted earlier, every peer group is tied, through kinship, friendship, or other connections to many other groups and individuals in a giant network that extends far beyond the West End. Thus, someone may have a report about someone else, even if he does not know the individual personally. For example, one evening, the conversation concerned a woman who had recently had a child, many years after having the last one. One of the women at the table reported that she had heard about the blessed event, though she had never met the mother, and did not know that she was the hostess' neighbor. As it turned out, she was friendly with a relative of the new mother, and had heard about it from her. That she did not know the mother personally was irrelevant; knowing her sister and some other relatives was quite sufficient.

The exchange of news has a number of functions. It keeps people up-to-date on what is going on among present and potential peer group members, and defines or redefines the place of the reporter and his audience in this large group. It also provides for social control, since deviant behavior is reported and evaluated quite fully. And, at the same time, it considers new ideas that might be useful to the group. Moreover, it supplies information about services and "experts" in a culture that suspects or rejects the professional expert provided by the outside world. Thus the constant flow of news holds the network of peer groups together and makes it easier for West Enders to do without formal community organizations—either their own or those of the outside world. Finally, the reportage and gossip provide entertainment and drama about one's own group of the kind that is available about other groups in soap operas and similar mass media fiction.

As the hours pass, the talk shifts back and forth. And while there are people who dominate the conversation, and others who contribute little, there is generally an opportunity during the long evening for everyone to talk, either to tell a story or to deliver an opinion. Conversation is interspersed with discussion and argument, although the arguments are generally over matters of current or past history rather than over opinions. Should there be radical disagreement about a substantive topic, say, race relations or birth control, the conversation comes to a sudden halt and the subject is changed. For reasons that will become apparent, West Enders are not attuned to the give-and-take of discussion, and, since the expression of highly diverse opinions on important issues could split the group, this is thus avoided by changing the subject.

The conversation therefore is cued to topics that will keep exchange and individual contributions flowing; those that do not lend themselves to this social function are quickly dropped. Midway in the study, for example, we spent two weeks in Puerto Rico, and, after our return, were invited to tell about the trip. As it turned out, however, there was little interest either in the trip, or in descriptions of Puerto Rico; West Enders were more curious as to how it felt being back in the group. The story that my wallet had been stolen on the last day of the trip did arouse great interest, and, for more than an hour afterwards, people talked about thefts which they had experienced or heard. This topic in turn led to some anecdotes about the honest poor, who gave rewards for the return of lost or stolen items, and the greedy rich, who did not.

On ceremonial and holiday occasions, the gathering of the group is more formal. On birthdays, saints' days, other religious holidays, and of course at weddings, christenings, and first communion celebrations, everyone in the entire family circle tries to be present, including members of the parental generation. At such times, the food is more lavish and gifts may be given. During the year, the group also may go out to restaurants or night clubs to watch a popular performer.

Peer group life also extends beyond the family circle, and some West Enders participate in informal cliques and in clubs made up of unrelated people. For example, unmarried men may spend their evenings at clubs in which they play cards during the week, and hold dances and parties on the weekends; married men may go out once or twice a week for a night with the boys. In addition, many women belong to informal

—and nameless—clubs that meet weekly, biweekly, or monthly at each other's houses on a rotating basis, and hold dinners at downtown restaurants on special occasions. Some of the clubs, many of whose members have known each other since adolescence, were formed after the women became wives, and have continued to meet regularly for more than a decade since then. In number, and in the amount of time devoted to them, however, these groups are much less important than the family circle. The remainder of the chapter refers mainly to the latter.

THE INDIVIDUAL AND THE GROUP

Although peer group sociability is prevalent in middle-class society, it is not as important as it is in the West End. I have already indicated the central role of the peer group throughout the life cycle, and I have hinted repeatedly at the emotional as well as social importance of the group in everyday life. One fact, then, should be obvious: West Enders live within the group; they do not like to be alone. Thus, what has been noted earlier about teenagers—that they are quiet and passive by themselves and burst into activity only with their peers—is true almost as much among adults. Indeed, for most West Enders, people who have been trained from childhood to function solely within the group, being alone brings discomfort and ultimately fear. The discomfort was expressed by housewives who got their housework done quickly so as to be able "to visit." It was expressed more strongly by people who feared that the destruction of the West End would tear them away from their group and leave them isolated. It was expressed perhaps most vividly by a corner boy who explained to his friends that a prison sentence was bad "because it separates you from friends and family."

Yet the peer group is important not only because it provides this much desired companionship and the feeling of belongingness, but because it also allows its members to be individuals, and to express that individuality. In fact, it is only within the peer group that people can do so. In the middle class, people can exist as individuals outside a group, and enter a group to accomplish personal as well as shared ends. Among the West Enders, however, people grow up within a group and use it to be individuals, with the result that this group cannot work together. This is the basic paradox of the peer group society. In unraveling it below, I hope to show also some of the differences between West End and middle-class social structure and personality.

Although the peer group is the most important entity in the West Ender's life, he is not merely a robot whose actions are determined by the group or the cultural tradition. In fact, peer group life in many ways is just the opposite of the cohesive and tightly-knit group that has served as a model for descriptions of primary relations in other societies. It is a spirited competition of individuals "jockeying" for respect, power, and status. Indeed, to the outside observer, West Enders appear to be involved in a never ending dialectic: individual actions take them out of the group momentarily and are followed by restraints that bring them back, only to be succeeded by more individuating talk or behavior. Peer group members act as if they were held together by ties of rubber, which they alternately stretch and relax, but rarely break.

This is most visible among the teenage and young adult action-seekers. Within the group their behavior is a series of competitive encounters intended to assert the superiority and skillfulness of one individual over the other, which take the form of card games, short physical scuffles, and endless verbal duels. Through bragging, teasing, wisecracking, and insulting, individuals express their own verbal strength and skill, while denigrating the characteristics and achievements of others. Only when there is a common opponent does the group coalesce, but even then this is not always likely to happen. For example, among the young adults whom I observed at a tavern where they hung out nightly, a basketball team broke up because the better players did not want to play on a team with the poorer ones, who would deny them the opportunity to display their individual talents.

While there is no physical competition among the adult groups, and even card games are rare, similar competition does exist, although in considerably muted form. One of the women's clubs in the area made an explicit agreement that members should not compete among each other in the purchase of house furnishings and furniture. At the same time, however, one of them told me that she spent more than a day to bake and clean house when the club met at her apartment. She did not consider this competitive activity. Most of the competitive play takes place in conversation, through an exchange of anecdotes that display the story teller's exploits, and of jokes and wisecracks that entertain the group while making one person stand out. The exchange is not vicious, nor is it used by self-centered people to call attention to themselves, or to make others look bad. In fact, any attempt by an insecure person to build himself up in the group at others' expense is considered out of place. It is politely ignored in his presence, and harshly criticized when he is out of earshot.

Group members—be they adult or adolescent—display themselves to the group, to show their peers that they are as good if not slightly better than the rest, but then they yield the floor to the next person and allow him to do likewise. The purpose of this is to create mild envy among the rest of the group. The settlement house worker who pointed this out to me was in charge of a kindergarten at the time, and illustrated her point by noting that whereas Jewish mothers came to find out how their children were doing, and what help the teacher could give them, Italian parents came to find out how well their offspring were doing compared with others, and to get praise about them from the teacher.

Individual display takes place not only in group interaction, but also in many other ways. One is conspicuous consumption. West Enders of both sexes like to display themselves in new clothes, which are bought regularly at Easter and Christmas and for other special occasions. The men do the same with their cars, either by purchasing new ones, or by continuously polishing the old ones. The women like to display their cooking and baking skills. And the most talented of both sexes try to become entertainers. Thus, although an interest in art is considered effeminate, there is nothing wrong if boys want to become singers of popular music, for this is an opportunity for self-display. In fact, most of the successful white singers today are Italians, and it is no accident that they are as much creators of a distinctive personal image as they are purveyors of songs. Italians have done well in contemporary popular music because it emphasizes the development of an individual image and style more than technical musical skill.[5]

The need for display within the group is so strong among West Enders, in fact, that they find themselves unable to save because of their high expenditures of food, clothing, and other expenses of group life. I heard some criticism of recent Italian immigrants who failed to participate in this pattern, and who saved their money to buy a house after living only a few years in America. Although redevelopment would force many renters to become homeowners, and the need to save money for the future had become apparent, the native-born West Enders were unable to withdraw sufficiently from the group display to put any money aside. Nor would they have seriously considered this alternative.

It should be noted that what I have called conspicuous consumption and display is not to be equated with the kind of consumption competition which has been noted among the *nouveau riche,* or among the American Indian tribes given to pot-latches. The West Enders do not seek to outdo all others, and thus be the best or numerically the greatest in these displays. Rather, they want to show themselves off, without questioning the right and ability of everyone else to do much the same.

Two other expressions of West End individualism are the rejection of formal dependence on the group, and the emphasis on the mutual nature of obligations. Despite the fact that West Enders live so much within a group, they feel that they cannot and do not want to depend on it for help. People say that "in the last analysis, you have to depend on yourself." They are loath to ask for favors from others, even within the family circle, and much more so from organized charity. The emphasis on independence is based partly on a realistic appraisal that others can extend only a limited amount of help, and that it would be unrealistic to depend on them. When economic deprivations strike one member of a low-income population, they are likely to hit others as well. Moreover, if other troubles arise, such as illness, they are apt to be serious ones. Although West Enders will offer and accept help, they do not cherish being dependent on others. They want to remain independent, for accepting aid is thought to reflect on the strength of the individual, and is thus a reflection on self-respect which places the dependent person in an inferior position.

---

[5] Incidentally, despite the popular stereotype, there was little interest in opera among the West Enders. If such interest had existed among Southern Italians and Sicilians, it disappeared with the first generation.

Moreover, giving and receiving—of help or gifts—involves the individual in a spiral of reciprocatory obligations. The obligation may be latent, in which case people feel a desire to give and receive, and enjoy the resulting reciprocity. Or it may be manifest, thus becoming a duty. In this case reciprocity can turn into a burden, and people try to escape involvement. This happens most often with representatives from the outside world, like welfare agencies and settlement houses, who want to give aid in exchange for deference or loyalty to institutions.

Among close friends and relatives, goods and services are exchanged freely and obligations remain latent, unless one or the other person falls seriously behind in reciprocating, or unless the exchange becomes competitive. Should someone reciprocate with a more expensive gift than he originally received, he may be suspected of showing off, or of trying to make the other person look bad. If it continues, this can lead to an eventual alienation from the group.

When relationships are not close, obligations are manifest. For example, after a man had done some electrical work for his sister, she invited him to dinner several times as payment for the work—which he had done for nothing. Although she was not formally required to reciprocate, since he was her brother, she wanted to do so because she felt it to be the proper thing. This brother had married an upwardly mobile woman, and was not part of the immediate family circle.

When obligations concern authority figures and hierarchical relationships, the rejection of dependence becomes stronger, and often evolves into fear of domination. Thus, whereas West Enders will subordinate themselves to someone whom they recognize as a leader, they will bitterly reject the individual who is imposed as a leader from the outside— or who tries to impose himself.

As relationships within the peer group society are expected to be equalitarian, no one is permitted to dominate anyone else. Someone who attempts to do so is suspected of wanting to exploit, to get something that he does not deserve and cannot get in any other way. This attitude, which governs almost completely relationships with the outside world, also crops up in dealings with other West Enders. For example, one morning, two cars approached each other on a West End street temporarily restricted to one lane and came so close that neither could pass the other. A five-minute discussion then followed of who would back up to let the other through. At the height of the argument, one said to the other, "We've been friends for years but you can't command me." Such struggles are frequent when West Enders relate to each other in roles that are outside the normal range of those encountered in peer group relations. Thus, if landlords who invited friends to take apartments in their buildings had to act as landlords, by raising the rent or by cutting down on maintenance, it was often done at the cost of broken friendships.

Although the peer group is a theater for individual expression, it is also characterized by strict control of deviant behavior. This is all the more important when individualistic striving is central to the group, for there is always the possibility that the group may be disrupted, which in turn would shut off further opportunity for individual display. The major mechanisms of social control are criticism, the expectation of criticism, and the not always successful attempts by individuals to maintain self-control.

Since everyone knows everyone else, life is an open book, and deviant acts are hard to hide. This means that such acts are committed either outside the reaches of the group—as in the case of adolescents who do their misbehaving outside the West End—or that they are not committed at all. As noted earlier, much of the group conversation is devoted to judging behavior, and any unusual behavior, whether deviant or innovating, is likely to be criticized. Jokes and wisecracks, a polite way of questioning deviant behavior, usually suffice to bring the individual back into line. Similarly, the individual is expected to keep up with the activities of the group, and the pattern of individual display. The person who is too noisy or dominating is suspect, but so is the one who is too quiet. The hostess who sets too lavish a table is criticized, but even more so is the person who is unwilling to entertain or feed the group in the style to which it is accustomed.

But as so much of life is based on routine, there is little incentive for nonconforming behavior. Thus most conformity is quite voluntary. But West Enders also regulate their conduct by involuntary conformity of the type expressed in the phrase "what will the neighbors think." Indeed, the expectations of what other people will think are extremely harsh; they assume the blackest thoughts and deeds possible. For example, a neighbor who had recently had a baby carried the baby carriage up several flights, rather than leaving it in an empty store that served as storage room for several adjacent apartment buildings. She justified her behavior by explaining that, since the storage room was not in her own building, people might think she was going in there to steal something. Similarly, the woman described earlier who had never entered her relative's apartment because she felt people would suspect them of having sexual relations, was certain that they believed this to be the case anyway. Politicians complain that they, too, are believed to act only on the basest motives. While the exaggerated expectations do constitute a potent control against deviant behavior, they create, at the same time, an unspoken atmosphere of mutual recrimination, in which everyone is likely to expect the worst from everyone else. It must be noted, however, that such expectations are usually not held about peer group members, but only about people who are less close—neighbors, for example.

It is clear that the ascription of evil motives and deeds stems not from observations of the neighbors' behavior or inferences from their conversations, but from the individual himself. He projects on the neighbors his underlying fear that he himself might do evil things or harbor evil motives. For although West Enders believe that fate regulates actions over which they have no say, their own behavior is thought to be self-determined. For example, crime, such deviances as homosexuality, overt forms of mental illness—and even fits of depression—are thought to be caused by lack of self-control.

The West Ender therefore is frequently concerned over his ability to control himself.[6] Among the adolescents and the action-seeking adults, the main concern is to stay out of "trouble"—which means not only to avoid getting caught by the police or by other agents of social control, but also not going out of control in episodic behavior, for this might detach the individual from the group. Among routine-seeking people, uncontrolled behavior is less of a problem. Their concern is to avoid getting into situations that could be misinterpreted. In short, the individual must control himself so that he cannot be suspected of negatively evaluated behavior, either by the group or by himself.

The definition of deviant behavior comes initially from the group itself, and the group encourages individuals to shame each other into conformity through overt criticism. As in all other groups, this criticism is often anticipated by expectations in the individual. Thus, one West Ender said one night, when he was eager to leave the female half of the family circle: "If I don't go back to the living room [and the male company] they'll start talking about me." West Enders seem to differ from middle-class people in that the individual's own preoccupation with self-control results in highly exaggerated—and sometimes unwarranted—expectations of what others think of him. This in turn is an effective device for limiting deviant behavior.

But whether social control is imposed from within or without, the middle-class stereotype of working-class society is in error. What the neighbors think is just as important to the West Ender as to the newest recruit to suburbia. If anything, social control is more strict than in the middle class, and nonconformity is not as easily excused.

In view of the severity of social control, it would be easy to caricature peer group life as a prison for its members. To the outsider, the concern with social control and self-control might indeed seem oppressive. But he must also take into account that there is little desire for voluntary nonconformity, and, consequently, little need to require involuntary conformity. Nor do people seem to be troubled by fears about the breakdown of self-control, or about the possibility that they may be suspected of misdeeds. Although these potentialities do lurk under the surface, they do not usually disturb the positive tenor of group relations. Such fears, of course, may be private preoccupations, less visible to the sociol-

[6] The concern with self-control is graphically illustrated in Joseph Caruso, *The Priest*, New York: Popular Library, 1958. This novel, written by a West Ender, deals with a priest whose unsuccessful attempt to control impulses of lust and violence drives him into renouncing his post. In the end, he returns to his duties because of peer group pressure. For empirical studies of Italian-American self-control problems, see M. K. Opler and J. L. Singer, "Ethnic Differences in Behavior and Psychopathology," *International Journal of Social Psychiatry*, vol. 2 (1956), pp. 11–22; and Ezra F. Vogel, "The Marital Relationships of Parents of Emotionally Disturbed Children," unpublished Ph.D. Dissertation, Harvard University, 1958, Chap. 6.

ogist than they would be to the clinical psychologist. Moreover, the people who are seriously troubled by these fears shun the kind of group I have discussed.

Tensions and problems exist in the peer group, as in every other group, but they are overshadowed by the gratifications that it provides for the individual. Perhaps the best illustration of this was given by a young man who was suffering from an ulcer, and was faced with a choice between his health and his group. As he explained it: "I can't stop drinking when I'm with my friends; I eat and drink like they do and when I'm alone I take care of my ulcer. But I don't care if it kills me; if it does, that's it."

In summary, social relationships within the peer group follow a narrow path between individualistic display and strictly enforced social control. The group is set up to provide its members with an opportunity for displaying, expressing, and acting out their individuality, as long as this does not become too extreme.

As a result, the peer group is unable to work together to achieve a common goal unless it is shared by all members of the group. Since the main function of the group is to provide an area for individual display, the members are less interested in activities that require working together than in impressing each other. Moreover, if group tasks, especially those of a novel nature, are suggested, people become fearful that they will be used as pawns by an individual who will gain the most from this activity. Consequently, the inability to participate in joint activities does inhibit community organization, even when it concerns the very survival of the group, as it did in the clearance of the West End.

. . .

FROM THE URBAN CONDITION:
GRIEVING FOR A LOST HOME

MARC FRIED

INTRODUCTION

For some time we have known that the forced dislocation from an urban slum is a highly disruptive and disturbing experience. This is implicit in the strong, positive attachments to the former slum residential area —in the case of this study the West End of Boston—and in the continued attachment to the area among those who left before any imminent danger of eviction. Since we were observing people in the midst of a crisis, we were all too ready to modify our impressions and to conclude that these were likely to be transitory reactions. But the post-relocation experiences of a great many people have borne out their most pessimistic pre-relocation expectations. There are wide variations in the success of post-relocation adjustment and considerable variability in the depth and quality of the loss experience. But for the majority it seems quite precise to speak of their reactions as expressions of *grief*. These are manifest in the feelings of painful loss, the continued longing, the general depressive tone, frequent symptoms of psychological or social or somatic distress, the active work required in adapting to the altered situation, the sense of helplessness, the occasional expressions of both direct and displaced anger, and tendencies to idealize the lost place.[1]

At their most extreme, these reactions of grief are intense, deeply felt, and, at times, overwhelming. In response to a series of questions concerning the feelings of sadness and depression which people experienced *after* moving, many replies were unambiguous: "I felt as though I had lost everything," "I felt like my heart was taken out of me," "I felt like taking the gaspipe," "I lost all the friends I knew," "I always felt I had to go home to the West End and even now I feel like crying when I pass by," "Something of me went with the West End," "I felt cheated," "What's the use of thinking about it," "I threw up a lot," "I had a nervous breakdown." Certainly, some people were overjoyed with the change and many felt no sense of loss. Among 250 women, however, 26 per cent report that they still feel sad or depressed two years later, and another 20 per cent report a long period (six months to two years) of sadness or depression. Altogether, therefore, at least 46 per cent give evidence of a fairly severe grief reaction or worse. And among 316 men, the data show only a slightly smaller percentage (38 per cent) with long-term

Excerpted from Chapter 12, "Grieving for a Lost Home," by Marc Fried, in *The Urban Condition*, edited by Leonard J. Duhl, M.D., © 1963 by Basic Books, Inc., Publishers, New York, pp. 151–164, 167–170.

grief reactions. The true proportion of depressive reactions is undoubtedly higher since many women and men who report no feelings of sadness or depression indicate clearly depressive responses to other questions.

In answer to another question, "How did you feel when you saw or heard that the building you had lived in was torn down?" a similar finding emerges. As in the previous instance, the responses are often quite extreme and most frequently quite pathetic. They range from those who replied: "I was glad because the building had rats," to moderate responses such as "the building was bad but I felt sorry," and "I didn't want to see it go," to the most frequent group comprising such reactions as "it was like a piece being taken from me," "I felt terrible," "I used to stare at the spot where the building stood," "I was sick to my stomach." This question in particular, by its evocative quality, seemed to stir up sad memories even among many people who denied any feelings of sadness or depression. The difference from the previous result is indicated by the fact that 54 per cent of the women and 46 per cent of the men report severely depressed or disturbed reactions; 19 per cent of the women and about 31 per cent of the men report satisfaction or indifference; and 27 per cent of the women and 23 per cent of the men report moderately depressed or ambivalent feelings. Thus it is clear that, for the majority of those who were displaced from the West End, leaving their residential area involved a moderate or extreme sense of loss and an accompanying affective reaction of grief.

While these figures go beyond any expectation which we had or which is clearly implied in other studies, the realization that relocation was a crisis with potential danger to mental health for many people was one of the motivating factors for this investigation.* In studying the impact of relocation on the lives of a working-class population through a comparison of pre-relocation and post-relocation interview data, a number of issues arise concerning the psychology of urban living which have received little systematic attention. Yet, if we are to understand the effects of relocation and the significance of the loss of a residential environment, it is essential that we have a deeper appreciation of the psychological implications of both physical and social aspects of residential experience. Thus we are led to formulations which deal with the functions and meanings of the residential area in the lives of working-class people.

THE NATURE OF THE LOSS IN RELOCATION: THE SPATIAL FACTOR

Any severe loss may represent a disruption in one's relationship to the past, to the present, and to the future. Losses generally bring about fragmentation of routines, of relationships, and of expectations, and

* This is implicit in the prior work on "crisis" and situational predicaments by Dr. Erich Lindemann under whose initiative the current work was undertaken and carried out.

frequently imply an alteration in the world of physically available objects and spatially oriented action. It is a disruption in that sense of continuity which is ordinarily a taken-for-granted framework for functioning in a universe which has temporal, social, and spatial dimensions. From this point of view, the loss of an important place represents a change in a potentially significant component of the experience of continuity.

But why should the loss of a place, even a very important place, be so critical for the individual's sense of continuity; and why should grief at such loss be so widespread a phenomenon? In order to clarify this, it is necessary to consider the meaning which this area, the West End of Boston, had for the lives of its inhabitants. In an earlier paper we tried to assess this, and came to conclusions which corroborate, although they go further, the results from the few related studies.

> In studying the reasons for satisfaction that the majority of slum residents experience, two major components have emerged. On the one hand, the residential area is the region in which a vast and interlocking set of social networks is localized. And, on the other, the physical area has considerable meaning as an extension of home, in which various parts are delineated and structured on the basis of a sense of belonging. These two components provide the context in which the residential area may so easily be invested with considerable, multiply-determined meaning. . . . the greatest proportion of this working-class group . . . shows a fairly common experience and usage of the residential area . . . dominated by a conception of the local area beyond the dwelling unit as an integral part of home. This view of an area as home and the significance of local people and local places are so profoundly at variance with typical middle-class orientations that it is difficult to appreciate the intensity of meaning, the basic sense of identity involved in living in the particular area.[2]

Nor is the intense investment of a residential area, both as an important physical space and as the locus for meaningful interpersonal ties, limited to the West End.[3] What is common to a host of studies is the evidence for the integrity of the urban, working-class, slum community as a social and spatial unit. It is the sense of belonging someplace, in a particular place which is quite familiar and easily delineated, in a wide area in which one feels "at home." This is the core of meaning of the local area. And this applies for many people who have few close relationships within the area. Even familiar and expectable streets and houses, faces at the window and people walking by, personal greetings and impersonal sounds may serve to designate the concrete foci of a sense of belonging somewhere and may provide special kinds of interpersonal and social meaning to a region one defines as "home."

It would be impossible to understand the reactions both to dislocation and to relocation and, particularly, the depth and frequency of grief responses without taking account of working-class orientations to residential areas. One of our primary theses is that the strength of the grief reaction to the loss of the West End is largely a function of prior orientations to the area. Thus, we certainly expect to find that the greater a person's pre-relocation commitment to the area, the more likely he is to react with marked grief. This prediction is confirmed again and again by the data.* † For the women, among those who had said they liked living in the West End *very much* during the pre-location interviews, 73 per cent evidence a severe post-relocation grief reaction; among those who had less extreme but positive feelings about living in the West End, 53 per cent show a similar order of grief; and among those who were ambivalent or negative about the West End, only 34 per cent show a severe grief reaction. Or, considering a more specific feature of our formulation, the pre-relocation view of the West End as "home" shows an even stronger relationship to the depth of post-relocation grief. Among those women who said they had no real home, only 20 per cent give evidence of severe grief; among those who claimed some other area as their real home, 34 per cent fall into the severe grief category; but among the women for whom the *West End* was the real home, 68 per cent report severe grief reactions. Although the data for the men are less complete, the results are substantially similar. It is also quite understandable that the length of West End residence should bear a strong relationship to the loss reaction, although it is less powerful than some of the other findings and almost certainly it is not the critical component.

More directly relevant to our emphasis on the importance of places,

* The analysis involves a comparison of information from interviews administered *before* relocation with a depth of grief index derived from follow-up interviews approximately two years *after* relocation. The pre-relocation interviews were administered to a randomly selected sample of 473 women from households in this area at the time the land was taken by the city. The post-relocation interviews were completed with 92 per cent of the women who had given pre-relocation interviews and with 87 per cent of the men from those households in which there was a husband in the household. Primary emphasis will be given to the results with the women since we do not have as full a range of pre-relocation information for the men. However, since a split schedule was used for the post-relocation interviews, the depth of grief index is available for only 259 women.

† Dr. Jason Aronson was largely responsible for developing the series of questions on grief. The opening question of the series was: Many people have told us that just after they moved they felt sad or depressed. Did you feel this way? This was followed by three specific questions on which the index was based: (1) Would you describe how you felt? (2) How long did these feelings last? (3) How did you feel when you saw or heard that the building you had lived in was torn down? Each person was given a score from 1 to 4 on the basis of the coded responses to these questions and the scores were summated. For purposes of analysis, we divided the final scores into three groups: minimal grief, moderate grief, and severe or marked grief. The phrasing of these questions appears to dispose the respondent to give a "grief" response. In fact, however, there is a tendency to reject the idea of "sadness" among many people who show other evidence of a grief response. In cross-tabulating the "grief" scores with a series of questions in which there is no suggestion of sadness, unhappiness, or dissatisfaction, it is clear that the grief index is the more severe criterion. Those who are classified in the severe grief category almost invariably show severe grief reactions by any of the other criteria; but many who are categorized as "minimal grief" on the index fall into the extremes of unhappiness or dissatisfaction on the other items.

it is quite striking that the greater the area of the West End which was known, the more likely there is to be a severe grief response. Among the women who said they knew only their own block during the pre-relocation interview, only 13 per cent report marked grief; at the other extreme, among those who knew most of the West End, 64 per cent have a marked grief reaction. This relationship is maintained when a wide range of interrelated variables is held constant. Only in one instance, when there is a generally negative orientation to the West End, does more extensive knowledge of the area lead to a somewhat smaller proportion of severe grief responses. Thus, the wider an individual's familiarity with the local area, the greater his commitment to the locality. This wider familiarity evidently signifies a greater sense of the wholeness and integrity of the entire West End and, we would suggest, a more expanded sense of being "at home" throughout the entire local region. It is striking, too, that while familiarity with, use of, and comfort in the spatial regions of the residential area are closely related to extensiveness of personal contact, the spatial patterns have independent significance and represent an additional basis for a feeling of commitment to that larger, local region which is "home."

THE SENSE OF SPATIAL IDENTITY

In stressing the importance of places and access to local facilities, we wish only to redress the almost total neglect of spatial dimensions in dealing with human behavior. We certainly do not mean thereby to give too little emphasis to the fundamental importance of interpersonal relationships and social organization in defining the meaning of the area. Nor do we wish to underestimate the significance of cultural orientations and social organization in defining the character and importance of spatial dimensions. However, the crisis of loss of a residential area brings to the fore the importance of the local spatial region and alerts us to the greater generality of spatial conceptions as determinants of behavior. In fact, we might say that a *sense of spatial identity* is fundamental to human functioning. It represents a phenomenal or ideational integration of important experiences concerning environmental arrangements and contacts in relation to the individual's conception of his own body in space.* It is based on spatial memories, spatial imagery, the spatial framework of current activity, and the implicit spatial components of ideals and aspirations.

It appears to us also that these feelings of being at home and of belonging are, in the working class, integrally tied to a *specific* place. We

* Erik Erikson . . . includes spatial components in discussing the sense of ego identity and his work has influenced the discussion of spatial variables. In distinguishing the sense of spatial identity from the sense of ego identity, I am suggesting that variations in spatial identity do not correspond exactly to variations in ego identity. By separating these concepts, it becomes possible to study their interrelationships empirically.

would not expect similar effects or, at least, effects of similar proportion in a middle-class area. Generally speaking, an integrated sense of spatial identity in the middle class is not as contingent on the external stability of place or as dependent on the localization of social patterns, interpersonal relationships, and daily routines. In these data, in fact, there is a marked relationship between class status and depth of grief; the higher the status, by any of several indices, the smaller the proportions of severe grief. It is primarily in the working class, and largely because of the importance of external stability, that dislocation from a familiar residential area has so great an effect on fragmenting the sense of spatial identity.

External stability is also extremely important in interpersonal patterns within the working class. And dislocation and relocation involve a fragmentation of the external bases for interpersonal relationships and group networks. Thus, relocation undermines the established interpersonal relationships and group ties of the people involved and, in effect, destroys the sense of group identity of a great many individuals. "Group identity," a concept originally formulated by Erik Erikson, refers to the individual's sense of belonging, of being a part of larger human and social entities. It may include belonging to organizations or interpersonal networks with which a person is directly involved; and it may refer to "membership" in social groups with whom an individual has little overt contact, whether it be a family, a social class, an ethnic collectivity, a profession, or a group of people sharing a common ideology. What is common to these various patterns of group identity is that they represent an integrated sense of shared human qualities, of some sense of communality with other people which is essential for meaningful social functioning. Since, most notably in the working class, effective relationships with others are dependent upon a continuing sense of common group identity, the experience of loss and disruption of these affiliations is intense and frequently irrevocable. On the grounds, therefore, of both spatial and interpersonal orientations and commitments, dislocation from the residential area represents a particularly marked disruption in the sense of continuity for the majority of this group.

THE NATURE OF THE LOSS IN RELOCATION:
SOCIAL AND PERSONAL FACTORS

Previously we said that by emphasizing the spatial dimension of the orientation to the West End, we did not mean to diminish the importance of social patterns in the experience of the local area and their effects on post-relocation loss reactions. Nor do we wish to neglect personality factors involved in the widespread grief reactions. It is quite clear that pre-relocation social relationships and intrapsychic dispositions *do* affect the depth of grief in response to leaving the West End. The strongest of these patterns is based on the association between depth of grief and pre-relocation feelings about neighbors. Among those women who had very positive feelings about their neighbors, 76 per cent show severe grief reactions; among those who were positive but less extreme, 56 per cent show severe grief; and among those who were relatively negative, 38 per cent have marked grief responses. Similarly, among the women whose five closest friends lived in the West End, 67 per cent show marked grief; among those whose friends were mostly in the West End or equally distributed inside and outside the area, 55 per cent have severe grief reactions; and among those whose friends were mostly or all outside, 44 per cent show severe grief.

The fact that these differences, although great, are not as consistently powerful as the differences relating to spatial use patterns does not necessarily imply the *greater* importance of spatial factors. If we hold the effect of spatial variables constant and examine the relationship between depth of grief and the interpersonal variables, it becomes apparent that the effect of interpersonal contacts on depth of grief is consistent regardless of differences in spatial orientation; and, likewise, the effect of spatial orientations on depth of grief is consistent regardless of differences in interpersonal relationships. Thus, each set of factors contributes independently to the depth of grief in spite of some degree of internal relationship. In short, we suggest that *either* spatial identity or group identity may be a critical focus of loss of continuity and thereby lead to severe grief; but if *both* bases for the sense of continuity are localized *within the residential area* the disruption of continuity is greater, and the proportions of marked grief correspondingly higher.

It is noteworthy that, apart from local interpersonal and social relationships and local spatial orientations and use (and variables which are closely related to these), there are few other social or personal factors in the pre-relocation situation which are related to depth of grief. These negative findings are of particular importance in emphasizing that not all the variables which influence the grief reaction to dislocation are of equal importance. It should be added that a predisposition to depression markedly accentuates the depth of grief in response to the loss of one's residential area. But it is also clear that prior depressive orientations do not account for the entire relationship. The effects of the general depressive orientation and of the social, interpersonal, and spatial relationships within the West End are essentially additive; both sets of factors contribute markedly to the final result. Thus, among the women with a severe depressive orientation, an extremely large proportion (81 per cent) of those who regarded the West End as their real home show marked grief. But among the women without a depressive orientation, only a moderate proportion (58 per cent) of those who similarly viewed the West End as home show severe grief. On the other hand, when the West End is not seen as the person's real home, an increasing severity of general depressive orientation does *not* lead to an increased proportion of severe grief reactions.

THE NATURE OF THE LOSS IN RELOCATION: CASE ANALYSES

The dependence of the sense of continuity on external resources in the working class, particularly on the availability and local presence of familiar places which have the character of "home," and of familiar people whose patterns of behavior and response are relatively predictable, does not account for all of the reaction of grief to dislocation. In addition to these factors, which may be accentuated by depressive predispositions, it is quite evident that the realities of *post*-relocation experience are bound to affect the perpetuation, quality, and depth of grief. And, in fact, our data show that there is a strong association between positive or negative experiences in the post-relocation situation and the proportions who show severe grief. But this issue is complicated by two factors: (1) the extent to which potentially meaningfully post-relocation circumstances can be a satisfying experience is *affected* by the degree and tenaciousness of previous commitments to the West End, and (2) the post-relocation "reality" is, in part, *selected* by the people who move and thus is a function of many personality factors, including the ability to anticipate needs, demands, and environmental opportunities.

In trying to understand the effects of pre-relocation orientations and post-relocation experiences of grief, we must bear in mind that the grief reactions we have described and analyzed are based on responses given approximately two years after relocation. Most people manage to achieve some adaptation to their experiences of loss and grief, and learn to deal with new situations and new experiences on their own terms. A wide variety of adaptive methods can be employed to salvage fragments of the sense of continuity, or to try to re-establish it on new grounds. Nonetheless, it is the tenaciousness of the imagery and affect of grief, despite these efforts at dealing with the altered reality, which is so strikingly similar to mourning for a lost person.

In coping with the sense of loss, some families tried to remain physically close to the area they knew, even though most of their close interpersonal relationships remain disrupted; and by this method, they appear often to have modified their feelings of grief. Other families try to move among relatives and maintain a sense of continuity through some degree of constancy in the external bases for their group identity. Yet others respond to the loss of place and people by accentuating the importance of those role relationships which remain. Thus, a number of women report increased closeness to their husbands, which they often explicitly relate to the decrease in the availability of other social relationships for both partners and which, in turn, modifies the severity of grief. In order to clarify some of the complexities of pre-relocation orientations and of post-relocation adjustments most concretely, a review of several cases may prove to be instructive.

It is evident that a very strong positive pre-relocation orientation to the West End is relatively infrequently associated with a complete absence of grief; and that, likewise, a negative pre-relocation orientation to the area is infrequently associated with a strong grief response. The two types which are numerically dominant are, in terms of rational expectations, consistent: those with strong positive feelings about the West End and severe grief; and those with negative feelings about the West End and minimal or moderate grief. The two "deviant" types, by the same token, are both numerically smaller and inconsistent: those with strong positive pre-relocation orientations and little grief; and those with negative pre-relocation orientations and severe grief. A closer examination of those "deviant" cases with strong pre-relocation commitment to the West End and minimal post-relocation grief often reveals either important reservations in their prior involvement with the West End or, more frequently, the denial or rejection of feelings of grief rather than their total absence. And the association of minimal pre-relocation commitment to the West End with a severe grief response often proves on closer examination to be a function of a deep involvement in the West End which is modified by markedly ambivalent statements; or, more generally, the grief reaction itself is quite modest and tenuous or is even a pseudo-grief which masks the primacy of dissatisfaction with the current area.

GRIEF PATTERNS: CASE EXAMPLES

In turning to case analysis, we shall concentrate on the specific factors which operate in families of all four types, those representing the two dominant and those representing the two deviant patterns.

1. The Figella family exemplifies the association of strong positive pre-relocation attachments to the West End and a severe grief reaction. This is the most frequent of all the patterns and, although the Figella family is only one "type" among those who show this pattern, they are prototypical of a familiar West End constellation.

Both Mr. and Mrs. Figella are second-generation Americans who were born and brought up in the West End. In her pre-relocation interview, Mrs. Figella described her feelings about living in the West End unambiguously: "It's a wonderful place, the people are friendly." She "loves everything about it" and anticipates missing her relatives above all. She is satisfied with her dwelling: "It's comfortable, clean and warm." And the marriage appears to be deeply satisfying for both husband and wife. They share many household activities and have a warm family life with their three children.

Both Mr. and Mrs. Figella feel that their lives have changed a great deal since relocation. They are clearly referring, however, to the pattern and conditions of their relationships with other people. Their home life has changed little except that Mr. Figella is home more. He continues to work at the same job as a manual laborer with a modest but sufficient income. While they have many economic insecurities, the relocation has not produced any serious financial difficulty for them.

In relocating, the Figella family bought a house. Both husband and wife are quite satisfied with the physical arrangements but, all in all, they are dissatisfied with the move. When asked what she dislikes about her present dwelling, Mrs. Figella replied simply and pathetically: "It's in Arlington and I want to be in the West End." Both Mr. and Mrs. Figella are outgoing, friendly people with a very wide circle of social contacts. Although they still see their relatives often, they both feel isolated from them and they regret the loss of their friends. As Mr. Figella puts it: "I come home from work and that's it. I just plant my-self in the house."

The Figella family is, in many respects, typical of a well-adjusted working-class family. They have relatively few ambitions for themselves or for their children. They continue in close contact with many people; but they no longer have the same extensiveness of mutual cooperation in household activities, they cannot "drop in" as casually as before, they do not have the sense of being surrounded by a familiar area and familiar people. Thus, while their objective situation is not dramatically altered, the changes do involve important elements of stability and continuity in their lives. They manifest the importance of externally available resources for an integral sense of spatial and group identity. However, they have always maintained a very close marital relationship, and their family provides a substantial basis for a sense of continuity. They can evidently cope with difficulties on the strength of their many internal and external resources. Nonetheless, they have suffered from the move, and find it extremely difficult to reorganize their lives com-pletely in adapting to a new geographical situation and new patterns of social affiliation. Their grief for a lost home seems to be one form of maintaining continuity on the basis of memories. While it prevents a more wholehearted adjustment to their altered lives, such adjustments would imply forsaking the remaining fragments of a continuity which was central to their conceptions of themselves and of the world.

2. There are many similarities between the Figella family and the Giuliano family. But Mrs. Giuliano shows relatively little pre-relocation commitment to the West End and little post-relocation grief. Mr. Giuliano was somewhat more deeply involved in the West End and, although satisfied with the change, feels that relocation was "like having the rug pulled out from under you." Mr. and Mrs. Giuliano are also second-generation Americans, of similar background to the Figellas'. But Mrs. Giuliano only moved to the West End at her marriage. Mrs. Giuliano had many objections to the area: "For me it is too congested. I never did care for it . . . too many barrooms, on every corner, too many families in one building. . . . The sidewalks are too narrow and the kids can't play outside." But she does expect to miss the stores and many favorite places. Her housing ambitions go beyond West End

standards and she wants more space inside and outside. She had no blood relatives in the West End but was close to her husband's family and had friends nearby.

Mr. Giuliano was born in the West End and he had many relatives in the area. He has a relatively high status manual job but only a modest income. His wife does not complain about this although she is only moderately satisfied with the marriage. In part she objected to the fact that they went out so little and that he spent too much time on the corner with his friends. His social networks in the West End were more extensive and involved than were Mrs. Giuliano's. And he missed the West End more than she did after the relocation. But even Mr. Giuliano says that, all in all, he is satisfied with the change.

Mrs. Giuliano feels the change is "wonderful." She missed her friends but got over it. And a few of Mr. Giuliano's hanging group live close by so they can continue to hang together. Both are satisfied with the house they bought although Mrs. Giuliano's ambitions have now gone beyond this. The post-relocation situation has led to an improved marital relationship: Mr. Giuliano is home more and they go out more together.

Mr. and Mrs. Giuliano exemplify a pattern which seems most likely to be associated with a beneficial experience from relocation. Unlike Mr. and Mrs. Figella, who completely accept their working-class status and are embedded in the social and cultural patterns of the working class, Mr. and Mrs. Giuliano show many evidences of social mobility. Mr. Giuliano's present job is, properly speaking, outside the working-class category because of its relatively high status and he himself does not "work with his hands." And Mrs. Giuliano's housing ambitions, preferences in social relationships, orientation to the class structure, and attitudes toward a variety of matters from shopping to child rearing are indications of a readiness to achieve middle-class status. Mr. Giuliano is prepared for and Mrs. Giuliano clearly desires "discontinuity" with some of the central bases for their former identity. Their present situation is, in fact, a transitional one which allows them to re-integrate their lives at a new and higher status level without too precipitate a change. And their marital relationship seems sufficiently meaningful to provide a significant core of continuity in the process of change in their patterns of social and cultural experience. The lack of grief in this case is quite understandable and appropriate to their patterns of social orientation and expectation. [Editor's note: The "deviant" examples have here been omitted.]

. . .

CONCLUSIONS

Grieving for a lost home is evidently a widespread and serious social phenomenon following in the wake of urban dislocation. It is likely to increase social and psychological "pathology" in a limited number of instances; and it is also likely to create new opportunities for some, and to increase the rate of social mobility for others. For the greatest number, dislocation is unlikely to have either effect but does lead to intense personal suffering despite moderately successful adaptation to the total situation of relocation. Under these circumstances, it becomes most critical that we face the realities of the effects of relocation on working-class residents of slums and, on the basis of knowledge and understanding, that we learn to deal more effectively with the problems engendered.

In evaluating these data on the effect of pre-location experiences on post-relocation reactions of grief, we have arrived at a number of conclusions:

1. The affective reaction to the loss of the West End can be quite precisely described as a grief response showing most of the characteristics of grief and mourning for a lost person.

2. One of the important components of the grief reaction is the fragmentation of the sense of spatial identity. This is manifest not only in the pre-location experience of the spatial area as an expanded "home," but in the varying degrees of grief following relocation, arising from variations in the pre-relocation orientation to and use of local spatial regions.

3. Another component, of equal importance, is the dependence of the sense of group identity on stable social networks. Dislocation necessarily led to the fragmentation of this group identity which was based, to such a large extent, on the external availability and overt contact with familiar groups of people.

4. Associated with these "cognitive" components, described as the sense of spatial identity and the sense of group identity, are strong affective qualities. We have not tried to delineate them but they appear to fall into the realm of a feeling of security in and commitment to the external spatial and group patterns which are the tangible, visible aspects of these identity components. However, a predisposition to depressive reactions also markedly affects the depth of grief reaction.

5. Theoretically, we can speak of spatial and group identity as critical foci of the sense of continuity. This sense of continuity is not *necessarily* contingent on the external stability of place, people, and security or support. But for the working class these concrete, external resources and the experience of stability, availability, and familiarity which they provide are essential for a meaningful sense of continuity. Thus, dislocation and the loss of the residential area represent a fragmentation of some of the essential components of the sense of continuity in the working class.

It is in the light of these observations and conclusions that we must consider problems of social planning which are associated with the changes induced by physical planning for relocation. Urban planning cannot be limited to "bricks and mortar." While these data tell us little about the importance of housing or the aspects of housing which are important, they indicate that considerations of a non-housing nature are critical. There is evidence, for example, that the frequency of the grief response is not affected by such housing factors as increase or decrease in apartment size or home ownership. But physical factors may be of great importance when related to the subjective significance of different spatial and physical arrangements, or to their capacity for gratifying different socio-cultural groups. For the present, we can only stress the importance of local areas as *spatial and social* arrangements which are central to the lives of working-class people. And, in view of the enormous importance of such local areas, we are led to consider the convergence of familiar people and familiar places as a focal consideration in formulating planning decisions.

We can learn to deal with these problems only through research, through exploratory and imaginative service programs, and through a more careful consideration of the place of residential stability in salvaging the precarious thread of continuity. The outcomes of crises are always manifold and, just as there is an increase in strain and difficulty, so also there is an increase in opportunities for adapting at a more satisfying level of functioning. The judicious use of minimal resources of counseling and assistance may permit many working-class people to reorganize and integrate a meaningful sense of spatial and group identity under the challenge of social change. Only a relatively small group of those whose functioning has always been marginal and who cannot cope with the added strain of adjusting to wholly new problems are likely to require major forms of intervention.

In general, our results would imply the necessity for providing increased opportunities for maintaining a sense of continuity for those people, mainly from the working class, whose residential areas are being renewed. This may involve several factors: (1) diminishing the amount of drastic redevelopment and the consequent mass demolition of property and mass dislocation from homes; (2) providing more frequently for people to move within their former residential areas during and after the renewal; and (3) when dislocation and relocation are unavoidable, planning the relocation possibilities in order to provide new areas which can be assimilated to old objectives. A closer examination of slum areas may even provide some concrete information regarding specific physical variables, the physical and spatial arrangements typical of slum areas and slum housing, which offer considerable gratification to the residents. These may often be translated into effective modern architectural and areal design. And, in conjunction with planning decisions which take more careful account of the human consequences of urban physical change, it is possible to utilize social, psychological, and psychiatric services. The use of highly skilled resources, including opportunities for the education of professional and even lay personnel in largely unfamiliar problems and methods, can minimize some of the more destructive and widespread effects of relocation; and, for some families, can offer constructive experiences in dealing with new adaptational possibilities. The problem is large. But only by assuring the integrity of some of the external bases for the sense of continuity in the working class, and by maximizing the opportunities for meaningful adaptation, can we accomplish planned urban change without serious hazard to human welfare.

REFERENCES

1. Abraham, K., "Notes on the Psycho-analytical Investigation and Treatment of Manic-Depressive Insanity and Allied Conditions" (1911), and "A Short Study of the Development of the Libido, Viewed in the Light of Mental Disorders" (1924), in *Selected Papers of Karl Abraham,* Vol. I, New York: Basic Books, 1953; Bibring, E., "The Mechanisms of Depression," in *Affective Disorders,* P. Greenacre, ed., New York: International Univ. Press, 1953; Bowlby, J., "Processes of Mourning," *Int. J. Psychoanal.,* 42:317–340, 1961; Freud, S., "Mourning and Melancholia" (1917), in *Collected Papers,* Vol. III, New York: Basic Books, 1959; Hoggart, R., *The Uses of Literacy: Changing Patterns in English Mass Culture,* New York: Oxford Univ. Press, 1957; Klein, M., "Mourning and Its Relations to Manic-Depressive States," *Int. J. Psychoanal.,* 21:125–153, 1940; Lindemann, E., "Symptomatology and Management of Acute Grief," *Am. J. Psychiat.,* 101:141–148, 1944; Marris, P., *Widows and Their Families,* London: Routledge and Kegan Paul, 1958; Rochlin, G., "The Dread of Abandonment," in *The Psychoanalytic Study of the Child,* Vol. XVI, New York: International Univ. Press, 1961; Volkart, E. H., with S. T. Michael, "Bereavement and Mental Health," in *Explorations in Social Psychiatry,* A. H. Leighton, J. A. Clausen, and R. N. Wilson, eds., New York: Basic Books, 1957.
2. Fried, M., and Gleicher, P., "Some Sources of Residential Satisfaction in an Urban Slum," *J. Amer. Inst. Planners,* 27:305–315, 1961.
3. Gans, H., *The Urban Villagers,* New York: The Free Press of Glencoe, 1962; Gans, H., "The Human Implications of Current Redevelopment and Relocation Planning," *J. Amer. Inst. Planners,* 25:15–25, 1959; Hoggart, R., *op. cit.;* Hole, V., "Social Effects of Planned Rehousing," *Town Planning Rev.,* 30:161–173, 1959; Marris, P., *Family and Social Change in an African City,* Evanston, Ill.: Northwestern Univ. Press, 1962; Mogey, J. M., *Family and Neighbourhood,* New York: Oxford Univ. Press, 1956; Seeley, J., "The Slum: Its Nature, Use, and Users," *J. Amer. Inst. Planners,* 25:7–14, 1959; Vereker, C., and Mays, J. B., *Urban Redevelopment and Social Change,* New York: Lounz, 1960; Young, M., and Willmott, P., *Family and Kinship in East London,* Glencoe, Ill.: The Free Press, 1957.

Chapter 4

THE MYTH OF SUBURBIA

Conventional wisdom about suburbs, those much-discussed residential areas ringing most American cities, suggests that much there can be described in terms of sickness and social pathology. In his now classic study, *Working-Class Suburb*, Bennett M. Berger was one of the first to argue that serious misconceptions about the social and cultural life of suburbanites had recently arisen, a set of misconceptions he termed "the myth of suburbia." [1] In the first selection in this chapter Herbert J. Gans provides a concise statement about some key elements of this myth:

> . . . the suburbs were breeding a new set of Americans, as mass produced as the houses they lived in, driven into a never ending round of group activity ruled by the strictest conformity. Suburbanites were incapable of real friendships; they were bored and lonely, alienated, atomized, and depersonalized. As the myth grew, it added yet more disturbing elements: the emergence of a matriarchal family of domineering wives, absent husbands, and spoiled children, and with it, rising marital friction, adultery, divorce, drunkenness, and mental illness. [2]

Attempting to sift out the truth in these assertions, Gans chose for careful study a famous suburb, a Levittown near Philadelphia. Taking up residence there during its first two years of development, Gans used the same participant observation technique as in his innercity study, *The Urban Villagers*, supplementing that live-in research approach with structured interviews taken from samples of new residents. As a participant-observer he spent many hours informally interviewing fellow homeowners, attending social gatherings and organizational meetings, and consulting with local informants.

The first portion of *The Levittowners* excerpted here outlines the research setting and basic theoretical arguments of Gans' study. In the chapters that follow this introduction, research findings are presented in great detail. Some of the most important are: (1) the majority of Levittown families were relatively young and were headed by white-collar workers; (2) although few families were nonwhite, there was much variation in ethnic, religious, and occupational backgrounds; (3) most residents had moved to Levittown from the surrounding area primarily in a search for new or more spacious housing and also with the desire to own a home; (4) on the average, time spent in traveling to work did not change significantly with the move; (5) for most families, time spent by parents with children increased or remained the same after the move; (6) in a sample which had moved from Philadelphia, more wives reported an increase in activities with their husbands than reported a decrease; (7) on the average, visiting with neighbors was greater after the move than before; (8) most residents reported *less* loneliness and boredom after the move; (9) unwanted conformity to neighborhood pressures and abdication of individuality seemed rare.[3]

These and other important findings are summarized and interpreted in the concluding chapter of *The Levittowners*, a major section of which is also reprinted here. Basically, Gans argues that his research contradicts many of the misconceptions associated with the myth of suburbia. Yet he does not give us a Pollyanna portrait of suburban life. Class conflict, difficulties in coping with the pluralism of life styles, and conflict over the direction of government in Levittown are also examined in this concluding chapter. In addition, the reader may find Gans' concluding discussion of the meaning and future of suburbanization in American cities provocative and unconventional.

In the second selection reprinted here Berger raises the important issue of diversity, for not all suburbs are white collar. Indeed, Berger's earlier book, *Working-Class Suburb*, not only developed the idea of the suburban myth, but also presented detailed data on the way of life common to a group of blue-collar families who had moved from the industrial city of Richmond, California, to a new suburb just outside San Jose. Berger carefully documented in that work his contention that the blue-collar families who had moved to the suburban fringe "had not been profoundly affected in any statistically identifiable or sociologically interesting way." [4] Thus, he found no evidence of status striving or status anxiety, but did find a general feeling of well-being. While couple-visiting and activity in formal associations were relatively rare (in contrast to patterns in some white-collar suburbs), there was a considerable amount of visiting with relatives and family activity. These important findings are further underscored in Berger's 1966 article, which is included in this reader, a paper in which Berger reviews the earlier arguments in the light of recent research and examines the sources and implications of misconceptions about suburban life. The role of a curious group of bedfellows—realtors, businessmen, city planners, intellectuals, the mass media—in the development of suburban stereotypes is suggested, and the serious implications of these stereotypes for present and future urban planning are carefully weighed. Moreover, in his policy-oriented concluding comments Berger seems to be developing arguments compatible with Gans' discussion of pluralism in suburban values and life styles. Social and cultural variety is a reality in the suburban fringe, as well as elsewhere in American cities, and in his view this pluralism should be recognized and taken seriously by those planners intent on shaping and reshaping the social and physical environments of American urbanites.[5]

NOTES

1. Bennett M. Berger, *Working-Class Suburb* (Berkeley: University of California Press, 1969).
2. Herbert J. Gans, *The Levittowners* (New York: Pantheon, 1967), pp. xv–xvi.
3. Ibid., especially pp. 22–240. Note that these generalizations are drawn from random samples of Levittown residents. An excellent report on Gans' methodology can be found in the Appendix to *The Levittowners.*
4. Bennett M. Berger, "Suburbia and the American Dream," *The Public Interest,* no. 2 (Winter 1966), p. 81.
5. Further discussions of pluralism and ethnicity can be found in the next chapter of this reader.

FROM **THE LEVITTOWNERS:**
THE SETTING, THEORY, AND
METHOD OF THE STUDY

HERBERT J. GANS

This study had its beginnings sixteen years ago when I concluded some research in the new town of Park Forest, Illinois, near Chicago. Having come to Park Forest when it was fourteen months old and already a community, I decided that someday I would study a new town from its very beginnings. Soon after I left Park Forest, it and other postwar suburban developments suddenly became a topic of widespread popular interest. Journalists and critics began to write articles suggesting that life in these new suburbs was radically different from that in the older cities and towns and that these differences could be ascribed both to basic changes in American values and to the effects of suburban life. In the first and most perceptive of these reports, Whyte's articles on Park Forest, the author described drastic increases in visiting and club activity, shifts in political party affiliation and church-going habits, and a more equalitarian mode of consumer behavior and status competition (keeping down with the Joneses) which he explained as a decline in individualism and the rise of a new Social Ethic—most evident in and partly created by the new suburbs.[1]

Later reports by less searching and responsible writers followed,[2] and so did a flood of popular fiction,[3] eventually creating what Bennett Berger has called the myth of suburbia.[4] Its main theme took off where Whyte stopped: the suburbs were breeding a new set of Americans, as mass produced as the houses they lived in, driven into a never ending round of group activity ruled by the strictest conformity. Suburbanites were incapable of real friendships; they were bored and lonely, alienated, atomized, and depersonalized. As the myth grew, it added yet more disturbing elements: the emergence of a matriarchal family of domineering wives, absent husbands, and spoiled children, and with it, rising marital friction, adultery, divorce, drunkenness, and mental illness.[5] In unison, the authors chanted that individualism was dying, suburbanites were miserable, and the fault lay with the homogeneous suburban landscape and its population. John Keats, perhaps the most hysterical of the mythmakers, began his book as follows: "For *literally nothing down* . . . you too can find a box of your own in one of the fresh-air slums we're building around the edges of American cities . . .

inhabited by people whose age, income, number of children, problems, habits, conversation, dress, possessions and perhaps even blood type are also precisely like yours. . . . [They are] developments conceived in error, nurtured by greed, corroding everything they touch. They . . . actually drive mad myriads of housewives shut up in them." [6]

Subsequently, literary and social critics chimed in. Although they wrote little about suburbia per se, articles and reviews on other subjects repeated what they had learned from the mass media, dropping asides that suburbia was intellectually debilitating, culturally oppressive, and politically dangerous, breeding bland mass men without respect for the arts or democracy. [7] They were joined by architects and city planners who accused the suburbs and their builders of ruining the countryside, strangling the cities, causing urban sprawl, and threatening to make America into one vast Los Angeles by the end of the century. [8]

I watched the growth of this mythology with misgivings, for my observations in various new suburbs persuaded me neither that there was much change in people when they moved to the suburbs nor that the change which took place could be traced to the new environment. And if suburban life was as undesirable and unhealthy as the critics charged, the suburbanites themselves were blissfully unaware of it; they were happy in their new homes and communities, much happier than they had been in the city. Some of the observations about suburbia were quite accurate, and the critics represented a wide range of political and cultural viewpoints, so that it is perhaps unfair to lump them all together—although I do so as a shorthand in the chapters that follow. Nevertheless, it seemed to me that a basic inaccuracy was being perpetrated by those who give American society its picture of itself, and when I learned that city planners also swallowed the suburban myth and were altering their professional recommendations accordingly, I felt it was time to do a study of the new suburbs. Lacking the grants to do a large comparative study of several communities that was—and still is—needed, and leaning toward participant-observation by my training, I decided the best way to do the research was to live in one such community. That community turned out to be Levittown, New Jersey.

THE SETTING

When I first began to think about the study, I learned that Levitt and Sons, Inc., then building Levittown, Pennsylvania, were planning to build yet another new community in the Philadelphia area. The firm was then, as now, the largest builder in the eastern United States, and Levittown was even then a prototype of postwar suburbia. [9] Hair raising stories about the homogeneity of people and conformity of life in the first two Levittowns made it clear that if any of the evils described by the critics of suburbia actually existed, they would be found in a Levittown. Moreover, Levitt was building communities and not just subdivisions, which meant that the entire range of local institutions and facilities typically associated with a community would be established *de novo;* the firm was offering relatively inexpensive houses, which meant that the community would attract both middle and working class people.[10]

In 1955, Levitt announced that he had purchased almost all of Willingboro Township, New Jersey, a sparsely settled agricultural area seventeen miles from Philadelphia, and that building would begin as soon as Levittown, Pennsylvania, was completed. The newest Levittown was to be a full-fledged community, with at least 12,000 houses, and because Levitt had bought almost the entire township, with its own government as well. Three basic house types, costing from $11,500 to $14,500, would be built on the same streets and organized into separate neighborhoods of about 1200 homes, each served by an elementary school, playground, and swimming pool. The complex of ten or twelve neighborhoods would be complemented by a set of communitywide facilities, including a large shopping center, some smaller ones, and of course high schools, a library, and parks; and some of these would be provided by the builder.

On a sunny Saturday in June 1958, Levittown was officially opened to potential purchasers, and that day my wife and I were among hundreds of others who looked over the houses. Since I wanted to be among the very first residents, we selected the model we liked best, a four-bedroom "Cape Cod," and made the required down payment of $100. A few weeks later, the first group of about 100 purchasers was asked to come to Levittown to pick a lot, and we chose one in the middle of a short block—to make sure that we would literally be in the middle of things. During the second week of October, we were among the first 25 families who moved into the new community—none of them, I was pleased to discover, coming to study it.[11]

THE THEORY OF THE STUDY

The study I wanted to do focused around three major but interrelated questions: the origin of a new community, the quality of suburban life, and the effect of suburbia on the behavior of its residents. Later, I added a fourth question on the quality of politics and decision-making.

My first task was to determine the processes which transform a group of strangers into a community, to see if I could identify the essential prerequisites for "community." But I also wanted to test the critics' charge that the Levittowns were inflicted on purchasers with little choice of other housing by a profit-minded builder unwilling to provide them with a superior home and community. Consequently, I intended to study how the community was planned: to what extent the plans were shaped by Levitt's goals and to what extent by the goals of the expected purchasers. For this purpose, I needed also to study the purchasers—why they were moving to Levittown and what aspirations they had for life in the new community. Once they had moved in, I wanted to observe the community formation process from the same perspective: how much specific groups were shaped by their founders, how much by their members, and how much by the group's function for the larger community. I hoped to know after several years to what extent the emerging community reflected the priorities of builder, founders, and other community leaders and to what extent the goals for which people said they had moved to Levittown.

These questions were grounded in a set of theoretical issues of relevance to both social science and public policy. Sociologists have long been asking what and who bring about innovation and social change, and what role elite leaders and experts, on the one hand, and the rank-and-file citizenry, on the other, play in this process. As a policy matter, the same question has been raised by the concept of mass society, which implies that many features of American society—whether television programs, Levittowns, or Pentagon policies—are imposed by an intentional or unintentional conspiracy of business and governmental leaders acting on passive or resigned Americans who actually want something entirely different.

This issue is of more than academic interest to makers of community policy, be they politicians or city planners. The city planner is an expert with a conception of the ideal community and good life, which he seeks to translate into reality through his professional activities. If a small number of leaders shape the community, he need only proselytize them effectively to establish his conception. If the residents themselves determine the community, however, he is faced with a more difficult task: persuading them of the desirability of his plans or somehow changing their behavior to accord with them. The further and normative issue is even more perplexing: whose values *should* shape the new community, the residents' or the planner's? [12]

The second question of the study sought to test the validity of the suburban critique, whether suburban ways of life were as undesirable as had been claimed. Are people status-seekers, do they engage in a hyperactive social life which they do not really enjoy, do they conform unwillingly to the demands of their neighbors, is the community a dull microcosm of mass society? Are the women bored and lonely matriarchs, and does suburban life produce the malaise and mental illness which the critics predicted? And if not, what dissatisfactions and problems *do* develop?

The third question followed logically from the second: were undesirable changes (and desirable ones too) an effect of the move from city to suburb or of causes unrelated to either the move or suburbia? My previous observations led me to suspect that the changes were less a result of suburban residence than of aspirations for individual and family life which encouraged people to move to the suburbs in the first place. Consequently, I wanted to discover whether the changes people reported after coming to Levittown were *intended,* planned by them before the move, or *unintended,* encouraged or forced on them afterwards by the community. If unintended changes outweighed intended ones, the community probably had significant effects on its residents. And if so, what *sources* and *agents* within the community created them—the physical environment of suburbia, the distance from urban facilities, the social structure and the people who made it, and/or the builder or organizational founder?

The theoretical issue about the impact of the community has long been debated within sociology, the ecologists arguing that the local economy and geography shape the behavior of the community's residents; the cultural sociologists suggesting that the community and its residents' behavior are largely a reflection of regional and national social structures.[13] The policy issue is related to the previous one. If there is no change in people's behavior when they move to the suburbs, then public policy which alters only the community, such as city planning, may be ineffective. The same is true if changes are mainly intended. If they are mainly unintended, however, and the community has impact on people's lives, then policy to change the community will also change their lives. And if the sources of change can be traced to the physical environment, the city planner's concern with altering that environment is justified; if they lie in the social environment, then social planning would be more effective. But if intended changes predominate, public policy would have to affect the aspirations with which people come to the community and the more fundamental sources of these aspirations. Of course, all this assumes that policy change is needed, which requires a prior determination of what is harmful or in need of improvement in suburban life.

As part of my study of the quality of life, I had intended to research political life as well, and as part of the inquiry into origins, to find out how much attention elected officials paid to feedback from the voters— whether the body politic was being created by political leaders on their own or in response to resident demands. In the course of my research I became aware of what should have been obvious all along: that the community was also being shaped by the decisions of its governing body, and that I needed to study who was making them and how, and to determine what role the planner and other kinds of experts played in the decision-making process. I wanted particularly to find out how much leeway the decision-makers had for unpopular decisions, especially those termed "in the public interest" by experts and planners. Underlying the empirical question was another normative one: whether government *should* be responsive and democratic, and when it should make unpopular decisions to preserve the public interest as well as the rights of powerless minorities.

All four questions ultimately boil down to a single one about the process of change and the possibility of innovation in a social system. They all ask how change can be brought about, whether the major initiators are the leaders or the led, and what role the planner or any other expert policy-maker can play. And they also ask, normatively speaking, what changes are desirable, particularly when they conflict with the actions or wishes of the majority of residents. These questions are, of course, relevant to any community, but they are raised more easily in a new community, where all social and political processes can be traced from their very beginning.

I should note that when I began my research, I had not formulated the questions as clearly or compactly as they are here written, and I had no intention of limiting myself only to them. One of the major pleasures of participant-observation is to come upon unexpected new topics of study, and these are reflected in the occasional tangential analyses that occur throughout the book.

. . .

NOTES

1. The articles appeared originally in *Fortune* in 1953, and in Whyte (1956), Part III. For full citation of works referred to in the notes by author's name only, see References, pages 106–107. Where several works by the same author are cited, the note reference is followed by the appropriate publication date.

2. Among the principal contributors to the popular image of suburbia were a 1950 novel by Charles Mergendahl, *It's Only Temporary* (perhaps the first of the flood of fiction and nonfiction about the suburbs) and Henderson, Allen, Burton, Spectorsky, Keats, and more recently, Wyden. A Sunday supplement, *Suburbia Today*, was filled with articles about suburbia, pro and con.

3. There were dramatic novels, mostly about upper middle class suburbs, like Otis Carney's *How the Bough Breaks;* melodramatic ones like John McPartland's *No Down Payment*, later made into a movie; and humorous ones like Mergendahl's; plays, for example, *Man in the Dog Suit;* and even an opera, Leonard Bernstein's *Trouble in Tahiti*. Levittown was often the site, by implication in Mergendahl's book, and explicitly in a half-hour television comedy series (never produced) called *The Man Who Came to Levittown*. While most of today's television situation comedies are set in the suburbs, they are not so identified and do not deal with problems they describe as suburban.

4. Berger (1960), Chap. 1. For other analyses of the popular image of suburbia, see Strauss, Chaps. 10 and 11; Dobriner (1963), Chap. 1; Riesman (1964); and Berger (1966).

5. On mental illness see James, and a full-length study which became a best-seller, by Gordon, Gordon, and Gunther. The myth of suburban adultery, which can probably be traced to century-old novels about upper and upper middle class unfaithfulness, has spawned a flood of strenuously erotic paperbacks which still keep coming, although the output of other suburban literature has now abated. See e.g., John Conway's *Love in Suburbia*, subtitled "They Spiced Their Lives with Other Men's Wives," or Dean McCoy's *The Development*, advertised as "a biting novel which strips bare the flimsy façade of decency concealing unbridled sensual desires of America's sprawling Suburbia."

6. Keats (1957), p. 7.

7. Although most sociologists doubted the   th, some accepted parts of it,

e.g., Gruenberg, Duhl, Riesman (1957), and Stein, Chaps. 9 and 12. Interestingly enough, "serious" novelists have not written about suburbia. George Elliott's *Parktilden Village* and Bruce Jay Friedman's *Stern* are set in suburban housing projects and reflect the suburban myth, but deal even less with representative and recognizable suburbanites than the popular novelists.

8. For example, Mumford, Chap. 16; Blake; and Gruen, Chap. 5.

9. Actually, most of the suburban building had taken the form of sub-divisions on the fringe of established communities rather than new communities, so that Levittown was in many ways atypical. It was a proto-type largely because it had become the symbol of modern suburbia among the critics, journalists, novelists, and moviemakers concerned with the subject.

10. My study was formulated in the affluent society of the mid-1950s and I was then especially interested in whether (and how) working class people were acculturating to middle class life styles. If the move from city to suburb created major changes in people's lives, I thought they would be most apparent among working class people moving to a middle class suburb and could best be studied there, provided one could distinguish between changes resulting from social mobility and changes resulting from the move. There were too few working class Levittowners to limit my research to them, but some years later, Berger (1960) studied a working class suburb, covering many of the topics in which I was interested.

11. Later, I would have welcomed sharing my task with other participant-observers, but at that time, I was unsure about people's feelings toward a resident researcher and thought that more than one sociologist in the community would make the research too visible. I was wrong, because the community was large enough and the neighborhoods separate enough, and because after a while the researcher became part of the daily scene and faded into invisibility.

12. This question was also evoked by a study I had just participated in: on the issue of whether municipal services ought to be planned according to the priorities of those who supplied them (the professional educators, recreationists, public health officials, and social workers), or of those who used them (their "clients"). My own research, which dealt with public recreation, concluded that parks and playgrounds ought to be planned for their users, and undoubtedly left an a priori bias in studying the larger issue in Levittown.

13. See, e.g., Duncan and Schnore.

. . .

LEVITTOWN AND AMERICA

I began this study with four questions, the answers to which can be generalized to new towns and suburbs all over America. *First,* a new community is shaped neither by the builder, the planner, and the organizational founder, nor by the aspirations with which residents come. A builder creates the physical shell of the community; a founder, the social one; but even when organizations and institutions are initiated by national bodies outside the community, they can only survive by attracting people and responding to their demands. If residents lack choice among churches or clubs, individual founders can impose their will or their vision of the community on the residents, but such lack of choice is rare. Aspirations of residents are usually limited to the house, family life, neighboring, and friendship; people have few that concern the larger community and the demands they make on it emerge after they have settled down. Only when they have lived on their blocks for a while can they decide what functions must be filled by the rest of the community, and only when they have met their fellow residents can they determine where compatible people are to be found and how they want to sort themselves. In short, their choices of (and within) community institutions are basically a function of the population mix they encounter.

These choices are not made in a vacuum, but involve values and preferences which people bring with them. Perhaps the most significant fact about the origin of a new community is that it is not new at all, but only a new physical site on which people develop conventional institutions with traditional programs. New towns are ultimately old communities on new land, culturally not significantly different from suburban subdivisions and urban neighborhoods inhabited by the same kinds of people, and politically much like other small American towns.

Second, most new suburbanites are pleased with the community that develops; they enjoy the house and outdoor living and take pleasure from the large supply of compatible people, without experiencing the boredom or malaise ascribed to suburban homogeneity. Some people encounter unexpected social isolation, particularly those who differ from the majority of their neighbors. Who will be socially isolated depends on the community; in Levittown, they were older couples, the well educated and the poorly educated, and women who had come from a cohesive working class or ethnic enclave or were used to living with an extended family. Such people probably suffer in every suburb; even though they want to escape from the close life of the "urban village," they miss their old haunts, cannot find compatible people, or do not know how to make new friends. But the least happy people are always those of lowest income and least education; they not only have the most difficulty in making social contacts and joining groups, but are also beset by financial problems which strain family tempers as well as family budgets. And if the suburb is designed for young adults and children, the adolescents will suffer from "nothing to do" and from adult hostility toward their youth culture and peer groups.

People's lives are changed somewhat by the move to suburbia, but their basic ways remain the same; they do not develop new life styles or ambitions for themselves and their children. Moreover, many of the changes that do take place were desired before the move. Because the suburb makes them possible, morale goes up, boredom and loneliness are reduced, family life becomes temporarily more cohesive, social and organizational activities multiply, and spare-time pursuits now concentrate on the house and yard. Some changes result from the move: community organizational needs encourage some people to become joiners for the first time, ethnic and religious difference demands more synagogue attendance, and social isolation breeds depression, boredom, and loneliness for the few who are left out. But change is not unidirectional; different people respond differently to the environment, and the most undesirable changes usually stem from familial and occupational circumstances.

Third, the sources or causes of change are not to be found in suburbia per se, but in the new house, the opportunity for home ownership, and above all, the population mix—the people with whom one now lives. They bring about the intended increase in social life, the unintended increase in organizational activity, and, of course, the equally unintended social isolation. Some changes can be traced to the openness of the social structure in a new community and people's willingness to accept and trust each other, as well as to the random settling pattern which requires them to make friends with strangers next door or to leave the block for the larger community to find compatible people. But most result from the homogeneity of age and class of the population that buys into a new suburb. Indeed, the basic sources of change come from goals for home ownership, a free-standing house, outdoor living, and being with people of similar age and class, which have long been basic aspirations of American working and middle class cultures.[1] Even unintended changes could be traced finally to national economic trends and cultural patterns that push people out of the city and provide incentives for builders to construct communities like Levittown. Ultimately, then, the changes people undergo in the move to the suburbs are only expressions of more widespread societal changes and national cultural goals.

Fourth, the politics of a new suburb is no more distinctive than the rest of its life. In any heterogeneous community, conflicting demands from the voters force the decision-makers to set up a performing government which observes democratic norms, freeing them to reconcile these conflicts in a backstage actual government. Their decisions are, more often than not, responsive to the majority of voters when that majority makes demands, but are unresponsive to powerless minorities, which therefore have to intervene—to upset the normal decision-making process in order to get satisfaction. Since they fail more often than they succeed, local government generally neglects minority demands and rights, and the public interest as well. Experts with sufficient consensus, skill, and power can implement decisions unpopular with the majority, but on the whole, such decisions have to be enforced by nonlocal agencies. Of course, suburbs like Levittown have few of the problems that face American cities, dying small towns, or stagnant rural areas, so that local governments can meet the limited needs of at least their dominant constituents. Supralocal governments must be developed, however, to deal with the problems generated by the myriad of suburban sovereignties and the artificiality of suburban boundaries.

THE POTENTIAL FOR INNOVATION AND CHANGE

My four initial questions were joined by a common theme: To what extent is a community made by its residents and to what extent by leaders, planners, and other experts who want to stimulate innovation and change? The findings, I would suggest, demonstrate again an important sociological truth and truism, that what happens in a community is almost always a reflection of the people who live in it, especially the numerical and cultural majority. That majority supports the organizations and institutions that define the community; it determines who will be enjoying life and who will be socially isolated; and it forms the constituencies to which decision-makers are responsive. In the last analysis, then, the community (and its origin, impact, and politics) are an outcome of the population mix, particularly of its dominant elements and their social structure and culture.

The processes by which this community outcome is achieved are conflict-ridden. A modern community is not like a folk culture, in which congruence between the community and its population is achieved by a widespread consensus about behavior and values. In Levittown, the congruence is much less perfect, and is produced by power struggles, which are constantly resolved by compromises so that institutions and organizations can function in an orderly manner. These struggles are unending, for every compromise solves only the immediate conflict, and new issues arise all the time. Whether the compromisers are parents, organizational leaders, or elected officials, they spend a great deal of time and energy in averting what they define as crises, and preserving the fragile equilibrium by which congruence between community and society is engineered. As a result, all other issues are pushed into the background, including innovation and change. And when decision-makers cannot satisfy everybody, there is rarely time or energy for any but the most numerous, powerful, or vocal constituents.

Under these conditions, founders, innovators, and individual "change agents," expert or otherwise, can do little. They may suggest new ideas, but before these are implemented, they have been altered to make them responsive to important constituencies. Without initiators, nothing can begin, but once the initiative has been taken, the social process transforms it. People who can initiate successfully and anticipate the re quired transformations are made leaders and often get credit for the workings of the social process—and those who want to be leaders learn quickly what will be successful. Only rarely is such a role awarded to innovators.

These findings could easily be used to justify the status quo, but that is not my conclusion or my purpose. The study suggests that change and innovation are always possible, but not easily achieved. No group or community is impervious to change, but neither is it an aggregate of open-minded people who do not know what they want and can be persuaded to shed their past. Consequently, advocates of innovation and change cannot be satisfied (as they so often are) with appealing for something new or demanding conformity to their ideas (as they so often do) because they are convinced of the superiority of what they propose. Groups and communities are fluid systems, with leaders who have some—but precious little—leeway in their decisions. If that lee-way is to be used for innovation, change agents who lack the power to insist on change or the resources with which to reward people for undertaking it must offer distinctly superior alternatives to present ar-rangements. No community and no social arrangement satisfies every-one, and as the data on Levittown make persuasively evident, even when most people are happy with their new community, some are not. The best approach to change, therefore, is to give up the single solution that compromises between the wants of different groups, and to experi-ment with new solutions for dissatisfied groups and cultures in the total population. This means a diversity of housing, living arrange-ments, and institutions, either within the same community or in sepa-rate ones, keyed to the diversity of background, culture, and aspirations relevant to community life.

Conflict, Pluralism, and Community. Although a part of my study was concerned with the possibilities of change and innovation, I do not mean to suggest that Levittown is badly in need of either. The com-munity may displease the professional city planner and the intellectual defender of cosmopolitan culture, but perhaps more than any other type of community, Levittown permits most of its residents to be what they want to be—to center their lives around the home and the family, to be among neighbors whom they can trust, to find friends to share leisure hours, and to participate in organizations that provide sociability and the opportunity to be of service to others.

That Levittown has its faults and problems is undeniable, and I have described them in previous chapters: physical and social isolation, familial and governmental financial problems, insufficient public trans-portation, less than perfect provision of public services, inadequate decision-making and feedback processes, lack of representation for minorities and overrepresentation for the builder, and the entire array of familial and individual problems common to any population. Many of them can be traced back to three basic shortcomings, none distinctive to Levittown or the Levittowners.

One is the difficulty of coping with conflict. Like the rest of the country, Levittown is beset with conflict: class conflict between the lower middle class group and the smaller working and upper middle class groups; generational conflict between adults, children, adolescents, and the elderly. The existence of conflict is no drawback, but the way conflict is handled leaves much to be desired. Levittowners, like other Americans, do not really accept the inevitability of conflict. Insisting that a consensus is possible, they only exacerbate the conflict, for each group demands that the other conform to its values and accept its priorities. When power is a valuable prize and resources are scarce, such a perspective is understandable, but in Levittown the exercise of power is not an end in itself for most people; they want it mainly to control the allocation of resources. Since resources are not so scarce, however, the classes and age groups could resolve their conflicts more constructively than they do, giving each group at least some of what it wants. If the inevitability of conflicting interests were accepted, differences might be less threatening, and this would make it easier to reach the needed compromises. I am not sanguine that this will happen, for if people think resources are scarce, they act as if they are scarce, and will not pay an extra $20 a year in taxes to implement minority demands. Even so, conditions to make viable compromises happen are more favorable in Levittown than in larger or poorer communities.

The second shortcoming, closely related to the first, is the inability to deal with pluralism. People have not recognized the diversity of American society, and they are not able to accept other life styles. Indeed, they cannot handle conflict because they cannot accept pluralism. Adults are unwilling to tolerate adolescent culture, and vice versa. Lower middle class people oppose the ways of the working class and upper middle class, and each of these groups is hostile to the other two. Perhaps the inability to cope with pluralism is greater in Levittown than elsewhere because it is a community of young families who are raising children. Children are essentially asocial and unacculturated beings, easily influenced by new ideas. As a result, their parents feel an intense need to defend familial values; to make sure that their children grow up according to parental norms and not by those of their playmates from another class. The need to shield the children from what are considered harmful influences begins on the block, but it is translated into the conflict over the school, the definitional struggles within the voluntary associations whose programs affect the socialization of children, and, ultimately, into political conflicts. Each group wants to put its cultural stamp on the organizations and institutions that are the community, for otherwise the family and its culture are not safe. In a society in which extended families are unimportant and the nuclear family cannot provide the full panoply of personnel and activities to hold children in the family culture, parents must use community institutions for this purpose, and every portion of the community therefore becomes a battleground for the defense of familial values.

This thesis must not be exaggerated, for much of the conflict is, as it has always been, between the haves and the have-nots. Even if Levittown's median income is considerably above the national average even for white families, no one feels affluent enough to let other people determine how their own income should be spent. Most of the political conflict in the community rages over how much of the family income should be given over to the community, and then, how it should be used. In fact, consensus about municipal policies and expenditures exists only about the house. Because many Levittowners are first-time homeowners, they are especially eager to protect that home against loss of value, both as property and as status image. But every class has its own status image and its own status fears. Working class people do not want to be joined by lower class neighbors or to be forced to adopt middle class styles. Lower middle class people do not want more working class neighbors or to be forced to adopt cosmopolitan styles, and upper middle class people want neither group to dominate them. These fears are not, as commonly thought, attributes of status-seeking, for few Levittowners are seeking higher status; they are fears about self-image. When people reject pluralism, they do so because accepting the viability of other ways of living suggests that their own is not as absolute as they need to believe. The outcome is the constant search for compatible people and the rejection of those who are different.

When the three class groups—not to mention their subgroupings and yet other groups with different values—must live together and share a common government, every group tries to make sure that the institutions and facilities which serve the entire community maintain its own status and culture, and no one is happy when another group wins. If working class groups can persuade the Township Committee to allocate funds for a firehouse, middle class groups unite in a temporary coalition to guarantee that a library is also established. When the upper middle class group attempts to influence school policy to shape education to its standard, lower middle class residents raise the specter of Levittown aping Brookline and Scarsdale, while working class people become fearful that the schools will neglect discipline or that taxes will rise further. Consequently, each group seeks power to prevent others from shaping the institutions that must be shared. They do not seek power as an end in itself, but only to guarantee that their priorities will be met by the community. Similarly, they do not demand lower taxes simply for economic reasons (except for those few really hard pressed) but in order to be sure that community institutions are responsive to their familial values and status needs. Obviously, power sought for these ends is hard to share, and decisions for levying and allocating public funds are difficult to compromise.

The third shortcoming of the community, then, is the failure to establish a meaningful relationship between home and community and to reconcile class-cultural diversity with government and the provision of public services. Levittowners, like other Americans, not only see government as a parasite and public services as a useless expenditure of funds better spent privately, but they do not allow government to adapt these services to the diversity among the residents. Government is committed to the establishment of a single (and limited) set of public services, and its freedom to do otherwise is restricted by legislation and, of course, by American tradition. Government has always been a minor supplier of services basic to everyday life, and an enemy whose encroachment on private life must be resisted. The primary source of this conception is the historic American prejudice against public services, which stems in part from the rural tradition of the individual and his family as a self-sufficient unit, but which is perpetuated by contemporary cultural values, and made possible by the affluence which enables at least middle class families to live with only minimal dependence on local government. The bias against public services does not interfere with their use, however, but only with their financing, and their extension and proliferation. Nor does it lead Levittowners to reject government outright, but only to channel it into a few limited functions. Among these, the primary one is the protection of the home against diversity.

Government thus becomes a defense agency, to be taken over by one group to defend itself against others in and out of the community. The idea that it could have positive functions, such as the provision of facilities to make life richer and more comfortable, is resisted, for every new governmental function is seen first as an attempt by one community group to increase its dominance over others. Of course, these attempts are rarely manifest, for the political dialogue deals mainly with substantive matters, but when Levittowners spoke against a proposal, they were reacting principally against those who proposed it rather than against its substance.

Until government can tailor its actions to the community's diversity, and until people can accept the inevitability of conflict and pluralism in order to give government that responsibility, they will prefer to spend their money for privately and commercially supplied services. Unlike city hall, the marketplace is sensitive to diversities among the customers and does not require them to engage in political conflict to get what they want. Of course, not all people can choose the marketplace over city hall, but Levittowners are affluent enough to do so. Moreover, until parents have steered their children safely into their own class and culture—or have given up trying—they are likely to seek out relatively homogeneous communities and small ones, so that they have some control over government's inroads against personal and familial autonomy. This not only maintains the sovereignty of hundreds of small local governments but also contributes to the desire to own a house and a free-standing one.

LEVITTOWN AS AMERICA

The strengths and weaknesses of Levittown are those of many American communities, and the Levittowners closely resemble other young middle class Americans. They are not America, for they are not a nu-

merical majority in the population, but they represent the major con-
stituency of the largest and most powerful economic and political
institutions in American society—the favored customers and voters
whom these seek to attract and satisfy. Upper middle class Americans
may spend more per capita and join more groups, but they are fewer
in number than the lower middle classes. Working and lower class people are more numerous but they have less money and power; and
people over forty, who still outnumber young adults, are already committed to most of the goods, affiliations, and ideas they will need in their
lifetime.

Even so, Levittowners are not really members of the national society,
or for that matter, of a mass society. They are not apathetic conform-
ists ripe for takeover by a totalitarian elite or corporate merchandiser;
they are not conspicuous consumers and slaves to sudden whims of
cultural and political fashion; they are not even organization men or
particularly other-directed personalities. Clearly inner-directed strivers
are a minority in Levittown, and tradition-directed people would not
think of moving to a new community of strangers, but most people maintain a balance between inner personal goals and the social adjustment
necessary to live with neighbors and friends that, I suspect, is prevalent
all over lower middle class America. Indeed, the inability to empathize
with diversity would suggest that inner-direction may still be a much
stronger pattern among the Levittowners than it was among the upper
middle class people studied by Riesman and his associates.[2] Although
ethnic, religious, and regional differences are eroding, the never ending
conflicts over other differences are good evidence that Levittowners are
far from becoming mass men.

Although they are citizens of a national polity and their lives are
shaped by national economic, social, and political forces, Levittowners
deceive themselves into thinking that the community, or rather the
home, is the single most influential unit in their lives. Of course, in one
way they are right; it is the place where they can be most influential,
for if they cannot persuade the decision-makers, they *can* influence
family members. Home is also the site of maximal freedom, for within
its walls people can do what they want more easily than anywhere else.
But because they are free and influential *only* at home, their dependence
on the national society ought to be obvious to them. This not being the
case, the real problem is that Levittowners have not yet become aware
of how much they are a part of the national society and economy.

In viewing their homes as the center of life, Levittowners are still
using a societal model that fit the rural America of self-sufficient farmers and the feudal Europe of self-isolating extended families. Yet the
critics who argue about the individual versus mass society are also
anachronistic; they are still thinking of the individual artist or intellectual who must shield himself from a society which either rejects him or
coopts him to produce popular culture. Both Levittowners and critics
have to learn that they live in a national society characterized by pluralism and bureaucracy, and that the basic conflict is not between indi-

vidual (or family) and society, but between the classes (and other interest groups) who live together in a bureaucratized political and cultural democracy. The prime challenge is how to live with bureaucracy; how to use it rather than be used by it; how to obtain individual freedom and social resources from it through political action.

Yet even though Levittowners and other lower middle class Americans continue to be home-centered, they are much more "in the world" than their parents and grandparents were. Those coming out of ethnic working class backgrounds have rejected the "amoral familism" [3] which pits every family against every other in the struggle to survive and the ethnocentrism which made other cultures and even other neighborhoods bitter enemies. This generation trusts its neighbors, participates with them in social and civic activities, and no longer sees government as inevitably corrupt. Even working class Levittowners have begun to give up the suspicion that isolated their ancestors from all but family and childhood friends. Similarly, the descendants of rural Protestant America have given up the xenophobia that turned previous generations against the Catholic and Jewish immigrants, they have almost forgotten the intolerant Puritanism which triggered attacks against pleasure and enjoyment, and they no longer fully accept the doctrine of laissez faire that justifies the defense of all individual rights and privileges against others' needs.

These and other changes have come about not because people are now better or more tolerant human beings, but because they are affluent. For the Levittowners, life is not a fight for survival any more; they have been able to move into a community in which income and status are equitably enough distributed so that neighbors are no longer treated as enemies, even if they are still criticized for social and cultural deviance. By any yardstick one chooses, Levittowners treat their fellow residents more ethically and more democratically than did their parents and grandparents. [4] They also live a "fuller" and "richer" life. Their culture may be less subtle and sophisticated than that of the intellectual, their family life less healthy than that advocated by psychiatrists, and their politics less thoughtful and democratic than the political philosophers' —yet all of these are superior to what prevailed among the working and lower middle classes of past generations.

But beyond these changes, it is striking how little American culture among the Levittowners differs from what De Toqueville reported in his travels through small-town middle class America a century ago. Of course, he was here before the economy needed an industrial proletariat, but the equality of men and women, the power of the child over his parents, the importance of the voluntary association, the social functions of the church, and the rejection of high culture seem to be holdovers from his time, and so is the adherence to the traditional virtues: individual honesty, thrift, religiously inspired morality, Franklinesque individualism, and Victorian prudery. Some Levittowners have retained the values of rural ancestors; some have only begun to practice them as affluence enabled them to give up the values of a survival-centered culture. Still other eternal verities remain; class conflict is as alive as ever, even if the struggle is milder and the have-nots in Levittown have much more than the truly poor. Working class culture continues to flourish, even though its rough edges are wearing smooth and its extended family and public institutions are not brought to the suburbs. Affluence and better education have made a difference, but they have not made the factory worker middle class, any more than college attendance has made lower middle class people cosmopolitan.

What seems to have happened is that improvements and innovations are added to old culture patterns, giving affluent Americans a foot in several worlds. They have more knowledge and a broader outlook than their ancestors, and they enjoy the advantages of technology, but these are superimposed on old ways. While conservative critics rail about technology's dehumanization of modern man, the Levittowners who spend their days programming computers come home at night to practice the very homely and old-fashioned virtues these critics defend.[5] For example, they have television sets, but they watch much the same popular comedies and melodramas their ancestors saw on the nineteenth century stage. The melodramas are less crude and vaudeville is more respectable; the girls dance with covered bosoms, but Ed Sullivan's program is pure vaudeville and "the Jackie Gleason Show" even retains traces of the working class music hall. The overlay of old and new is not all good, of course; the new technology has created methods of war and destruction which the old insularity allows Americans to unleash without much shame or guilt, and some Levittowners may find work less satisfying than their ancestors. But only some, for the majority's parents slaved in exhausting jobs which made them too tired to enjoy the advantages of suburbia even if they could have afforded them. On the whole, however, the Levittowners have only benefitted from the changes in society and economy that have occurred in this century, and if they were not given to outdated models of social reality, they might feel freer about extending these benefits to less fortunate sectors of American society. But whether people's models are anachronistic or avant-garde, they are rarely willing to surrender their own powers and privileges to others.

LEVITTOWN AND THE FUTURE OF SUBURBIA

Presently available data make it certain that another suburban housing boom will take place during the next ten years. As the children born during the period of high family formation and fertility after World War II become parents, they will need housing to raise their own children, and will almost surely want to find it in the suburbs.[6] Unless a sharp economic downturn reduces middle class employment opportunities and either slows down the rate of family formation or forces young families to double up with their parents, yet another ring of suburban communities will spring up around most American cities.

The form the newest suburbia will take is as yet unknown. In most metropolitan areas, the current building of subdivisions, one by one, will probably continue. Where land for suburban development is running short, the single-family house may give way to the row house; where land is plentiful (as in the West) more comprehensively planned new towns with their own sources of employment are possible.[7] In big cities like New York and Chicago, where the remaining vacant land is more than forty miles from downtown, future suburban growth may be reduced by the unwillingness of commuters to travel over an hour each way, although this may in turn generate more support for high-speed mass transit. But the present trend of industrial decentralization is likely to increase as well, so that more job opportunities will be available in the suburbs themselves, bringing yet more vacant land into the range of an acceptable journey to work. And if the decentralization of industry is accompanied by the decentralization of offices, nothing should impede further suburbanization in all American cities.

This likelihood is already being viewed with alarm in some quarters. Advocates of the city are fearful that further suburban development can only result in added physical, financial, cultural, and political deterioration of the cities. They are joined by opponents of urban sprawl and by conservationists who are afraid that new suburbanization will further reduce rural acreages and may even cut into the forests and wildernesses that now provide recreational opportunities and land reserves at the edges of many metropolitan areas. In this coalition can also be found the critics of suburbia, concerned that an undesirable way of life will proliferate even further in the next generation.

Some of these fears may be reasonable, but none justify halting suburbanization. The inaccuracy of the suburban critique indicates that if the suburbs have positive consequences for the present generation of young parents, they will have similar ones for the next generation. Although suburbanization may further increase residential segregation by class and race, class segregation may be reduced as class lines within the middle class and between the lower middle and working class are blurred. And if future suburbanization takes the form of new towns and large subdivisions, these will be (like Levittown) more heterogeneous than small subdivisions and urban neighborhoods—which have often been one-class and one-race areas.

The fear of more urban sprawl also seems exaggerated. Urban sprawl is an inefficient use of land rather than the absolute evil it has been labeled, but it also promotes flexibility of growth.[8] If employment opportunities continue to decentralize, the wasteful features of urban sprawl may be reduced, partly because vacant areas will be filled in, but mostly because new suburban centers with industry and offices as well as shopping centers will develop all over the metropolitan area.[9] Indeed, in the future, the present mononuclear metropolis, with a downtown center surrounded by a disordered mass of urban and suburban areas of low density, is likely to become a multinuclear one with many centers, of which downtown is only the oldest and most important.

Probably the major disadvantage of urban sprawl is the proliferation of small local government.[10] Although it provides people with considerable control over their own destinies, it discourages public action on the many metropolitan-wide problems. A logical case can be made for some form of metropolitan government, and the case has been made logically since the beginning of the twentieth century. Unfortunately, its advocates often see only the advantages for the larger area, but ignore the very real disadvantages for local communities. These have opposed metropolitan government in the past as a trespass on local autonomy, and for fear of domination by predominantly white Catholic or nonwhite working class urban voters. (On the other hand, as suburbanization continues, city residents may begin to oppose it for fear of domination by white middle class suburbanites.) If the elements of metropolitan government can be separated into those badly needed and universally wanted, those which only increase governmental efficiency and economy at the cost of local autonomy, and those which are made unworkable by intense class and race conflicts, it may be possible to promote the first. Federal subsidies, now already beginning to flow, may make it worthwhile for suburbs to band together with other suburbs and with the city on selected problems and public services. But further suburbanization would not affect the chances of metropolitan government. The suburbs of the next decade and generation may strengthen existing small communities, but they will not add many new ones to the welter of local government. They will not cut down governmental sprawl, but neither will they increase it.

The reduction in open space is even less serious. Despite the uproar over "megalopolis," there is an immense amount of vacant land even within that alleged belt of city running from Boston to Norfolk. Most of America is less densely settled than the Eastern seaboard, and as Hans Blumenfeld once pointed out, the country is so rich in land that all Americans could be housed at suburban densities in the buildable parts of California. The disappearance of farmland near the big cities is irrelevant now that food is produced on huge industrialized farms, and the destruction of raw land and private upper class golf courses seems a small price to pay for extending the benefits of suburban life to more people.

More recreational acreage will be needed with increasing leisure time, but principally as small parks in the dense portions of the city and as larger ones for weekend and vacation trips. The latter can be located at the edge of the metropolitan area, where they can be made accessible by expressways and mass transit. Moreover, parks are much less important than beaches, lakes, amusement areas, camping sites, and motels with adjacent recreation facilities. Wildernesses provide a desirable recreation resource, but they are used by relatively few people per acre. Making inexpensive and efficient transportation available to distant wildernesses would be more sensible than preventing many people from living in the suburbs in order to retain a wilderness nearby in which a handful can seek solitude a few times a year.

Actually, the conservationist opposition to further suburbanization rests less on the need for recreational land than on a desire to reserve vacant land for future generations, and this in turn is based less on accurate predictions of actual land needs than on a value judgment that the preservation of open land is more important than the current needs of people. Although land should be saved for requirements of ecological balance and for the use of future generations if current needs are not urgent, I believe that restricting current development for an unpredictable future is undesirable. We do not know today how Americans will want to live fifty years from now, or where. By then work and play patterns may have changed so much that many people will want to live a hundred miles or more beyond the city limits. Transportation methods may be available to bring a wilderness five hundred miles away within easy and cheap reach of every metropolitan area resident, and economic and technological devices for rapid land-use changes may have been created. Consequently, ignoring the present demand for land in order to save it for an unknown future demand by our grandchildren cannot easily be justified.

For this reason, I suspect that conservationist opponents of suburbanization are less concerned with future land needs than with a desire to preserve land from people. Many—although not all—of the advocates of wilderness preservation are ideological descendants of the nineteenth century conservatives who opposed European immigration because they did not want America to become a country of non-Puritan city dwellers. In preserving open land, they also wanted to preserve America as a predominantly rural, predominantly Protestant society in which they held political and cultural power. The idea that America ought to be a country of open spaces rather than one of people deriving maximum utility and pleasure from the land still exists today and is manifested by opposition to proposals that virgin lands (note the phrase) be opened up for intensive recreational use. Opponents fear that the land will be "spoiled" by unappreciative (read urban middle and working class) populations. They choose to bar people instead of demanding sufficient funds to remove the garbage left behind by people who have engaged in the very "constructive and wholesome" recreational pursuits that wilderness advocates also favor.

The final source of opposition to further suburbanization comes from the defenders of the city. As the white middle class continues to leave the cities, these become more and more the residence of a small number of rich people—at least in the biggest metropoli—and of a large number of poor people, many of them nonwhite. This trend is alleged to destroy cities as centers of civilization, on the assumption that culture can be created only in the city. Cities were centers of culture in the past, not because they were cities, but because they housed the upper-income populations who supported the creators of culture. The current flourishing of culture in many American cities denies the traditional assumption, for while its supporters have been living in the suburbs for more than two generations, they have not only returned to the city to use its cultural facilities, but have also generated suburban facilities, a trend that will increase more rapidly in the next decades. Whether or not the dominance of poor people in the cities will affect the creators of culture is harder to judge, but many who supply the middle class with culture are already living in suburbs and exurbs without loss of creativity, while new urban (but not middle class) culture is coming into being for the ever larger pool of poor people.

. . .

NOTES

1. There is some evidence that the desire for the single-family house is international, and even exists in countries which cannot afford to satisfy it. I found it among Swedes who must live in apartment complexes (albeit well-planned ones); it is reported in England by Orlans, pp. 106–107 and in Ghana by Tetteh, p. 25.
2. Riesman (1950).
3. The term is borrowed from Banfield (1958), p. 10.
4. Compare, for example, the picture of late nineteenth century class relationships in a small New England town. Thernstrom, Chaps. 1 and 2.
5. See, for example, Ellul.
6. If one assumes that parents become first-home buyers at about age twenty-five, the new suburban building boom can be expected to begin in earnest about 1972, twenty-five years after the start of the postwar increase in family formation and fertility.
7. For example, two sizeable new towns, Columbia, Maryland, and Reston, Virginia, are now being built near Washington, D.C. For a study of these and of the many proposed California new towns, see Eichler.
8. Lessinger, Greer (1962), Chap. 7.
9. See, e.g., Gutkind.
10. See, e.g., Banfield and Grodzins, Wood (1961), and Greer (1963).

REFERENCES

Allen, Frederick L. "The Big Change in Suburbia," *Harper's Magazine,* Vol. 208, June 1954, pp. 21–28, and Vol. 209, July 1954, pp. 47–53.

Banfield, Edward C. "The Case for Scatteration," *Journal of the American Institute of Planners,* Vol. 28, August 1962, pp. 159–169.

Banfield, Edward C., and Grodzins, Morton. *Government and Housing in Metropolitan Areas.* New York: McGraw-Hill, 1958.

Berger, Bennett M. *Working Class Suburb.* Berkeley and Los Angeles: University of California Press, 1960.

Berger, Bennett M. "Suburbia and the American Dream," *The Public Interest,* No. 2, Winter 1966, pp. 80–92.

Blake, Peter. *God's Own Junkyard.* New York: Holt, Rinehart and Winston, 1963.

Burton, Hal. "Trouble in the Suburbs," *Saturday Evening Post,* Vol. 228, September 17, 1955, pp. 19–21, 113–118.

Dobriner, William M. *Class in Suburbia*. Englewood Cliffs: Prentice-Hall, 1963.

Duhl, Leonard J. "Mental Health and Community Planning," in *Planning 1955*. Chicago: American Society of Planning Officials, 1956, pp. 31–39.

Duncan, Otis D., and Schnore, Leo F. "Cultural Behavioral and Ecological Perspectives in the Study of Social Organization," *American Journal of Sociology*, Vol. 65, September 1959, pp. 132–155.

Eichler, Edward P. (with Marshall Kaplan). *The Community Builders*. Berkeley and Los Angeles: University of California Press, 1967.

Ellul, Jacques. *The Technological Society*. New York: Knopf, 1964.

Gordon, R., Gordon, K., and Gunther, M. *The Split Level Trap*. New York: Geis, 1961.

Greer, Scott. *Governing the Metropolis*. New York: Wiley, 1962.

Greer, Scott (with Norton Long). *Metropolitics*. New York: Wiley, 1963.

Gruen, Victor. *The Heart of our Cities*. New York: Simon and Schuster, 1964.

Gruenberg, Sidonie M. "Challenge of the New Suburbs," *Marriage and Family Living*, Vol. 17, May 1955, pp. 133–137.

Gutkind, Erwin A. *The Twilight of Cities*. New York: Free Press of Glencoe, 1962.

Henderson, Harry. "The Mass Produced Suburbs," *Harper's Magazine*, Vol. 207, November 1953, pp. 25–32, and December 1953, pp. 80–86.

James, T. F. "Crackups in the Suburbs," *Cosmopolitan*, Vol. 149, October 1960, pp. 60–65.

Keats, John. *The Crack in the Picture Window*. Boston: Houghton Mifflin, 1956 (Ballantine Books paperback 1957).

Lessinger, Jack. "The Case for Scatteration," *Journal of the American Institute of Planners*, Vol. 28, August 1962, pp. 159–169.

Mumford, Lewis. *The City in History*. New York: Harcourt, Brace and World, 1961.

Orlans, Harold. *Utopia Limited: The Story of the English Town of Stevenage*. New Haven: Yale University Press, 1953.

Riesman, David (with N. Glazer and R. Denney). *The Lonely Crowd*. New Haven: Yale University Press, 1950.

Riesman, David. "The Suburban Dislocation," *The Annals*, Vol. 314, Fall 1957, pp. 123–146. Reprinted in David Riesman, *Abundance for What?* Garden City: Doubleday, 1964, pp. 226–257.

Riesman, David. "Flight and Search in the New Suburbs," in David Riesman, *Abundance for What?* Garden City: Doubleday, 1964, pp. 258–269.

Spectorsky, A. C. *The Exurbanites*. Philadelphia: Lippincott, 1955.

Stein, Maurice. *The Eclipse of Community*. Princeton: Princeton University Press, 1960.

Strauss, Anselm L. *Images of the American City*. New York: Free Press of Glencoe, 1961.

Tetteh, Austin. "Social Background of the Kumasi Plan," *Ekistics*, Vol. 14, July 1962, pp. 22–25.

Thernstrom, Stephan. *Poverty and Progress*. Cambridge: Harvard University Press, 1964.

Whyte, William H., Jr. *The Organization Man*. New York: Simon and Schuster, 1956.

Wood, Robert C. *1400 Governments*. Cambridge: Harvard University Press, 1961.

Wyden, Peter. *Suburbia's Coddled Kids*. Garden City: Doubleday, 1960.

FROM **THE PUBLIC INTEREST:**
SUBURBIA AND THE AMERICAN DREAM

BENNETT M. BERGER

Americans have never been other than ambivalent in their commitment to cultural variety, as against their longing for cultural uniformity. Today, this ambivalence is becoming a central concern of public policy. For, as urban planning becomes an increasingly visible and legitimate part of the activity of the public sector, its power will grow to support or to undermine cultural diversity in the traditional seat of that diversity— the cities. Like the myth of a homogeneous "suburbia," which for a long time obscured, and to some extent still obscures, the actual variety of suburban life, complacence about the cultural diversity of cities may blind us to the conditions which sustain it. My aim in this essay is to take what I and others have learned about the variety of suburban styles of life, and to relate this knowledge, first to some of the more pervasive pluralisms of American culture, and then to a few of the problems of planning for urban diversity.

THE PERSISTENCE OF THE MYTH OF SUBURBIA

Some years back, I undertook a study (reported in *Working-Class Suburb*, Univ. of Calif. Press, 1960) in order to observe the transformation of a group of automobile assembly line workers into the "suburbanites" who had become stock figures in American popular culture in the 1950's through the satirical and other efforts of a variety of popular magazines. It seemed to me that, having found a working class population more than two years settled in a new suburb, I was provided with an almost natural experimental setting in which to document the processes through which "suburbia" exercised its profound and diffuse influence in transforming a group of poorly educated factory workers into those model middle-class Americans obsessed with the problems of crab-grass and "conformity."

Well, it is now a matter of public record that my basic assumption was wrong. As the interview evidence piled up, it became clearer and clearer that the lives of the suburbanites I was studying had not been profoundly affected in any statistically identifiable or sociologically in-

From Bennett M. Berger, "Suburbia and the American Dream," in *The Public Interest*, No. 2 (Winter 1966). Copyright © National Affairs, Inc., 1966. Reprinted by permission, pp. 80–91.

teresting way. They were still overwhelmingly Democrats; they attended church as infrequently as they ever did; like most working class people, their informal contacts were limited largely to kin; they neither gave nor went to parties; on the whole they had no great hopes of getting ahead in their jobs; and instead of a transient psychology, most of them harbored a view of their new suburban homes as paradise permanently gained.

But (appropriately enough for a Ph.D. candidate) I was cautious in the general inferences I drew from that study. It was, after all, based only on a small sample, of one suburb, of one metropolitan area, in one region, and it suffered from all of the methodological limitations inherent in small case studies. None of my findings gave me any reason to doubt the truth of what William H. Whyte, for example, had said of his organization men; but it also seemed to me that there was little reason *not* to believe that my findings in San Jose would be repeatedly confirmed in many of the less expensive suburbs around the country whose houses were priced well within the means of unionized workers in heavy industry, and of lower white collar employees as well. I did, in short, question the right of others to generalize freely about suburbia on the basis of very few studies of selected suburbs which happened to be homogeneously middle or upper class in character—especially when it seemed apparent that suburban housing was increasingly available to all but the lowest income levels and status groups.

The considerable bulk of research that has been done on suburbs in the years since I did my work has given me no reason to alter the conclusions I drew then. Indeed, none of this research can be expected to give much comfort to those who find it convenient to believe that a suburb exercises some mysterious power over its residents, transforming them into replicas of Whyte's practitioners of "The Outgoing Life." There seems to be increasing consensus among students of suburbia that suburban development is simply the latest phase of a process of urban growth that has been going on for a long time, that the cultural character of suburbs varies widely in terms of the social make-up of its residents, and of the personal and group dispositions that led them to move to suburbs in the first place; that the variety of physical and demographic differences between cities and suburbs (and there *are* some) bears little significance for the way of life of their inhabitants, and that some of these differences, although statistically accurate, are sociologically spurious, since the appropriate comparisons are not between residential suburbs and cities as wholes, but between suburbs and urban residential neighborhoods. In general, the reported changes in the lives of suburbanites were not *caused* by the move to suburbia, but were reasons for moving there in the first place. In suburbs, as in city apartments, social class, the age-composition of residents, the age of the neighborhood, etc., are much more profound predictors of the style of life than is residential location with respect to the city limits. Analysis of national samples has provided confirmation neither of a trend to Republicanism in politics nor a return to religion. Suburbs, in short, seem—as Reissman and Ktsanes have characterized them—to be "new homes for old values."

It appears, then, that there are no grounds for believing that suburbia has created a distinctive style of life or a new social character for Americans. Yet the myth of suburbia persists, as is evident from the fact that it is still eminently discussable over the whole range of our cultural media, from comic books to learned journals. One should not be surprised at this, for myths are seldom dispelled by research; they have going for them something considerably more powerful than mere evidence. And though nothing I say here can change this fact, it may give us some comfort to understand the sources of the myth, the functions it performs for the groups by whom it is sustained, and the nature of its appeal to America's image of itself.

In my book, and then, again, later in an article, I undertook a functional explanation of the myth of suburbia. I pointed first to the fact that suburbs were rich with ready made visible symbols: patios and barbecues, lawnmowers and tricycles, shopping centers, station wagons, and so on, and that such symbols were readily organizable into an image of a way of life that could be marketed to the non-suburban public. I also pointed out that this marketing was facilitated by the odd fact that the myth of suburbia conveniently suited the ideological purposes of several influential groups who market social and political opinion—odd because these groups could usually be found disagreeing with each other, not only about matters of opinion, but about matters of fact as well. Realtor-chamber-of-commerce interests and the range of opinion represented by the Luce magazines could use the myth of suburbia to affirm the American Way of Life; city planners, architects, urban design people and so on could use the myth of suburbia to warn that those agglomerations of standardized, vulgarized, mass-produced cheerfulness which masqueraded as homes would be the slums of tomorrow. Liberal and left-wing culture-critics could (and did) use the myth of suburbia to launch an attack on complacency, conformity, and mass culture, and found in this myth an up-to-date polemical vocabulary with which to rebuke the whole slick tenor of American life: what used to be disdained as "bourgeois" was now simply designated as "suburban." In short, the *descriptive* accuracy of the myth of suburbia went largely unchallenged because it suited the *prescriptive* desires of such a wide variety of opinion, from the yea-sayers of the right to the agonizers of the center to the nay-sayers of the left.

But though I still think this analysis of the myth makes good sense, I think too that there is something more—something, if I may be permitted to say so, deeper, profounder, and which I was only dimly aware of then. I think now that the myth can be understood also as our society's most recent attempt to come to terms with the melting pot problem, a problem that goes straight to the heart of American ambivalence about cultural pluralism.

CULTURAL PLURALISM AND THE MELTING POT

America has never really come to terms with the legend of the melting pot. That legend, if I may quote the windy text of its original source, saw America as the place where "Celt and Latin, Slav and Teuton, Greek and Syrian, Black and Yellow, Jew and Gentile, the palm and the pine, the pole and the equator, the crescent and the cross" would together build "the Republic of Man and the Kingdom of God." Despite the hope that a unified American culture might emerge from the seething cauldron, it didn't happen; instead, the formation of ethnically homogeneous communities—ghettoes—helped the immigrants preserve large segments of their cultures, and the tendency to endogamy helped them preserve it beyond the first generation. But in spite of the evident facts of our cultural pluralism (by which I mean the persisting correlation of significant differences in values and behavior with ethnic, regional, and social class differences), attempts are continually made to create an image of *the* typical or representative or genuine American and his community. These attempts have usually succeeded only in creating stereotypes—most familiarly, perhaps, a caricature of one or another variety of Our Town: white, anglo-saxon, Protestant, and middle class. *Saturday Evening Post* covers, white picket fences, colonial houses, maple hutches and the like have historically played an important role in such attempts. *The myth of suburbia is the latest attempt to render America in this homogeneous manner*, to see in the highly visible and proliferating suburban developments a new melting pot which would receive the diverse elements of a new generation from a society fragmented by class, region, religion, and ethnicity, and from them create *the* American style of life. Suburbia as America is no more false a picture, probably, than Babbitt or Our Town as America; but it fails as a melting pot for the same reason that the original melting pot idea failed: like many other urban neighborhoods, specific suburbs developed a tendency to homogeneity, almost always in terms of social class and very often in terms of ethnicity.

The myth of American cultural homogeneity and the stubborn fact of heterogeneity reflect a persistent ambivalence in American society regarding cultural unity and diversity, between the melting pot idea and the pluralist idea. During and after the period of rapid immigration into the "teeming cities," for example, free public education expressed the need for some minimum "Americanization," whereas the ghetto expressed the impulse to cultural self-preservation (both by the natives who excluded and the immigrants who segregated themselves). In the rest of the country, 4th of July style patriotic rhetoric expressed the gropings toward an elementary national identity, whereas provincial arrogance—and hostility to "the government" and to centers of cosmopolitan influence—expressed the affirmation of narrow local autonomies. The ambivalence was really a double ambivalence; each polar position was itself unstable: to be truly tenable, a pluralist ideology must accord intrinsic honor and value to a diversity of life styles, and this it has never completely done. The salient features of minority sub-cultural styles have more often than not been regarded as stigmata by dominant groups, tolerable so long as they were temporary, that is, *transitional* to something approaching the dominant cultural style. On the other hand, the attempts of provincial, nativist ("WASP") groups to secure their own style as *the* American style stopped short of supporting the emergence of broadly inclusive *national* institutions which would have facilitated that transition. The most enthusiastic celebrators of "Americanism" were precisely the groups who were most wary of in-tegrating the varieties of the national life into a unified culture.

Indeed, a unified national culture has until quite recently been a most improbable prospect, since the United States has traditionally been a society without very powerful national institutions with which to pro-mote that unity and pass it on down the generations. Without an estab-lished church or a powerful federal government, without national politi-cal parties or a standardized educational system, enormous distances and poor communications enabled local economies to breed a highly differentiated system of *native* subcultures—in addition to those created by the immigrants. Even today, there are probably dozens of distinctive American types, to some extent stereotypes, perhaps, but which never-theless call attention to the wide variety of *native* styles: Vermont farmers and Boston Brahmins, Southern Bourbons and Tennessee hill-billies, Beatniks and organization men, Plainvillers, Middletowners, and cosmopolitan intellectuals, to say nothing of teenagers, the jet set, and many, many more, all American, all different, and none probably very eager to be integrated into an idea of "*the* American" at a level of com-plexity suitable for a *Time* cover story or a patriotic war movie.

It is not surprising, then, that when one tries to abstract from Amer-ican life a system of values which can be called distinctively or repre-sentatively American, the task is immensely difficult. The most system-atic attempt by a sociologist, that of Robin Williams in his book *American Society,* is foiled by the fact that important groups in Amer-ican society do not share the 15 or 16 values which he offers as basically American. There is no question that values such as "achievement," "work," "efficiency," "equality," and the rest have played a significant role in creating the quality of American life, but important parts of the lower and working classes (important because of their numbers) do not share them, and important parts of the upper class (important be-cause of their influence) do not share them—although they may affirm them when a journalist is nearby.

MYTHS AND STYLES OF LIFE

The persistent attempts to find some transcendent principles or values which define the unity of American culture have been defeated by the persistence of important class and ethnic differences. Even under natural or "organic" conditions, then, "American" patterns of culture are enormously difficult to describe with any accuracy. This difficulty is exacerbated when a society becomes sophisticated enough to be self conscious about its culture and rich enough to do something about it. The maturity and the luxury of our civilization constrain its elites to define an "American" style, and the miracle of our technology arms us to manufacture it. Our society is wealthy enough to support a substantial class of intellectuals devoted to staying on top of contemporary events to "spot the trend," "see the pattern," "find the meaning," "discover the style." And our media are such that these spottings and seeings are more or less instantaneously communicated to audiences of millions, whose demand upon the marketers of opinions and interpretations for sensible and coherent syntheses is greater than the available supply.

Under such conditions, we do not get serious historical interpretation of contemporary events; we do not even get responsible journalism; we get myths, which themselves become part of the forces shaping what is happening, and which hence function ideologically. The myth of suburbia fosters an image of a homogeneous and classless America without a trace of ethnicity but fully equipped for happiness by the marvelous productivity of American industry: the ranch house with the occupied two-car garage, the refrigerator and freezer, the washer and dryer, the garbage disposal and the built-in range and dishwasher, the color TV and the hi-fi stereo. Suburbia: its lawns trim, its driveways clean, its children happy on its curving streets and in its pastel schools. Suburbia, California style, is America.

Most American intellectuals have sustained this myth in order to hate it; but the bases of their antipathy have never really been made clear. Somehow associated with these physical symbols of suburbia in the minds of most intellectuals are complacency, smugness, conformity, status anxiety, and all the rest of the by now familiar and dreary catalogue of suburban culture. But the causal connection between the physical character and the alleged cultural style of suburbia has never been clearly established. It is almost as if American intellectuals felt, like some severe old Calvinist prophet, that physical comfort necessarily meant intellectual sloth. Perhaps it is because we have been too well trained to believe that there is somehow a direct relationship between the physical structure or the esthetic shape of a residential environment and the sort of values and culture it can possibly engender— so that the esthetic monotony of suburbia could house nothing but a generation of dull, monotonous people, and its cheerful poverty of architectural design could breed nothing but a race of happy robots. The only trouble with this view is that there is little evidence and less logic to support it. Most of the adult suburbanites were *urban* bred, and hence presumably already shaped by the time they became suburbanites. And although it is still a little too early to tell what kind of culture will be produced by the generation bred in the manufactured environment of suburbia, we might remember that the generation bred in the endless and prison-like New York tenements did not do badly.

But becoming aware of the myth of suburbia, and pointing to the disparities between it and what we actually know of suburbs we have closely studied, should not be confused with a *defense* of suburbia. Nor should anything I have said about the critics of suburbia be interpreted as an expression of my personal bias in favor of suburbia. As I suggested earlier, myths are potent enough to survive evidence; they are not disarmed by understanding. Quite the contrary. Once myths gain currency, once they go, as we say, "into the cultural air," they *become real*, and function frequently as self-fulfilling prophecies. Life copies literature; fact is affected by fiction; history is constrained by myth. "If a situation is defined as real," said William I. Thomas, "it is real in its consequences," and I have no doubt (though I have no data) that family decisions regarding whether to move to the suburbs have been affected (both pro and con) by the myth of suburbia. And despite everything reasonable I have said about suburbs, I *know* that the fact that I unreasonably dislike them has been conditioned, *beyond the possibility of redemption by mere research*, by the very myth of suburbia I have helped explode.

In the sense in which I have been speaking of them, myths are more or less noble fictions; fictions in that they are *made*, and noble depending on the art with which they are made, the extent to which one is in favor of the consequences they foster, and, most particularly, the forms of solidarity they promote. In the context of the debate over "suburbia," what is usually at stake is whose version of America shall become "American."

PLURALISM AND PLANNING

Whose shall? I want to suggest that the question is relevant to the way in which the future quality of urban life is planned. Like Emile Durkheim, who suggested that the punishment of crime was significant less as a deterrent or as simple revenge than as a collective reaffirmation of cultural values, I want to suggest that we look more closely at the images of solidarity which inform the proposals for dealing with social problems in general, and with urban problems in particular. For social problems, of course, have no objective existence—although the facts to which they refer may. It is objectively true that some people have always lived in dilapidated, unsafe, unheated, vermin-infested residences, but "slums" have not always been a social problem. Slums become a social problem when a large enough group of important people decide that poor people ought not to live in such places.

Americans have a propensity to find social problems. By defining them as real and hence setting ameliorative forces into action, we affirm our liberal heritage. To find problems, to mobilize opinion about them, to shake our social structure by its metaphorical shoulders and force it to *pay attention* to these matters, nourishes our beliefs in progress and perfectibility. America is a country dedicated to the propositions that no evils are ineradicable, no problems insoluble, no recalcitrance beyond conciliation, no ending need be unhappy; we are a most un-Greek democracy. Finding and dealing with problems, then, are necessary conditions for the verification of these propositions; the very existence of social problems to ameliorate, reaffirms our principles more than any imaginable utopia could. But not just any problems at any time. Because at any given moment there is an indefinitely large number of social problems which are theoretically identifiable, public concern with some (to the exclusion of others) can be understood not only in terms of the salience of the difficulties of those who *have* the problems but also in terms of the relevance of proposed solutions to the dominant forms and rhetoric of solidarity.

When we set out to improve the quality of urban life, what we are most likely to be doing is altering the conditions under which weak and vulnerable sections of the population live. The wealthy, who also have problems, are protected from the welfare impulses of others. The strong and the autonomous grant no one the right to alter the conditions of their lives—that is what strength and autonomy are about. Public concern over, and desire to plan for, "the problem of" the increasing proportions of aged persons in our society, for example, do not extend to Dwight Eisenhower, Harry Truman, or H. L. Hunt, all of whom qualify for the statistical category "aged," but not for our image of those who need help—although, if consulted, I might have several suggestions as to how they might spend their declining years more wholesomely. The people who have the problems which are defined as "real" are those who are vulnerable to public action, and thus to the implicit images of solidarity which underlie that action. I think it is essential that we be very clear about these images, for to plan for the *quality* of urban life is to be concerned with the *culture* of urban life, and hence with the forms of human solidarity which planning is likely both to foster and discourage.

I see three broad alternatives for those who are confronted with the problem of planning the quality of urban life. First of all, planners can simply abdicate from any concern for the cultural consequences of what they do, and instead interpret their mandate narrowly—for example, the improvement of the physical environment for the poorly housed. To the extent that they have been planned at all, most new, inexpensive suburbs have been developed in this way—with occasional exceptions, as in the gestures by the Levittowns toward the provision of some institutional facilities. More centrally located urban residential development for the poor and the less-than-affluent has also been dominated by considerations such as square footage, hygiene, and domestic technology. Now to provide room, cleanliness, comfort, and convenience to people who have previously been without them is an important achievement; but it is not planning for the quality of urban life. Quite the contrary; the *quality* of urban life is precisely what is usually left out of consideration—perhaps as a luxury rendered expendable by the need to bring large numbers of people up to some minimum physical standard. Under these conditions of planning, images of human solidarity seem limited exclusively to *households* within which *family* solidarity may be symbolized by culinary and recreational technology (refrigerators, freezers, barbecues, TVs, etc.), whereas solidarities beyond that of the family and household seem irrelevant, alien, or distant. There is a sense in which this alternative is evasive because such planning *does* engender a quality in urban life, but it is the quality that most cultivated foreign observers complain about in most American cities.

Planning's second alternative, it seems to me, is to make a conscious effort to alter the environments of certain groups, with the overt intention of bringing their culture closer to some monolithic or homogeneous ideal. Presumably, this would be some more advanced version of the melting pot idea, in which either a bureaucratic or entrepreneurial version of a middle class life-style would be given as an ideal toward which the poor should be encouraged to reach. Here the aim would be to make the society more monolithically what it already dominantly is. This alternative founders on its utopianism, on its assumption that a cultural consensus can be engineered or induced in a society in which conflict is endemic and which will remain so as long as the interests of groups and classes remain opposed. In the absence of any ability by planners to wipe out class differences, we must expect, in any multi-class community, controversy not only over the appropriate means to reach agreed-upon goals but over the goals themselves and the priorities to be assigned to them. This is the stuff of politics and culture, and where interests and norms are rooted in a class-based style of life, the attempt by one group to elicit the commitment of the entire community to a specific goal will very likely threaten another group and elicit its opposition. Moreover, these political and cultural diversities have a right to exist and persist. We can be reasonably sure that the vulnerable and dependent groups most readily affected by planning would gladly be rid of their slums, their poverty, and the discrimination against them. Beyond this it is difficult to assume anything with great assurance except, perhaps, that groups develop an attachment to those aspects of their culture which have not been imposed by necessity, an attachment made evident by their tendency to take the culture with them when they move from one environment to another, and to preserve whatever of it that circumstances permit. On the other hand, utopian planning dominated by visions of profound cultural changes is always interesting, and such planners might well devote more energy to making these visionary ideals manifest and rhetorically vivid, if only in order to help others to know whether to be for or against the form of solidarity they envision.

THE PLURALIST ALTERNATIVE

Finally, there is the pluralist alternative, an alternative perhaps best expressed in the recent work of Herbert Gans, and, to a lesser extent, of Jane Jacobs. Whatever reservations one may have about the work of either, each of them projects an unambiguous image of the kind of human solidarity they would like to see fostered by urban planning. This solidarity is loose and heterogeneous, composed of more or less autonomous groups and neighborhoods formed on the basis of ethnicity and social class; communities attached, perhaps, to the notion that good fences make good neighbors, but necessarily related to one another through those political and economic accommodations long characteristic of urban life. If they are open to criticism as "romanticists" (although it is not clear to me why a preference for dense street life, or an insistence that an ethnic working-class neighborhood is not necessarily a slum, renders one vulnerable to such criticism), it should at least be said in their defense that they obviously care enough about the *quality* of urban life to evoke a strong and clear image of it (something their critics do not always do)—strong enough in Mrs. Jacobs' case and clear enough in Professor Gans' case to make it easy for a reader to be for or against them.

I am mostly for them, since planning for pluralism seems to me not only the most sensible way of responding to the fact of persisting cultural diversities but the most honorable way as well. In making their assumptions, planners might first of all assume (it is the most reasonable assumption) that most groups which are displaced by planning *will take their culture with them* if they can. Planners would do well to anticipate this, and to modify their plans accordingly, to facilitate the preservation of those parts of their culture that the groups want preserved. This means that planning would have to be done *for specific types of people with distinctive cultural styles,* that is, for a variety of specific, known tastes rather than for faceless densities with a given amount of disposable income for housing. A working class group with a durable pattern of sexual segregation (husbands and wives living largely separate extra-familial lives) requires for its sustenance residential and community facilities different from those required by a middle class group with a culture pattern emphasizing companionable family togetherness.

If the strain put upon the middle class biases of professional planners by such considerations seems excessive, I ask only that you think of the problem of the Negro ghetto and the potential controversy about whether *its* subculture ought to be preserved. People as different as a sociologist like Lee Rainwater and a Negro leader like James Baldwin have remarked (without clearly deploring it) upon the Dyonisianism prevalent in the Negro ghetto. Now, this is a culture pattern which clearly is both at once an adaptation to the trapped character of ghetto life, and a means of providing compensatory satisfactions for that blocked access to middle class life. If the satisfactions are not only compensatory but real, planners might think about providing facilities for the nourishment of this psycho-cultural pattern—even as they think about eliminating the enforced segregation and demoralization which make it more attractive.

Even after discrimination on the basis of race disappears, however, we have no evidence to suggest that segregation will ever disappear. If the experience of other ethnic groups is any guide (and I know of no better guide), many Negroes will choose to live among their own "kind" even after they have formally free choice of housing. However "kind" may be defined in the future, there is no reason *not* to expect social class and ethnicity to continue to play an important role—although it is quite conceivable that color may eventually not have much to do with ethnicity. We know little enough about the nature of ethnicity—and even less, perhaps, about which members of an ethnic group *prefer* to live in ghettoes, or why, even after they can live almost wherever they please. But the *fact* that many of them do is beyond question. We have no reason *not* to expect this to be true of Negroes also, particularly of those whose views are represented by the most militant Negro leaders, insistent upon the acceptance of Negroes into American society *as Negroes*—with all that this historically implies.

I hope it is clear that these remarks are not the elaborate rationalizations of a conservative searching for an acceptable rhetoric to defend the *status quo*. Quite the contrary; they are the remarks of a sociologist who, being for the extension of the widest possible range of choice to all segments of the population, nevertheless knows that choices are hardly ever random, and that no man is so free that he is not constrained by the norms of the groups to which he belongs or would like to belong. This is as it should be; but the sense of choice rests on the existence of real alternatives. Cultural diversity has somehow been maintained in the suburbs without much help from planners. We may not be so lucky in the cities unless planners begin to understand the conditions of cultural distinctiveness and to design for it.

Chapter 5

MIDDLE AMERICANS

At least for the last half-century many Americans have adopted a "melting-pot" perspective in describing or prescribing the social and cultural adaptations made by the millions who migrated to the United States from other countries. The melting-pot theme is found not only in the speeches of presidents but also in the conversations of ordinary Americans, and it was given an influential formulation by Zangwill in an early twentieth-century play about the struggle of a Russian immigrant, who at one point argues that

> America is God's Crucible, the great Melting-Pot where all the races of Europe are melting and re-forming! Here you stand, good folk, think I, when I see them at Ellis Island, here you stand in your fifty groups, with your fifty languages and histories, and your fifty blood hatreds and rivalries. But you won't be long like that, brothers, for these are the fires of God. . . . A fig for your feuds and vendettas! Germans and Frenchmen, Irishmen and Englishmen, Jews and Russians—into the Crucible with you all! God is making the American.[1]

While America-the-Crucible ideas have taken a variety of forms and have been countered with alternative interpretations, they still maintain a powerful grip on American thinking about the assimilation process—past, present, and future.

For example, many would argue that the current trend is—and ought to be—toward a precipitous decline in the significance of ethnicity in American society. While there has been debate over the character and operation of this adaptive process, until quite recently few seemed to question the view that ethnic differences were no longer of any real consequence.

In *Why Can't They Be Like Us?* sociologist Andrew Greeley argues

convincingly for the survival of meaningful ethnic differences in contemporary American society. In addition to the data cited in the excerpts
from Greeley's book reprinted here, extensive research evidence for the
persistence of ethnic differentials is provided throughout the book. To
illustrate, examination of survey research (opinion poll) materials on
Catholic immigrant groups (including the Irish, Germans, Italians, and
Poles) revealed very important variations among white ethnics not only
in socioeconomic status but also in racial attitudes and general outlook
on life. Particularly important, too, was the reported tendency for these
white Americans to socialize and marry within their own ethnic groups.
Thus, Greeley argues that the ethnic neighborhood is still very much a
part of urban society:

> Considerable numbers of human beings continue to live in neighborhoods
> and continue to be deeply attached to their social turf, to view the geog-
> raphy and the interaction network of their local communities as an ex-
> tension of themselves and to take any threat to the neighborhood as a
> threat to the very core of their being.[2]

Rejecting the view that there is really a "blue-collar ethnic problem,"
Greeley further proposes that existing ethnic diversity, as well as the apparent resurgence of ethnic self-consciousness among whites, can be
viewed positively. Thus, the intimate primary ties of these predominantly
urban groups provide a social location and a context for the development of strong personal identity. From this perspective ethnic groups do,
and in the future can, provide cultural richness and liveliness in an
urban environment, perhaps preventing the emergence of the much-
feared specters of "mass society" and the "lonely crowd."

In the second selection in this chapter we are introduced in a rather
intimate way to a few of those Americans often maligned in discussions
of "blue-collar ethnic" or "hard-hat" Americans. Similarly rejecting the
notion that these middle Americans should be viewed as a "problem,"
Robert Coles provides vivid verbal portraits, the result of long hours
spent interviewing a number of Americans who described themselves
simply as "plain people" or "average people." Relatively little analysis
accompanies Coles' ethnographic sketches, but the surprising diversity
and complexity of the views represented are particularly underscored.
In the excerpt reprinted here the variety and inconsistency of working-
class perspectives are conspicuously evident. At times Joe—a man who
works at several blue-collar jobs—certainly seems to fit the image of a
hard-hat bigot, espousing negative views of college students and black
Americans. However, a few minutes later Joe confounds those who
would neatly classify him with unexpected comments like the following: "If I was a Negro, I'd be madder than hell. I'd stand up to anyone
who tried to keep me away from my share." [3] Nor is his view of students
as monolithic or inflexible as some might make it out to be. "And soon
Joe switches, says maybe, says yes, says it is true that some of the
students are good, mean well, are on the workingman's side against the
big corporations." [4]

While Coles' interviews reflect views that many have come to associate with popular images of blue-collar Americans, including firm commitment to the work ethic, entrenched patriotism, devotion to home and family, and strong criticism of students and black Americans, they also accentuate the confusion, the complexity, the honesty, and even the *radicalism* of middle Americans. Perhaps most striking is the strain of economic radicalism, which is often mixed with more conservative points of view; the comments of a young Vietnam veteran, a welder, are instructive:

> We argue during the coffee break. One guy will say that Nixon is cracking down on nigger-bums, and the welfare-bleeders. . . . But pretty soon the next guy will open up with a reminder that the Negro is only trying to get *his,* just like we tried to get *ours,* the working man did. And who won't give anyone an extra dime, unless he's pushed? I'll tell you. It's the banker and the big businessman. . . . I've never been asked what I think in a poll, and no one I know has ever been asked. If they did come around and talk with us at work and ask us their questions, I'll bet we'd confuse them. One minute we'd sound like George Wallace, and the next we'd probably be called radicals or something.[5]

NOTES

1. Israel Zangwill, *The Melting Pot* (New York: Macmillan, 1925), p. 33.
2. Andrew M. Greeley, *Why Can't They Be Like Us?: America's White Ethnic Groups* (New York: Dutton, 1971), p. 100. See also Bennett Berger's discussion in Chapter 4.
3. Robert Coles and Jon Erikson, *The Middle Americans* (Boston: Atlantic-Little, Brown, 1971), p. 9.
4. Ibid., p. 6.
5. Ibid., pp. 138–139.

FROM **WHY CAN'T THEY BE LIKE US?:** THE FUTURE OF ETHNIC GROUPS

ANDREW M. GREELEY

It is now time to address ourselves to three general questions: 1) Are ethnic groups likely to survive in American society? 2) Can anything be done to mitigate ethnic conflicts? and 3) What kind of research would help shed some of the light we need on this subject?

As to the first question—whether ethnic groups have a future in American society—the previous chapters have, I hope, provided sufficient answer. There is no reason to think they will not continue to play an important role, at least for the rest of this century, despite the fact that the compositions of the groups are changing, as well as the kind of identification they provide for their members. (Joshua Fishman, in his large and impressive study of language loyalty,[1] indicates that there is apparently an inevitable decline across generation lines in the use of a foreign tongue, although he and many of his coauthors entertain some hope that the decline can be arrested and even reversed.)

Although immigration has by no means come to an end, and hundreds of thousands of immigrants enter the United States each year, the ratio of immigrants to the total population is obviously much smaller than it was at the turn of the century. And while the new immigrants do provide clients for the hard core of purely ethnic services (especially the press and radio programs identified with the mother tongue), they no longer represent the major focus of concern for most American ethnics.

Poles, Norwegians and Italians, for example, are far more concerned with shaping their future within the American environment than preserving their cultural links with the past. The cultural links are preserved, however, in two fashions—first, by the unconscious transmission of role expectations, some rooted in the past and others in the early experience in this country; and second, through a scholarly or artistic interest in the customs of the past. Thus, though the ethnic groups in this country have taken on a life of their own, more or less independent of the national cultures and societies where their roots lie, many of the old links survive, indirectly and undeliberately, or in a highly self-conscious academic fashion.

Again we can see how blurred the picture is and how difficult it is to be confident in the absence of more careful research. The American Irish are different, let us say, from the American Poles in part because they come from different cultural backgrounds, in part because they came to the United States at different times, in part because the two groups have had vastly different experiences in the American society, and in part because there are conscious efforts—at first from an intense determination to survive, and later out of leisurely academic and artistic interests—to keep a lot of the traditions and customs of the past.

The American Irish, I suspect, are only slightly moved by the current Londonderry riots in which Catholics in the north of Ireland have adopted some of the tactics of American blacks in their own civil rights movement. Not long ago, during a visit to a Catholic girls' college in the heartland of America, I noticed a sign on the bulletin board announcing that the Irish Club of the college would shortly hold its monthly meeting. I asked the young lady who was showing me through the college if she belonged to the Irish Club; it turned out that she not only belonged, she was its president. "Peggy," I asked her, "do you know what the six counties are?" She admitted that she did not. "Have you ever heard of the Sinn Fein?" She had not. "Have you ever heard of the Easter rising, or the I.R.A.?" She conceded her ignorance. Finally, I said "Peggy, do you know who Eamon de Valera is?" She brightened. "Isn't he the Jewish man that is the Lord Mayor of Dublin?" she asked.

And yet Peggy is Irish, and proudly so, though she is part of the fourth generation. She might be hard put to say specifically how she differs from her Polish classmates, but the political style of her family, the shape of its commitment to Roman Catholicism, perhaps even its interpretation of the meaning of the good life, are rooted in the Irish past; and even though Peggy later married a boy with a German name (it was all right, her relatives assured me, because his mother was Irish), she continues to be Irish, and I suspect her children will too, no matter what their name happens to be.

For Jews, the issue of ethnic identity is, it seems to me, even more subtle and complex. The horrifying disaster of the Second World War made most Jews much more explicitly conscious of their background and cultural traditions, and the existence of Israel as a modern nation state embodying these traditions reinforces this consciousness. Thus, while Jews are one of the most thoroughly acculturated groups in American society, they are also extremely conscious of their origins and history, and even in the third and fourth generation they make greater efforts to preserve their own culture than any other major immigrant group.

INTERMARRIAGE AND IDENTITY

Those who doubt that ethnic groups have much of a future usually point to intermarriage as proof that ethnicity is vanishing on the American scene. The truth is, however, that there is almost nothing in the way of detailed literature on ethnic intermarriage except the studies on intermarriage between Jews and gentiles.[2]

Harold Abramson's study, referred to in Chapter 7 [not reprinted here], finds that ethnic intermarriage does, indeed, increase with generation, education and occupational success. But ethnic intermarriage hardly seems to be a random event. A typical ethnic in Abramson's population was some two and one-half times more likely to choose a mate from his own ethnic group than he would if ethnicity were irrelevant in a choice of spouse. Furthermore, even intermarriage seems to take place along certain ethnically predictable lines—that is to say, if someone does marry outside his ethnic group, he is more likely to choose someone from a group considered relatively close to his own. Thus an Irishman, for example, is much more likely to marry a German than a Pole or an Italian.

Abramson's data, which were collected for another purpose, do not supply the answers to two critical questions. First, what sort of ethnic identification, if any, does the new family choose for itself? While there is not much in the way of precise data, impressionistic evidence (reported by Moynihan and Glazer) seems to indicate that a choice of ethnic identity is made either by the spouses themselves or by their children.

The second and more complicated question is: Which traits are passed on to which children in an ethnic intermarriage? Let us consider, for example, the apparent political liberalism of the Irish in comparison with the other Catholic groups described in the previous chapter. In a marriage between an Irish male college graduate and a Polish female college graduate, holding all the other variables constant, whose social attitudes are likely to affect the children? Will the father, rather than the mother, prevail because the father is political leader of the family? Will the father influence his sons and the mother her daughters, or will the flow of influence be vice versa? Or will it all cancel out, with the Polish-Irish children assuming positions on social issues somewhere between those of the two ethnic groups?

Of course we also have no way of knowing whether the social attitudes reported in the previous chapter will survive into the next generation, even in ethnically endogamous marriages. These complicated questions simply underscore how precious little we know about the later stages of acculturation and assimilation. What we do know, however, scarcely justifies the popular assumption that the ethnic groups are disappearing.

But if they are likely to persist, how is society to cope with the problems that ethnicity generates? For it seems to me we must, above all, recognize that ethnic problems are also likely to persist, and that it does little good to lament them or moralize about them. We must also be carefully aware of our own ethnic biases and not permit ourselves the luxury of superior attitudes towards behavior which, if the truth be told, we dislike mostly because it's not the sort of thing "our kind of people" might do. And thirdly, we must be wary of turning correlations into causes. In Chapter 6 [not reprinted here], for example, we described correlations between "Polishness" and certain ethnocentric attitudes. It would be quite easy to make a leap and say that being Polish "causes" the ethnocentric attitudes—and some Polish critics of the data I've discussed have assumed I was making such a leap, even though there were no grounds for such an assumption. There may be something in the Polish cultural background to explain anti-Semitism, but there is nothing I can think of that would explain racism. Thus, I would be much more inclined to see the conflict between the Poles and the blacks in terms of the particular stage in the ethnic assimilation process that the Poles happen to have reached at the time when the black group has become militant. In other words, I am inclined to think we can explain the conflict between the Poles and the blacks almost entirely in economic, social and psychological terms, without having to fall back on cultural traditions at all.

The problem is not much easier with respect to the somewhat less intense controversies separating white ethnic groups, one from another. I have no clear notions of how to cope with an apparent increase in Jewish animosity toward Catholics in recent years . . . or with the antagonism between Irish Catholics and other Catholic groups. I suspect we need intergroup dialogue, cultural exchanges and serious interest in the cultural institutions of those groups with which we are most likely to compete. I am also inclined to think we need leaders who are less demagogic since ethnic groups seem to have a genius for flocking to demagogic leadership. And we must show great self-restraint in attacking the leadership of other groups, even though that leadership is likely to leave itself wide open to such attacks. But having repeated suggestions which must be considered as little more than truisms of intergroup work, I am at a loss as to how to proceed further. We simply do not know enough; not enough data are available, not enough experiments have been done, and all too few theories have been advanced to enable us either to understand what is going on or to prescribe remedies for the pathology we may observe.

It does seem to me, however, that it is essential for political leaders, social planners and influential figures in the ethnic communities to abandon the rather foolish controversy of whether ethnicity is a good thing or a bad thing—particularly since it clearly has both good and bad effects—and settle down to a better understanding of what it means and how we may live with it, not merely tolerably, but fruitfully.

A number of people have made some concrete suggestions for helping to "cool" the tensions among America's ethnic groups. Some try to deal with the problems "where they're at," that is, at the actual point of collision. The American Arbitration Association, for example, has organized a new Center for Dispute Settlement which will offer free mediation and arbitration services to help resolve differences between racial and ethnic groups, students and school administrators, landlords and tenants, businessmen and consumers, and other groups involved in clashes that might otherwise escalate into dangerous confrontations.

Others address themselves to efforts to get at the underlying causes. If competition for scarce, or presumably scarce, opportunities and services is at the root of much of the conflict among ethnic groups, they reason, one way to reduce such conflict is to "enlarge the pie" through economic and social programs aimed at improving the overall quality of life for all Americans. Such proposals have come from a variety of sources, including the carefully detailed Freedom Budget, outlined a few years ago by economists Leon Keyserling and Vivian Henderson and others, and the broad *Agenda for the Nation* published by the prestigious consultants of the Brookings Institution. All of these proposals envision a shift in national priorities to channel some of our enormous productive capacities into programs to provide jobs, schools, housing, recreation, health services and other essentials, not only for the hard-core poor who, in our less affluent past, have been consistently squeezed out in the competition for these needs, but also for the many millions of hard-working lower middle-class ethnics embittered by poor schooling, dead-end jobs and an unrelenting, unfair tax burden.

. . .

NOTES

1. Joshua Fishman *et al., Language Loyalty in the United States* (London and The Hague: Mouton, 1966).
2. Marshall Sklare, "Intermarriage and the Jewish Future," *Commentary,* April 1964, and Erich Rosenthal, "Studies of Jewish Intermarriage in the United States," *American Jewish Year Book,* Vol. 64 (1963), two of the best research reports on this subject.

CONCLUSION:
PROBLEM OR PROMISE

As someone who has insisted for a decade and more that American social science ought to be concerned about the continuation of ethnicity in American society I have mixed feelings about the current fascination with the subject in academic, governmental, foundation and mass media offices. Obviously, I am delighted that people don't look at me as though I were crazy when I say that ethnic groups have survived in American society, but I am considerably less than pleased to discover that from a state of nonexistence white ethnic groups have become a social problem without anybody bothering to do any careful study in between. My feeling is that most members of American ethnic groups are going to be unpleasantly surprised to discover that they are a problem or that they are a "blue-collar problem" and, much worse, a "hard hat problem." As much of a shock as it may be to elite groups in American society, there are considerable numbers of white ethnics who are not blue-collar workers, and even substantial numbers who are college graduates and professionals; but they still have some recollection of what it was like to be a social problem, to be an object of the ministrations of welfare workers and settlement house do-gooders and they are, unless I am mistaken, quite disinclined to become that once again. Nor are they to be bought off by an increase in real income or by "community services." Indeed, the American white ethnics realize almost as much as do their black brothers that when the elite groups define you as a problem you are in for trouble. There was a time when the white ethnics had no choice but to be a "problem," but they have a choice now and I think they want no part of it.

Nonetheless, the elites persist in talking about the "blue-collar ethnic problem" and find themselves now joined by some of those alienated ethnics who only recently were seeking their own self-validation by crusading for rights for blacks. When the blacks made clear to them that they no longer could play their paternalistic roles, some of these leaders—most notably Catholic clergymen—rediscovered their own ethnic heritage and, with barely a change in vocabulary, they are now crusading for white ethnic rights. Indeed, one of them went so far recently as to observe that in a couple of years white ethnics would catch up to the blacks in matters of ethnic self-consciousness—a statement well calculated to offend, if possible, everyone.

In the final analysis, I suspect more harm will be done by this "social problem" approach than was done by simply ignoring the existence of white ethnic groups. It should be obvious by now that the perspective of this book assumes that ethnic diversity is an opportunity rather than a problem. Why the social problem approach is being emphasized and the "positive contribution" approach largely ignored is in itself a subject for further investigation.

The great theme of classical sociology is that in the last centuries Western society has moved from *gemeinschaft* to *gesellschaft,* from community to association, from primary group to secondary group, from mechanical solidarity to organic solidarity, from traditional authority to bureaucratic authority, from primordial drives to contractual drives. Weber, Durkheim, Tonnies, Toreltsch and Talcott Parsons have merely arranged different orchestrations on this architectonic theme. Under the impact of rationalization, bureaucratization, industrialization and urbanization, it is argued, the old ties of blood, faith, land and consciousness of kind have yielded to the rational structural demands of the technological society. In the conceptual framework of Professor Parsons's famous pattern variables, the immense social changes of the last two centuries have moved the race or at least the North Atlantic component of it from the particularistic to the universal, from ascription to achievement, from the diffuse to the specific. And other observers see a shift from the mythological to the religionless, from the sacred to the profane to the secular, from the folk to the urban. In other words, in organized society at the present time, the rational demands of the organization itself—or the organizations themselves—provide the structure that holds society together. Nonrational and primordial elements, if they survive at all, survive in the "private sphere" or in the "interstices." The old primordial forces may still be somewhat relevant in choosing a wife or a poker or bridge partner, but they have no meaning in the large corporate structures—business, labor, government, education, or even, for that matter, church. In the private sphere and in the interstices, the nonrational and primordial ties are seen as everywhere in retreat. Ethnic groups are vanishing, religion is losing its hold, men and women are becoming so mobile that they need no geographic roots. Professor Bennis[1] argues that there is emerging a "temporary society" made up of those members of the social elite for whom geographic, institutional and interpersonal stability are no longer necessary. These men, according to Bennis, move from place to place, occupation to occupation, and relationship to relationship without feeling any sense of personal or physical dislocation. Wherever they go, they are immediately able to relate intensely to their fellows, and when the time comes to terminate a set of relationships, they then enter into a new set that is equally intense but equally transitory. There is some suggestion in *The Temporary Society* that these new elites might even be capable of temporary marriage relationships. Whatever is to be said about the merits, moral, biological or aesthetic, of the temporary society, it is certainly the ultimate in the pilgrimage from *gemeinschaft* to *gesellschaft.* The lives of the denizens of the temporary society are completely shaped by the functional necessities of technological industrialism.[2]

In this official model of classical sociology, then, the primordial is seen to be on the way out. There may be some disagreement as to the speed of the evolutionary process, but nonetheless, secular man, technological man, religionless man, temporary man is seen as the man of the future. He is the one who occupies the critical positions in the government, in the media, in the university faculties, in the large corporate businesses. He needs little in the way of roots, nothing in the way of transcendental faith, and, as far as the technostructure is concerned, precious little in the way of emotion. Professor John Schaar ironically describes the cognitive ideology of such a man. "Reality is that which is tangible, external, measurable, capable of being precisely conveyed to others; everything that is left over—and some might think that it is half of life—becomes curiously unreal or epiphenomenal. If it persists in its intrusions on the 'real' world, then it must be treated as trouble and those whose acts or motives are imbedded in the unreal world are treated as deviant cases in need of repair or reproof." [3]

Even if one does not wish to go quite that far in describing the pilgrimage from community to association, one still must admit that the implicit basic premises of most contemporary social analysis assume that the "public sphere" is the real world, that what goes on in corporate structures is what holds society together. The primordial or the tribal is limited to certain reactionary segments within the society and, even there, will be eradicated by the college educated in a generation or two.

The old right and the new left may disagree, but I think that an implicit value premise runs through much of this analysis: the rationalized society is not only the way things are but the way things should be. The primordial or prerational ties are seen as "unenlightened" and "reactionary." One need not discuss the current resurgence of interest in white ethnic groups very long without realizing that among many liberal academics there is a strong moral revulsion against ethnic groups. The term "white ethnic racist" is used much the same way as "damn Yankee" is used in the South. It becomes one word and indeed an epithet. An official of a national social work organization inviting me to give a speech at a meeting on the subject noted that "as far as I'm concerned, these people [white ethnics] are simply a barrier to social progress, though I suppose they have their own problems, too." And at the same conference a panel discussion about white ethnics labels them as "social conservatives." Serious discussions are held under the sponsorship of government agencies or private foundations in which the white ethnic "problem" is discussed as something about which "something must be done." One cannot speak to an academic group on the subject of ethnicity without some timid soul rising in the question period to inquire whether it might not be immoral to discuss the question of ethnic groups since ethnicity stresses the things which separate men and we ought to be concerned about those things which unite them. The bias in these reactions is apparent: the survival of the primordial is a social problem. The evolution from the nonrational to the rational, the sacred to the profane, the primordial to the contractual, the folk to the urban is seen not merely as a useful analytic model, but as profoundly righteous moral imperative. As some people have not completed their pilgrimage through this simple evolutionary model, obviously they are a social problem and "something must be done about them," such as, for example, seeing that their real income goes up at the rate of 5 per cent a year or providing day care centers for their neighborhoods. If one does enough of such things for them, maybe then they or at least their children will someday become more enlightened and be just like us.

It is certainly not my intention to deny the great utility of the official model of classical sociology. Obviously, a great transformation has come over the North Atlantic world since 1750. I need only to visit Ballendrehid, County Mayo, Ireland, to know that it is different from Chicago, Cook County, Illinois. The insight of the great sociologists is extraordinarily valuable but the trouble with their model as a tool for analysis is that the temptation is strong either to ignore or to treat as residual phenomena whatever can't be made to fit the model. I would contend that it is the very elegance of the official model of classical sociology that has blinded us to an incredibly vast range of social phenomena which must be understood if we are to cope with the problems of contemporary America.

I would suggest, then, that another model must be used either in conjunction with the official one or as the component of a more elaborate model which will integrate the two. According to this model, the basic ties of friendship, primary relationship, land, faith, common origin and consciousness of kind persist much as they did in the Ice Age. They are the very stuff out of which society is made and in their absence the corporate structures would collapse. These primordial, prerational bonds which hold men and women together have of course been transmuted by the changing context. The ethnic group, for example, did not even exist before the last of the nineteenth century. It came into existence precisely so that the primordial ties of the peasant commune could somehow or other be salvaged from the immigration experience. But because the primordial ties have been transmuted does not mean that they have been eliminated. They simply operate in a different context and perhaps in a different way. They are, according to this second model, every bit as decisive for human relationships as they were in the past. In fact, a strong case could be made that one primordial relationship—that of marriage—has in one respect become far stronger than it ever was in the past, because prospective marriage partners now require more rather than fewer ties of interpersonal affection; and while such ties of affection may appear structurally tenuous, they can be far more demanding on the total personality than were the structural ties of the past.

To the extent that this model has validity, a simple, unidimensional and unidirectional evolution from *gemeinschaft* to *gesellschaft* has not taken place. What has happened, rather, has been a tremendous increase in the complexity of society, with vast pyramids of corporate structures being erected on a substratum of primordial relationships. Since the primordial ties tend to be the infrastructure, or at least to look like the infrastructure to those who are interested primarily in corporate bureaucracies, it is possible to ignore them or at least to give them minimal importance. One does not, after all, think about the foundation of the Empire State Building when one sees it soaring into the air above Manhattan Island—not at least unless one happens to be an engineer.

From this second model, if it has any validity, one would conclude that the persistence of primordial bonds is not merely a social problem, but also a social asset. Communities based on consciousness of kind or common faith or common geography would be seen in this model not merely as residues of the past, but rather as a basic subcomponent of the social structure. Membership in such communities would be seen as providing personal identity and social location for members as well as making available a pool of preferred role opposites whose availability would ease stress situations at critical junctures in modern living. In other words, collectivities grouped around such primordial bonds would be seen not merely as offering desirable cultural richness and variety, but also as basic pillars of support for the urban social structure. A city government would view itself as fortunate in having large and diverse ethnic groups within its boundaries because such collectivities would prevent the cities from becoming a habitat for a "lonely crowd" or a "mass society." Psychologists and psychiatrists would be delighted with the possibilities of ethnic group membership providing social support and self-definition as an antidote to the "anomie" of the mass society. Another way of putting the same matter would be to say that to the extent the second model is a valid one, the lonely crowd and the mass society do not really exist.

But to what extent does the second model have any validity? My inclination would be to say that, if anything, much more research data can be fitted into the second model than into the first one. This is not the appropriate place to review in detail all the available evidence about the survival of the primordial, but one can at least list the principal research efforts. The now classic Hawthorne experiments of Elton Mayo and his colleagues demonstrated how decisive in the supposedly rationalized and formalized factory was the influence of informal friendship groups. Ruby Jo Reeves Kennedy proved in the early 1940's that there had been no change in patterns of religious intermarriage for a half century and thirty years later the research done at the National Opinion Research Center on young college graduates indicates that denominational (which includes Baptists, Lutherans, Methodists, etc., as separate denominations) intermarriage is still not increasing in the United States. The *American Soldier* [1] showed how decisive personal loyalty was in holding together the combat squad. The work of Morris Janowitz and Edward Shils proved that the Wehrmacht began to fall apart only when the rank and file soldier began to lose faith in the paternalistic noncom who held his unit together. The voting studies of Paul Lazarsfeld and his colleagues proved that voting decisions were not made by isolated individuals but rather by members of intimate primary groups; and the similar studies of Elihu Katz and others on marketing decisions and the use of innovative drugs showed how such decisions were strongly influenced by informal personal relationships. Will Herberg's classic, *Protestant, Catholic, Jew,* suggested a model explaining that religion is so important in the United States precisely because it provides self-definition and social location. James Q. Wilson's study of police discovered that sergeants of different ethnic groups have different administrative styles and the work of Edward Levine and others on the Irish as politicians has made clear—to those who are yet unaware of it —that the Irish have a highly instinctive political style (a political style, be it noted, that assumes the persistence and importance of primordial groups).

Manpower research done at NORC indicates that ethnicity is a moderately strong predictor of career choice. (Germans go into science and engineering, Jews into medicine and law, Irish into law, political science and history and the foreign service.) Studies of hospital behavior show that different ethnic groups respond differently to pain in hospital situations. (The Irish deny it and the Italians exaggerate it.) The Banfield and Wilson school of political science [5] emphasizes urban politics as an art of power brokerage among various ethnic and religio-ethnic groups. More recent research at NORC has shown that there is moderately strong correlation between ethnicity and a number of behavioral and attitudinal measures—*even when social classes have held constant.* Other research studies suggest that in large cities professional practices —medical, dental, real estate, construction—tend to be organized along religious or ethnic lines, and yet other work would indicate that some groups choose to create a form of self-segregation, even in the suburbs. Louis Wirth was right; there would indeed be a return to the ghetto but the ghetto would not be in Douglas Park (Chicago), it would be in Skokie and Highland Park (the suburbs).

I could go on, but it hardly seems necessary. Weep not for *gemeinschaft;* it is still very much with us. On the contrary, the burden of evidence ought to be on those who claim to see it vanishing. When it is argued that at least among the social elites secular, technological, religionless man seems to dominate, we need only point out that precisely the offspring of these elites seem presently most interested in recreating the tribal in the world of the psychedelic, neo-sacral communes. The model of classical sociology obviously is not to be abandoned, but it must be freed from a simple-minded, evolutionary interpretation. Furthermore, it is even more necessary to divest the model from the moralistic overtones which it has acquired in popular sociology and, unless I am very much mistaken, in professional sociology as well. To assume that religious or ethnic or geographic ties are unenlightened, reactionary, benighted or obscurantist is to make a moral judgment for which there are no grounds in serious social analysis.

The issue of the two models is not by any means just a theoretical one for, if one uses only the first model, then the angry white ethnic groups are seen basically as a social problem. But if one uses also the second model, one might conclude that ethnic loyalty could be a strong, positive force which might make available vitality and vigor for the preservation and enrichment of urban life for all members of the city.

Thus, I would hypothesize that taking the propensity to desert the city as a dependent variable, one would find a strongly ethnic neighborhood scoring much lower on that variable than a cosmopolitan neighborhood. I would even go further and suggest that in an ethnic neighborhood under "threat" there would be less inclination to desert the city than in a less threatened cosmopolitan neighborhood. In one study of the 1969 mayoral election in Gary, Indiana, it was discovered that Poles who are more strongly integrated into the Polish community were more likely to vote for Mayor Hatcher than Poles who were less integrated into the ethnic community (though, obviously, in absolute numbers not many were likely to vote for him). There has been so little positive research done on the subject of white ethnic groups that one hesitates to state conclusively that ethnic identification and loyalty might be a positive asset for promoting social change in the city. Unfortunately, the rigid theoretical limitations of the official model have made it difficult to persuade funding agencies that such research might be appropriate. We are now faced with the rather bizarre situation in which many funding agencies are almost pathetically eager to do something about "the white ethnic problem," without ever having established that it is in fact a problem. It might be a distinct advantage.

If the second model has any utility at all, one could also call into question much of the romantic criticism and equally romantic utopianism of contemporary American society. It may turn out that there is, after all, rather little anomie. It may be that the mass society does not exist beyond Los Angeles and the university campuses around the country. It may be that the young who are seeking to create new clans, new tribes or new communes could achieve the same goals by moving back into their grandparents' neighborhood—an experiment which would also have the happy advantage of revealing to them that intimate communities can be narrow, rigid, doctrinaire and, in many instances, quite intolerant of privacy, creativity and diversity. If such romantic utopians would at least spend some time in their grandparents' neighborhood, they would be a bit more realistic about the problems that they will encounter in the Big Sur or along the banks of the Colorado River.[6]

American social scientists have to put aside their underlying assumptions if they are intelligently to investigate and understand ethnic pluralism in the large cities of our Republic. Social policy makers must likewise put aside most of *their* underlying assumptions. A considerable number of both the social scientists and social policy makers are currently announcing that black is beautiful (whether they really believe it or not is another matter) but if black is beautiful (and it is) then so is Irish, Polish, Italian, Slovenian, Greek, Armenian, Lebanese and Luxembourger.[7] All these represent valid and valuable cultural heritages. They all represent sources of identification and meaning in a vast and diverse society. They all have a positive contribution to a richer and more exciting human community.

Let me conclude with a story whose point I think I need not elaborate. I was standing in front of a church in the west of Ireland, camera in hand, attempting to record the church which I thought just possibly was the place of my grandfather's baptism. The parish priest, who was out cutting his hedge despite the rain, approached me, noted that I was a new man around here, and introduced himself. I must say I was a bit surprised when, on hearing my name, he remarked, "Ah, yes, you'd be the sociologist fellow from Chicago." Then he added, "Would you be wantin' your grandfather's baptismal record now?"

I admitted that the idea hadn't occurred to me. He shook his head in discouragement. "Ah," he said, "fine sociologist you are."

"Do a lot of people come seeking such records?" I asked.

He nodded gravely. "Indeed they do," he said, "indeed they do. Those poor people, you know, they've been in the States now for three generations and they come seeking roots; they want to know who they are; they want to know all about their past and their ancestors. The poor people, I feel so sorry for them. That's why I had all their baptismal records put on microfilm. It makes it a lot easier for people to find their roots."

NOTES

1. Warren G. Bennis and Philip E. Slater, *The Temporary Society* (New York: Harper & Row, 1968).
2. To make my own biases in the matter perfectly clear, if I had to choose between the temporary society and a commune, I wouldn't have much difficulty choosing the latter.
3. John Schaar, "Reflections on Authority," *New American Review,* vol. 8, 1970, p. 671.
4. Samuel A. Stouffer et al., *The American Soldier: Adjustment During Army Life* (Princeton, N.J.: Princeton University Press, 1949).
5. See E. C. Banfield and J. Q. Wilson, *City Politics* (Cambridge: Harvard University Press, 1963).
6. I here rely heavily on a paper of mine, "The Positive Contributions of Ethnic Groups in American Society," which was done for the American Jewish Committee, 1968.
7. In Chicago we have a colony of Luxembourgers.

FROM **THE MIDDLE AMERICANS**

ROBERT COLES AND JON ERIKSON

"We are proud of ourselves, that's what I'd like to say. We're not sure of things, though; we're uncertain, I'm afraid, and when you're like that —worried, it is—then you're going to lose a little respect for yourself. You're not so proud anymore." There he goes, like a roller coaster; he is up one minute, full of self-confidence and glad that he is himself and no one else, and the next minute he is down, enough so to wish he somehow could have another chance at his life, start in again and avoid the mistakes and seize the opportunities and by God, "get up there."

Now, where is "there" for him? In the observer's mind the question is naturally asked, but the man who speaks like that about his destination would not understand why anyone would feel the need to do so, require a person to say the most obvious things in the world. In fact, if the question were actually asked, the man would have one of his own in return, which out of courtesy he might keep to himself: you mean you don't know? And that would be as far as the man would want to take the discussion. He has no interest in talking about life's "meanings," about his "goals" and his "values." At least, he has no interest in a direct and explicitly acknowledged discussion of that kind. He feels more comfortable when he slides into such matters, when he is talking about something quite concrete and of immediate concern and then for a few minutes finds himself "going off." It is not that he minds becoming introspective or philosophical or whatever; he likes to catch himself "getting carried away" with ideas and observations. What he dislikes is the self-consciousness and self-congratulation and self-display that go with "discussions." Perhaps he is "defensive" about his lack of a college education. Perhaps he feels "inferior," suffers from a poor "self-image." Sometimes a visitor slides into that way of looking at a person, even as sometimes the person being branded and pinioned comes up with considerably more than the self-justifications he at first seems intent upon offering: "Maybe we should ask ourselves more questions, Doris and me, like you do. I don't have time for questions; and neither does my wife. Mind you, I'm not objecting to yours. They're not bad questions. I'll have to admit, there'll be a few seconds here and there when I'll put them to myself. I'll say, Joe, what's it all about, and why in hell kill yourself at two jobs? I'll ask myself what I want out of life. My dad, he'd do the same, I can remember."

He can indeed remember. At forty-three he can remember the thirties, remember his father's vain efforts to find work. He can remember those three letters, WPA; he can remember being punished, shouted at, and grabbed and shouted at some more, because he dropped an ice-cream cone. Did he know what a nickel meant, or a dime? Did he know how few of them there are, how hard they are to come by? Now, his youngest son has a toolbox, and once in a while tries to pound a nail through a nickel or a dime, or even a quarter. The father gets a little nervous about such activities, but soon his apprehension gives way to those memories—to an amused, relaxed moment of recall. Indeed, it is just such ironies, both personal and historic, that get him going. And that is how he often does get going, with an ironic disclaimer: "I don't want to go on and on about the depression. My dad will do that at the drop of a hat. We've never had another one so bad since the Second World War started, so I don't believe we're in danger. But you can't forget, even if you were only a kid then. When my kids start complaining, I tell them they should know what their grandfather went through. I start telling them what it was like in America then; but they don't take in what you say. They listen, don't get me wrong. No child of mine is going to walk away from me when I'm talking. I have them looking right at me. But they think I'm exaggerating. I know they do. My wife says it's because they were born in good times, and that's all they've ever known. Maybe she's right. But even now for the workingman, the average guy, it's no picnic. That's what I really want my kids to know: it's no picnic. Life, it's tough. You have to work and work and work."

Then he adds that he likes work. No, he *loves* work. What would he do without it? He'd be sitting around. He'd go crazy. He'd last maybe a few weeks, then go back and be glad to be back. True, he'd like to get rid of his second job. That's not work, what he does in the evenings— after supper, or on weekends and some holidays. He needs the extra money. The bills have mounted and mounted. Prices are not merely "up"; they are "so high it's a joke, the kind of joke that makes you want to cry." So, he finds "odd jobs," one after the other, but when he talks about them he doesn't talk about his *work;* he refers to the *jobs,* and often enough, the damned jobs.

He can even be heard talking about the "slave time" he spends, and his mind is as quick as anyone else's to pursue that particular image: "You've got to keep ahead of the game, or you drown. The more money you make, the more you spend it, even if you're careful with money; and we are. We've so far kept up, but it's hard. I get odd jobs. I'll work around the clock sometimes, with just a few hours off to nap. I wire a building. I can do plastering and painting. I'm a steam fitter, but I'm handy at anything. A man wants some work on his house and he gets me to do it. He doesn't want to pay high union wages and doesn't want to register every change he makes in his house with the city officials, who'll make him lose his shirt doing unnecessary things—or paying them off. If he could do the work himself, like I can, he wouldn't hire anyone—because he's in the same tight squeeze I'm in, we're all in. But he's a schoolteacher, you see, or he works in an office, and he can't do anything with his hands, so I get the work. I feel bad taking the

money from them, I mean it. But I do the job good, real good, and I've
got to have the extra money. I get a good salary every week. We live in
a real good house. We live as comfortably as anyone could ever want.
I work for one of the biggest real estate companies in the city. They
keep me going. I'll be in one building, then I move on to the next one.
I put in heating systems, fix boilers. I do everything. In the winter there's
emergencies, a pipe has frozen, you know. In the summer we get ready
for the winter. Even so, with good wages, we can barely keep our heads
up over the water. Doris and I, we go wild with those bills. I tell her we've
got to stop buying everything. Once I said we're going into the woods
and live in a tent and hunt our food and grow it. She said that was fine
with her, and I had no argument. So, I laughed; and she did, too.

"No, I guess we're where we are and we have to stay here, and so long
as I've got my health, my strength, we'll do all right; we'll get by. The
niggers are moving toward us, you know. They're getting big ideas for
themselves. I hear they're making more money than ever before. They're
pushing on us in the unions. They want to be taken in fast, regardless
of what they know. A man in the trades, he's got to prove himself. You
can't learn to be a good steam fitter or electrician overnight. But they're
pushing for quickie jobs, that's what. I say to hell with them. Let them
take their turn, like everyone else. That's another reason to make more
money on the side. If we ever had to leave here, because they started
coming in, then we could. There are times when I feel like a nigger
myself; I'll admit it. I've been going all day, and I'm back at work after
supper, and I'll be sweating it with a pipe or a radiator, and I'll say to
myself: Joe, you're a goddamn slave, that's what you are; you might as
well be picking cotton or something like that. And my face is black, too,
from the dirt in the cellar!"

He smiles and moves toward a cup of coffee nearby. He stretches
himself on a leather chair, the kind that unfolds in response to the
body's willful selective pressure and has the occupant no longer sitting
but lying back, "in the perfect position for television." He watches television when he can, and if he were home more he would watch more
television. He likes to view sports—football, basketball, hockey. He will
watch golf, but not very enthusiastically. He has never played golf. The
game is too slow for him, and there is, too, a touch of the fancy in those
clubs and the carts and the caps a lot of golfers wear. So he thinks,
anyway; and he knows why. His father used to tell him that golf was a
rich man's game. He now knows better; even his father knows better.
But knowing is not being convinced. In his words: "You can know something, but you can't change the way you feel." (So much for whole textbooks of psychology and psychiatry.)

As a matter of fact, the game of golf can prompt him to reflect. He
has a friend who plays golf. The city golf course is crowded, though. In
order really to enjoy the game one must belong to a club, have access
to a first-rate, uncrowded course. The friend has a friend—his lawyer,
in fact—who takes him to a fine country club. Every Saturday morning
the two men play golf, then go home and meet again the next Saturday.

They don't have lunch afterwards, or breakfast beforehand. They don't talk much to each other. What they have in common is golf, period. And there is a lesson in that. It's hard to "move away from your own kind of people."

Joe and Doris see no reason to make lists of "criteria" that characterize the people they feel comfortable with, or on the contrary don't; but upon occasion they will spell things out rather clearly. Joe will talk about "brainy people." One of his friends has a son who is just studying and studying, not in order to become a doctor or a lawyer (which is fine) but to stay out of the draft (Joe thinks) and "because he's so shy he can't talk to people, so he lives in the library." The subject of libraries and the universities that own them leads to other matters. Joe and Doris want those libraries and universities for their children, and indeed, their oldest son is in his first year of college. But no one can be snobbier, more arrogant and condescending than "a certain kind of professor" or a lot of those "professional students," which mean students who are not content to study and to learn, but make nuisances of themselves, flaunt themselves before the public, disrupt things, behave like fools. He gets angry as he gets further into the discussion, but his wife slows him down, and even manages to cause a partial reversal of his views. After all, she insists, he is always complaining about certain things that are wrong with the country. He is always saying that the rich are getting richer, and the ordinary man, he can barely keep up with himself. Someone has to do more than complain; someone has to say unpopular things. Doris herself does so, says unpopular things, at least at certain times—though only to her husband, when they are having a talk. And soon Joe switches, says maybe, says yes, says it is true that some of the students are good, mean well, are on the working-man's side against the big corporations.

They don't like those big corporations; Joe and Doris don't, and their neighbors don't. If the students are at different times called vulgar, wild, crazy, insulting, and obscene, the corporations are declared clever, wily, treacherous, dishonest, and powerful beyond belief. Doris believes in "balancing things," and she believes in keeping her cool. She wants her husband, also, to have a certain distance on events. When he takes after college students, she reminds him that they have one in the family, hope to have more in the family as the years go by. And she brings up the corporations, and the way they "behave." They are decorous and restrained, but in Doris's mind they are no less outrageous than "the bad element" among the students, the ones who "look so awful" and make her and everyone she knows feel uncomfortable and puzzled and really, at a loss.

After a while one can see that Doris and Joe are just that: at a loss to figure certain things out, at a loss to know how their own various opinions can ever become reconciled into some consistent, believable and coherent viewpoint. To some extent, they well know, the task is hopeless, because like the proudest, most knowing social critic, they are thoroughly aware of the ambiguities and ironies they, we, everyone must face: "I try to slow Joe down. He'll be watching the news, and he shouts at the demonstrators, you know. He doesn't like the colored very much. He says they're pushing too hard on the rest of us. I agree, but I think we ought to be careful, because the children will hear, and they'll repeat what they listen to us saying in Sunday School, and that's no good. Our son wants to be an engineer. He is in college. He is a sensible boy. He'll never be a radical or a militant. But he tells his father to go easy, and I agree. Where I go wild is on prices. They go up and up and no one seems to want to stop them. I voted Republican for the first time last year, because I thought they'd do something. But they're like the Democrats. They're all the same. They're all a bunch of politicians, every one of them. Joe says I'm as nutty when I talk about politicians and the prices in the supermarket as he is when he talks about the colored and the college students.

"There are times when I wonder who really runs this country. It's not people like us, that I know. We vote, we do what we're supposed to do and we go fight in the wars—I lost a brother in the Second World War and a cousin in the Korean War, and I hope to God my son doesn't end up in Vietnam, like my nephew, his cousin—but we don't get any place for being good citizens. There are some big people, in Washington I guess, and they make all the decisions; and then it's left for us to go and send our boys to fight, and try to pay the high prices that the politicians have caused us to have. Don't ask me more. I don't know who the big people are. But it's a clique. They own the stocks in the banks and the corporations. It's up to them, what the country does. We get these letters from our congressman, that he sends around, and it's just a lot of talk. Why, even my thirteen-year-old daughter knows better. She read the newsletter and she said he was just talking out of both sides of his mouth. Well, I went up and hugged and kissed her. I put my name on a list at the supermarket, protesting high prices. I guess that's how he got my name in the first place, that congressman. To tell the truth, I don't remember his name, and I don't want to."

Not that she or her husband spend much time talking about such frustrating, mystifying and upsetting issues. By and large they shun what Doris calls "current events." There is more than enough to do from day to day. Joe works almost all the time. Doris does, too. She has four children to look after. She has a house to keep clean, very clean. She has her aged mother to visit, who lives nearby with Doris's older sister. And then of late Doris has also had to find work. She doesn't "always" work, but she "helps out" at a luncheonette for two hours, eleven to one, five days a week. Her husband did not want her to do so, but she insisted, and she got her way. She rather likes the work, serving the crowded tables. She gets a view of the outside world. She meets people. She hears people talk, and she learns what is on their minds. She makes a few dollars. She feels more independent. She feels that time goes by more quickly. And much as she dislikes talking about all the world's problems, she finds herself listening rather intently to what others have to say about those problems: "I can't help it. I'll be coming over to a table with food, and serving it, and I'll hear them, the men on their lunch hour, and the women, too. They all talk the same way, when you come right down to it. They're worried about where the country is going. Yesterday I waited on a man who lost his son in Vietnam. You know how I know? I heard him telling his friend that the boy died so we could be safe over here. I'm sure he's right. I couldn't help wondering what I'd say if it happened to me, if I lost my son. I guess I'd say what he did, that man. My husband says there's nothing else you *can* say. You have to believe your own government. I mean, if you start turning on your own country, then what have you got left? The answer is nothing, I guess.

"I don't think the country is being run the way it should be. Don't ask me how I'd do better, but everyone I know agrees we're in trouble: boys dying every day over there in the jungle, and here the criminals taking over. There's the big gangsters, the Mafia, and there's the demonstrators, and downtown there's the colored—little boys, no more than ten or twelve a lot of them, looking for things to steal. I've seen them steal in the department stores. They knock down women and run away with their pocketbooks. I don't even carry one any more when I go shopping in town. And I only go there to do holiday shopping, because most of the stores have branches out in our plaza. Why don't the students and the college people demonstrate against the criminals? My sister-in-law was knocked down by three colored boys. They had a knife! They said they'd kill her. They took her pocketbook and ran. And you hear the Negro people asking for more, more, more!"

She would go so far and no further. She would never use the word "nigger." Her husband does, all the time he does; but when he goes further, starts cussing and swearing, starts sending people to hell, starts making sweeping, utterly unqualified judgments, she tries to stop him, and usually manages to succeed. She even gets him to reverse himself somewhat—which means, she gets him to say a number of *other* things he believes. For example, he believes that at birth "we're all just about the same," and he believes "it's the education a child gets that makes the difference," and he believes that "if a child is born poor and he doesn't get good food, then he's going to pay for it later."

As a matter of fact when he is feeling reflective and not pushed into a liberal corner by anyone, Joe will come up with some rather strong-minded rebuttals of his own assertions: "I can see how the niggers feel cheated out of things. If I was a Negro, I'd be madder than hell. I'd stand up to anyone who tried to keep me away from my share. We have a couple of them, carpenters, working with us on the job now. They're the best guys you could want. They work hard, and they're smart. They speak good, as good as anyone I know. If all the Negro people were like those two, then I can't believe we'd be having the trouble we are. A man is a man, that's what I believe; I don't care what his skin color is, or where he goes to church. This country has every kind of people in it; and it's all to the good, because that way no one group runs the show. The thing that bothers me about the Negro people is this: they're not like the rest of us, and I don't mean because their skin is a different color. I drive through their neighborhood. I've worked in the buildings where they live. I'd be working on the pipes and I'd hear them from another apartment or down in the cellar. (The sound carries!) If you ask me, they're slow, that's what I think. They're out for a good time. They want things made easy for them—maybe not all of them, but plenty of them. They actually want relief. They think they're entitled to it!"

He stops. He lifts his head up, ever so slightly but noticeably nevertheless, and significantly. He is about to reminisce. After several years of visiting his home and getting to know him and his family, one can anticipate at least that much, the several directions his mind will pursue, if not the particular message he will deliver on a given day. So, he takes a slightly longer swallow of beer, and waits a few seconds, as if to pull them all together, all his memories. And then he is on his way: "I remember my father, how it killed him to take money from the government, the WPA, you know. I remember him crying. He said he wished he was never born, because it's not right that a man shouldn't be able to earn a living for his family. He could have stayed on relief longer, but he got off as fast as he could. He hated every day he didn't work. I guess they made some work for people, the WPA did; but no one was fooled, because it was phony work. When a man really wants to do something, and instead he's raking leaves and like that, he's even worse off than sitting on his porch all day—except that without the money, I guess we all would have starved to death.

"Now with the niggers it's different. They want all they can get—for free. They don't really like to work. They do work, a lot of them, I know. But it's against their wish, I believe. They seem to have the idea that they're entitled to something from the rest of us. That's the big thing with them: they've suffered, and we should cry our heads off and give them the country, lock, stock and barrel, because we've been bad to them, white people were. I have friends, a lot of them; and let me tell you, not one of them goes along with that way of thinking. You know why? It's an insult, it's an insult to you and me and everyone, including the niggers themselves. If I was a Negro, and someone came up to me and told me how sorry he was—sorry for what he'd done, his people had, and sorry for the Negro people—I'd tell him to get away fast, real fast, if he wanted to keep his good health. Pity is for the weak; my grandfather used to tell us kids that. But your niggers, a lot of them want pity; and they get it. You know who gives it to them? The rich ones out in the fancy suburbs, they're the ones—the bleeding hearts, always ready to pat people on the head and say you're wonderful, and we love you, and just sit back, we'll take care of you, with welfare and the rest, just like we do with our pet dogs."

There is more, much more. He fires himself up as he gets deeper and deeper into the subject, the issue, the argument he is setting forth. He reaches for more beer, and his wife gets slightly worried, then obviously nervous, then somewhat alarmed. She wants him to stop. She wants us to change the subject. She doesn't necessarily disagree with the thrust of his remarks; but the more he speaks, the longer the exposition, the more explicit the references and criticisms and illustrative examples, the more uncomfortable she feels. Why? What bothers her about her husband's ideas? He asks her that. She has told him that he is getting "carried away." He says yes, he is getting carried away with the truth, and if that is wrong, it is also rare "in this country, today." He invokes the "credibility gap." He reminds us that politicians and businessmen tell lies all the time. He insists that "a lot of very proper types" delude themselves and fool others. It is hard to be honest, and for that reason most of us shirk saying what we know "in our hearts" is true. People are afraid to speak out, say certain things, because they know they'll be called "prejudiced," and in fact they are not at all that; rather they are "letting the chips fall where they do."

But yes, he goes on to acknowledge, she is right, his wife; she always is, as a matter of fact. What is the point of working oneself up into a virtual frenzy over people who themselves never let anything really trouble them? In his own words and manner he says that he actually rather accepts his wife's disapproval—and anticipates exactly why she "really" was made anxious: "She doesn't want the kids to hear that kind of talk. They admire this minister, and he's always worrying out loud over someone, or some problem." Joe dislikes all those sermons; they make him feel uncomfortable, accused, a criminal of sorts. The minister can talk as he wishes, and if need be, move on to another church; whereas people like Joe and Doris have to stay—or so Joe feels. And anyway, ministers have a way of making things much too simple and stark and apocalyptic: "To hear him talk on Sunday, you'd think we were on the verge of ruin, America, unless we solve every problem we have and especially the race problem. He's got the Negro people on his brain, our minister. He must dream about them every night. He says we're to blame, the white people, for all that's happened. I went up once after the sermon and asked him what I've done that's to blame. He said he didn't mean any one person, just the whole white world. I didn't know how I could answer him. I said I'd never wanted to hurt a Negro, all I wanted was for them to leave me alone and I'd leave them alone. But that got him going again, and I pretended that I had to leave, because we had to be somewhere. On the way home I told Doris I'm ready to start shopping for a new church, but she and the children like him, the minister. They say he's 'dynamic.' He either makes me mad or puts me to sleep. So you see, we don't agree on *everything* in this house."

Joe is at times envious. His sister is married to a schoolteacher who is a Catholic. In the Catholic Church, he believes, one is spared those sermons. In the Catholic Church one goes for mass, for communion, not to be lectured at over and over again. But his sister and brother-in-law disagree. They have also had to sit through sermons, and they have their misgivings about the direction the church is taking. Here is what his sister says: "It's not any one church, it's them all. I listen to my neighbors talk. A lot of church people are always scolding the ordinary

man. If you ask me, the rich people and the college professors have too
much influence with the cardinal. Even the Catholic Church can be
pushed around. All of a sudden, these last few years, we've been hearing these letters from him, the cardinal. He tells us this is wrong and
that is wrong, and it seems all he has on his mind is the colored people.
I'm sick and tired of them and their complaining. And they've stirred
up everyone; my husband tells me the children in junior high school
are 'organizing.' That's what they call it. They have 'grievances,' and
they want to talk about them with the teachers and the principal. I'd
give them the back of my hand. I'd read them the riot act. But no, the
principal is afraid that if they get 'too strict,' the teachers, then the kids
will get even more aroused, and there will be more trouble. Can you
imagine that? And he's talking with them—hour after hour, I hear.

"There's something wrong, that's what I say; and it all started with
this civil rights business, the demonstrations, and then the college radicals and on and on. It used to be that you could go to church and pray
for your family and country. Now they're worried about colored people
and you even get the feeling they care more about the enemy, the people killing our boys in Vietnam, than our own soldiers. And the schools,
the radicals and the colored are both trying to destroy the schools—I
mean, take them over, that's what. They don't like what's being taught,
and they don't like the teachers, and a day doesn't go by that they don't
have something bad to say, or a new threat for us to hear. My husband
says he'd quit tomorrow if he didn't have so much seniority, and if he
could get another job. It's pretty bad for you these days if you're just a
law-abiding, loyal American and you believe in your country, and in
people being happy with their own kind, and doing their best to keep us
the first in the world. And, God forbid, if you say we need to keep the
streets safe, and stop those riots and marches, then the priest will pull
you aside and tell you that you don't 'understand.' But I do, that's the
point. I understand what's happening. We're losing our freedom. We
can't be ourselves anymore. There are those that want to change the
country completely. They are dictators. A lot of priests are with us; but
some have been fooled, and two of them are in our parish, I'll tell you."

There are differences, of course, in the two families. A teacher is not
a steam fitter. Once the teacher felt himself "higher," a man of education, a man who wears a suit to work. Now the teacher feels hard
pressed and bitter. His salary has for a decade been inadequate, and for
half a decade he has had to work in the evenings and on weekends, even
as his brother-in-law does. The high school children seem harder to control. The educational critics are constantly saying bad things about
people like him, or so he feels. And everyone's sympathy seems to go
elsewhere: "The priests, a lot of them feel sorry for the Negroes and
the North Vietnamese. The college students love Asians and Africans,
love to go work in the ghetto. Their professors keep on saying how bad
our schools are. College professors make three and four times what we
do, and they have the nerve to say we're not 'motivated' enough, and we
don't teach the way we should. They can cry with sympathy for some

insolent, fresh-talking Negro demonstrator, who wants the world delivered into his hands within twenty-four hours, but if we even try to explain our problems, they start telling us how wrong we are, and how we need to learn how to be 'open' with the children, and 'accepting,' and how we are 'rigid' and 'prejudiced,' and everything bad. I've heard them on television.

"No one asks people like me to be on television. I'm a teacher, but no educational television people come and ask me my opinion. They get these writers and 'experts' and let them say one bad thing after the other, and we're supposed to say: that's right, that's absolutely right. Not one of them impresses me as anything but a sensationalist. They love tearing things down. And you know who eats it all up, don't you: the intellectuals, the rich people out in the suburbs, the people who send their children to private schools, and then say it's awful, how we're treating the Negroes, and not keeping up with all those 'progressive' ideas, which (mind you) change every other year."

One can, of course, go on and on with tape-recorded conversations such as these, toned down here, edited there, abbreviated necessarily. One can call upon a bank teller or a barber or a repairman for the telephone company or a truck driver or a man who works in a large factory or a man who works in a small warehouse. One can call upon the electricians and carpenters who work with Joe, or other teachers who work with his brother-in-law in a high school. And then, there are clerks, accountants, salesmen, bus drivers, firemen, and policemen. If an observer wants to lump them all together, millions and millions of men, women and children, he can resort to labels and phrases, some of them more traditional than others. For a long time there have been "blue-collar workers" and "white-collar workers"; and there has been the "lower middle class." More than any other expression, though, the people themselves (as we have mentioned) like to use "ordinary man" or "average American" or "plain person." Again and again one hears those words, all the time spoken with pride and conviction and a touch of sadness, a touch of worry—as if the country has not learned to appreciate such people, and maybe even makes them pay for the sins of others, pay with their lives, their savings, their energies. And they have indeed paid. They have seen their savings mean less, or disappear, as inflation gets worse and worse. They have had to take second jobs to keep up with prices. They have sent their sons abroad, and thousands of them have died—all of which an observer knows and reads and repeats to himself from time to time and then is likely to forget.

Is it, then, a certain vulnerability that they share, those "ordinary people"? Are they best thought of as socially insecure, economically marginal, politically unorganized, hence weak? Ought we be talking about millions and millions of people in such a way; that is, do they all lend themselves to the generalizations that social scientists, journalists and politicians persist in using? Needless to say, statistics and indices of one kind or another certainly do tell a lot; they quite precisely tell us how much money comes into homes, how much is spent and by whom

—that is, people employed where and of what educational "level" or background. But again, one must ask whether expressions like "social class" quite explain what it **is t**hat so many Americans have in common when they call themselves "ordinary." Money is part of the answer; they have some, enough to get by, *just* get by, *barely* get by, *fairly* comfortably get by. (Qualifications like "just" or "barely" or "fairly" are always there and say a good deal.) But there are other things that matter to people. How much schooling did I get? How much do I wish I'd had? How much do I want for my children? What kind of work do I do, apart from the money I make, and what kind would I like to do? Where do I live? Where would I prefer to live, if I could have my choice? Which church do I attend? How do I like to dress? And finally, do I feel at ease about my life and my future, even though I live in a good, strong house, well supplied with gadgets and appliances on the inside and surrounded by a nicely tended lawn on the outside?

Chapter 6

PERSPECTIVES ON POVERTY IN AMERICA

Perhaps one of the most serious problems in American cities is persisting poverty. In 1970 more than 24 million Americans were counted as poor using the government poverty line of $4,000 for an urban family of four. The majority of these persons resided in urban places. Over the years a variety of interpretations of poverty have been developed in both popular and scholarly writings. Popular perspectives have usually blamed poverty *on the poor themselves*. Doubtless the most famous scholarly conceptualization has been that of Oscar Lewis, an anthropologist whose ethnographies of the Mexican and Puerto Rican poor are widely read. Developing the concept of a "culture of poverty" in the book *Five Families*, Lewis argues that this culture is "a way of life which is passed down from generation to generation along family lines."[1] In class-stratified, capitalistic societies—including the United States—the poor adapt in distinctive ways to their oppressive conditions, and these adaptations are transmitted from one generation to the next through the socialization process. The culture of poverty transcends national differences; it consists of at least seventy distinctive traits, such as chronic unemployment, the lack of saving, a short childhood and early initiation into sex, a high rate of illegitimacy and family disorganization, authoritarianism, and a pervasive sense of marginality and fatalism. As for policy implications, Lewis has noted that "by the time slum children are age six or seven they have usually absorbed the basic values and attitudes of their subculture and are not psychologically geared to take full advantage of changing conditions or increased opportunities which may occur in their lifetime."[2]

147

One of the numerous critics of the culture-of-poverty approach is Hyman Rodman, whose recent book *Lower-Class Families* argues that, while this approach can provide a useful way of cataloging poverty characteristics, it often leads to a stereotyped view of the poor that emphasizes negative aspects. Problematical, too, for culture-of-poverty theorists is the heterogeneity of life styles among the poor. Indeed, Rodman contends that there are at least four major responses made by lower-class persons in adapting to deprivation: (1) they may reject middle-class values and adhere only to distinctive lower-class values; (2) they may adhere only to middle-class values and not pursue lower-class values; (3) they may share middle-class values and at the same time develop alternative values; and (4) they may reject all values in given areas and act pragmatically in these areas.[3]

In the first selection in this chapter Rodman discusses the third response noted above, the "lower-class value stretch." Many poor individuals share dominant middle-class aspirations while at the same time adhering to alternative lower-class values; thus, the repertoire of values in a given area is usually greater for lower-class individuals. If this "biculture" of poverty is actually characteristic of more of the poor than is the culture of poverty, then Rodman's policy-oriented argument in *Lower-Class Families* seems particularly relevant to government programs: "Opening up opportunities, rather than changing the values of the poor, may therefore be the crucial practical problem in attacking poverty." [4]

The second selection, an excerpt from Charles A. Valentine's *Culture and Poverty*, delineates three important models or conceptualizations of poverty. One perspective depicts the lower class as a "self-perpetuating subsociety with a defective, unhealthy subculture." A second model describes the lower class as an "externally oppressed subsociety with an imposed, exploited subculture." Yet a third approach synthesizes certain points made in the other two perspectives: the lower class is seen as a "heterogeneous subsociety with variable, adaptive subcultures." The first model, basically similar to Lewis' culture of poverty, seems to be the prevailing orientation toward the poor among the majority of academic analysts and social planners and has shaped numerous governmental attempts to grapple with the problem of poverty. Yet much of the evidence relevant to this first model is contradictory, and Valentine asserts that "in this form it is little more than a middle-class intellectual rationale for blaming poverty on the poor and thus avoiding recognition of the need for radical change in our society."

Valentine's preference is for the synthesis model, which like Rodman's concept of the lower-class value stretch depicts the poor as having some distinctive subcultural values, positive and negative, but also as sharing middle-class patterns. Very important is the emphasis on the role of external social factors in determining poverty. Further, arguing that the subculture of poverty is not the main determinant behind the perpetuation of poverty, Valentine is sharply critical of various anti-poverty programs directed either at maintaining dependency or altering the values of the poor. As an alternative policy, he suggests that positive discrimination on behalf of low-income workers in the job market would be a way of providing the poor with expanded resources and thereby reducing poverty in America—basically a proposal for major *structural* change.

More recently, Valentine has responded to some of the critics of *Culture and Poverty* by admitting that problems exist in his conceptualization of culture, particularly in his acceptance of the assumption that the continuity of cultural patterns can be explained solely in terms of the socialization process; thus he has subsequently admitted that "many replicated patterns are the result of the response of successive generations to similar conditions of social life." [5] In addition, he has expressed the view that more attention should have been given in his analysis to the critical economic factors that determine the situation of poor Americans—those given some stress in Model 2—and to the fact that many Americans actually profit from the perpetuation of an unequal distribution of resources.[6] Apparently for this reason, Valentine has become less hopeful in regard to the prospects for his positive-discrimination proposal for eradicating poverty. Perceiving this proposal as a last appeal for change within the existing system, he asserts that "my answer today is that a fundamental and revolutionary restructuring of society is the only solution, that to support anything short of this is effectively to defend a grossly inhumane status quo, and that there are some grounds for cautious hope that national and world conditions may be moving toward a point at which this necessary solution will come about." [7] Whether Valentine is correct in this new assessment, and whether the provocative positive-discrimination proposal might still be more viable or likely than revolutionary restructuring, we can only leave for the reader to ponder and determine.

NOTES

1. Oscar Lewis, *La Vida* (New York: Random House, 1965), p. xliii.
2. Ibid., p. xlv.
3. Hyman Rodman, *Lower-Class Families* (New York: Oxford University Press, 1971), pp. 4–5, 192–193.
4. Ibid., p. 6. For discussion of social life in a "slum," see Chapter 3 above.
5. Charles A. Valentine, "Models and Muddles Concerning Culture and Inequality: A Reply to Critics," *Harvard Educational Review*, Vol. 42, no. 1 (February 1972), p. 98. He continues: "The programming received may even be different from the actual patterns; in other words people may be enculturated to behave in one way but be obliged by situational or functional factors beyond their control to behave in another way."
6. See Charles A. Valentine, "Black Studies and Anthropology: Scholarly and Political Interests in Afro-American Culture," in *Addison-Wesley Modular Publications*, no. 15 (1972), pp. 39–40.
7. Valentine, "Models and Muddles," pp. 101–102.

FROM **SOCIAL FORCES:**
THE LOWER-CLASS
VALUE STRETCH*

HYMAN RODMAN

There are sharp disagreements about the nature of the values held by members of the lower class, and correspondingly, about whether a society is based upon a common value system, or a class-differentiated value system.[1] Some writers assert that the basic values of a society are common to all social classes within that society, while others assert that the values differ from class to class. Similarly, in discussing problems such as illegitimacy and juvenile delinquency, some writers assert that the lower-class values that center about these phenomena are similar to the middle-class values, while others assert that the lower-class values differ from those of the middle class. In this paper I propose to delineate these contradictory points of view, as well as to suggest that through a consideration of what I will refer to as the lower-class value stretch we can resolve some of the apparent contradictions.

A Common Value System. The assumption that a common value system underlies a system of stratification has been made by Parsons, as in

From Hyman Rodman, "The Lower-Class Value Stretch," *Social Forces*, 42 (December 1963). Reprinted by permission, pp. 205–215.

* Revision of a paper read at the annual meetings of the Eastern Sociological Society, April 1961. Although they do not necessarily agree with what I am saying, I gratefully acknowledge the help I received in writing this paper from Reinhard Bendix, Oswald Hall, George C. Homans, Everett C. Hughes, Frank E. Jones, Sally Snyder, Katherine Spencer, and Marvin B. Sussman. Talcott Parsons was especially helpful and encouraging. In addition, an unrestricted research grant from the Social Research Foundation provided the assistance needed to bring this paper to completion.

[1] One could illuminate the discussion about a common or a class-differentiated value system by focusing upon any class rather than just the lower class. For example, do members of the upper class share the general values of society, or do they hold values unique to themselves? Indeed, the whole question of the parallels between the upper class and lower class deserves a good deal more attention. Deviations from the conventional standards of society are said to occur in both of them. And there are some related and interesting findings in small group research that both low-ranking and high-ranking members of a group have greater leeway, in certain respects, to deviate from the norms of the group: See John W. Thibaut and Harold H. Kelley, *The Social Psychology of Groups* (New York: John Wiley and Sons, 1959), pp. 250–251; George C. Homans, *The Human Group* (New York: Harcourt, Brace, 1950), p. 144; Henry W. Riecken and George C. Homans, "Psychological Aspects of Social Structure," in Gardner Lindzey, ed., *Handbook of Social Psychology*, Vol. II (Cambridge, Mass.: Addison-Wesley, 1954), pp. 793–794. For an excellent discussion of the subject, which I first read after writing the above, see George C. Homans, *Social Behavior: Its Elementary Forms* (New York: Harcourt, Brace & World, 1961), pp. 336–358 *et passim*.

his reference to "a single more or less integrated system of values" in any society.[2] Merton has also assumed that a society is based upon a common value system:

It is . . . only because behavior is typically oriented toward the basic values of the society that we speak of a human aggregate as comprising a society. Unless there is a deposit of values shared by interacting individuals, there exist social relations, if the disorderly interactions may be so called, but no society.[3]

When we turn to those who have dealt specifically with illegitimacy and juvenile gang delinquency we find that certain writers imply the existence of a common value system by their contention that middle-class norms [4] are also effective within lower-class groups. For example, Blake and Goode have discussed illegitimacy in Jamaica and the Caribbean generally, and while taking note of a high rate of illegitimacy in the area (typically more than 50 percent) they nevertheless conclude that even from the point of view of the lower class this represents deviant behavior.[5] According to their interpretation the norm of legitimacy is the only norm to be found within the lower class as well as within the middle class. Although they do not address themselves to the question of whether a society is characterized by a common value system or a class-differentiated value system, we can nevertheless take their interpretation as indicative of a belief in the existence of a common value system.

[2] Talcott Parsons, "General Theory in Sociology," in Robert K. Merton, Leonard Broom, Leonard S. Cottrell, Jr., editors, *Sociology Today* (New York: Basic Books, Inc., 1959), p. 8.

[3] Robert K. Merton, *Social Theory and Social Structure,* revised and enlarged edition (Glencoe, Ill.: Free Press, 1957), p. 141.

[4] No formal distinction is made in this paper between values, norms, aspirations, and (desirable) goals. I realize that they can be distinguished from each other and that several volumes could be devoted to the task. I realize also that some authors may complain, and with some justice, that by using their statements about norms, aspirations, or goals as an index of their position on "values" I am distorting their point of view. (Most authors, I should add, themselves use some of these concepts interchangeably.) But it is because I want to focus on the common element of *desirability* that lies behind all these concepts, as I use them, that I am running that risk. At the same time, there is the advantage of being able to suggest that the "stretch" concept also applies to norms, aspirations, and goals, and does not necessarily have to be tied to the lower class. Since some of these points are incidental to this paper, which focuses upon the lower-class value stretch, I do want to state outright here a methodological point that is only implied in other parts of the paper. When a subject is asked for a single "value" (or norm, aspiration, goal) response among a number of alternatives, and he selects a single alternative, this cannot be taken as evidence that he holds only the selected value and no other values. Regardless of the care taken in constructing a questionnaire, value alternatives that are mutually exclusive in a psychological sense cannot be set up.

[5] Judith Blake, "Family Instability and Reproductive Behavior in Jamaica," *Current Research in Human Fertility* (New York: Milbank Memorial Fund, 1955), pp. 34–39; William J. Goode, "Illegitimacy in the Caribbean Social Structure," *American Sociological Review,* Vol. 25 (February 1960), pp. 21–30.

In somewhat the same vein, a number of writers on juvenile gang delinquency have implied the existence of a common value system. Taft, for example, holds that juvenile delinquents share the basic values of our society.[6] Sykes and Matza have agreed with this viewpoint, but they also point out that through techniques of neutralization (e.g., projecting blame upon outside forces that propel one into action, or denying one's actions have harmed anyone) the delinquent is often able to spare himself the anguish of guilt.[7] This position that the delinquents share the conventional values of the society can also be taken as evidence for a belief in the existence of a common value system.

A Class-Differentiated Value System. In contrast to the authors cited above, who support the notion that a common value system underlies a stratified society, there are others who support the notion that a class-differentiated value system underlies a stratified society. Herbert H. Hyman,[8] in a paper that is in considerable measure a reaction to Merton's paper "Social Structure and Anomie," gives empirical evidence that there are differences in the value systems of different classes. He examines the educational, income, and occupational aspirations of various classes, showing that, in general, level of aspiration is correlated with class level. Thus, he concludes that we have a class-differentiated value system.

Allison Davis has also, for a long time, been emphasizing the differentiated values that are to be found within a society, particularly as exemplified by lower-class persons who have adapted their values to their deprived circumstances. As he says, individuals of different classes are "reacting to different realistic situations. . . . Therefore their values and their social goals are different." [9]

In writing of illegitimacy in the Caribbean, Henriques has stated

---

[6] Donald R. Taft, *Criminology,* revised edition (New York: Macmillan, 1950), pp. 181–182.

[7] Gresham M. Sykes and David Matza, "Techniques of Neutralization: A Theory of Delinquency," *American Sociological Review,* Vol. 22 (December 1957), pp. 664–670. [Cf. Fritz Redl and David Wineman, *Children Who Hate* (Glencoe: Free Press, 1951), pp. 158–174.] In a more recent paper Matza and Sykes have taken a somewhat different tack. In the earlier paper their position was that the delinquents shared the conventional values. In this paper they address themselves to specifically delinquent values but stress the striking similarities of these to certain subterranean values that are to be found within the society at large. This raises the question of public versus private values and the greater efficiency of the higher classes in maintaining the privacy of their private values. David Matza and Gresham M. Sykes, "Juvenile Delinquency and Subterranean Values," *American Sociological Review,* Vol. 26 (October 1961), pp. 712–719.

[8] Herbert H. Hyman, "The Value Systems of Different Classes: A Social Psychological Contribution to the Analysis of Stratification," in Reinhard Bendix and Seymour M. Lipset, editors, *Class, Status and Power* (Glencoe: Free Press, 1953), pp. 426–442.

[9] Allison Davis, "The Motivation of the Underprivileged Worker," in William Foote Whyte, editor, *Industry and Society* (New York: McGraw-Hill, 1946), p. 104.

flatly that from a social point of view this does not represent deviance within the lower class. Rather, the values of the lower class differ from those of the middle class, and illegitimacy is acceptable and in no way stigmatized within the lower class. He believes that those who assess "the lower-class forms of the family" in terms of middle-class norms are committing a "fundamental error." [10]

In a similar vein, Walter Miller's major point about juvenile delinquency within the lower class is that it is congruent with the values to be found within the lower class, and that these lower-class values are very different from those to be found within the rest of the society. According to Miller, "the cultural system which exerts the most direct influence" upon members of delinquent gangs "is that of the lower-class community itself—a long established, distinctively patterned tradition with an integrity of its own." [11] Or again, with more clarity for our purposes, Miller states:

> There is a substantial segment of present-day American society whose way of life, values, and characteristic patterns of behavior are the product of a distinctive cultural system which may be termed "lower class." [12]

Here, too, it is clear that Miller does not specifically address himself to the general question of whether a society is characterized by a common or a class-differentiated value system, but we can readily see that he believes that values are differentiated by class.

Common or Class-Differentiated Values? To what shall we attribute these different positions? Are we to believe that we have a common or a class-differentiated value system? That illegitimacy and juvenile delinquency are deviant or normative within the lower class? Should we go along with Parsons, Taft, and Goode, or with Davis, Miller, and Henriques?

I am certain that some of the writers will complain about the pigeonhole I have assigned them to, and in fairness to them it must be pointed out that they do not all fit comfortably into their assigned slots. By examining their writings carefully it can be seen that, from my point of view, most of them have second thoughts about their major position, or make statements that qualify their major position. For example, Parsons talks of "secondary or subsidiary or variant value patterns" [13] in addition to the basic value pattern. On the other hand, Allison Davis

[10] Fernando Henriques, *Family and Colour in Jamaica* (London: Eyre & Spottiswoode, 1953), p. 162.

[11] Walter B. Miller, "Lower Class Culture as a Generating Milieu of Gang Delinquency," *Journal of Social Issues*, Vol. 14, No. 3, 1958, p. 5.

[12] *Ibid.*, p. 6.

[13] Talcott Parsons, *The Social System* (Glencoe: Free Press, 1951), p. 169. See also his discussion of the need for patterning as well as flexibility in adapting to changing situations: Talcott Parsons, "The Point of View of the Author," in Max Black, editor, *The Social Theories of Talcott Parsons: A Critical Examination* (Englewood Cliffs, New Jersey: Prentice-Hall, 1961).

says that "each social class has developed its own differentiated and adaptive form of the basic American culture." [14] In these statements, Parsons and Davis, who perhaps best exemplify the contrasting positions taken on this question, are practically in agreement. There must be something here that calls for further examination and clarification.

It will be useful to follow the progression of Merton's thoughts on these questions in some detail, for Merton, in his recent writings, has completely broken out of his assigned pigeonhole. In his first paper on "Social Structure and Anomie" Merton's tone strongly suggests that he once assumed the existence of a common value system. In this extremely influential paper Merton made the point that the basic problem faced by members of the lower class is that they are structurally in a position that makes it exceedingly difficult for them to attain the cultural goals of the society by legitimate means, and therefore "the greatest pressures toward deviation are exerted upon the lower strata." [15] This suggests that the members of the lower strata typically share the common values of the society,[16] and in the statement of Merton's that I have already quoted (p. 151) he becomes even more explicit about the existence of a common value system.

In fairness to Merton, however, it must be pointed out that even in his first paper, despite the strong inference that we can draw, he scrupulously refrains from stating outright that members of the lower class actually internalize the general values of the society. The cultural values are presented as external to the (lower-class) individuals, as in his following statement:

> To say that the goal of monetary success is entrenched in American culture is only to say that Americans are bombarded on every side by precepts which affirm the right or, often, the duty of retaining the goal even in the face of repeated frustration.[17]

In his second paper on "Continuities in Social Structure and Anomie," Merton takes direct cognizance of the question as to whether all members do in fact share the same system of values:

> But if the communications addressed to generations of Americans continue to reiterate the gospel of success, it does not follow that all Americans in all groups, regions, and class strata have uniformly assimilated this set of values.[18]

Merton's conclusion on the question of common or class-differen-

---

[14] Allison Davis, *Social-Class Influences Upon Learning* (Cambridge: Harvard University Press, 1948), p. 10.

[15] Robert K. Merton, *op. cit.*, p. 144.

[16] Cf. Herbert H. Hyman, *op. cit.*, p. 427: "It is clear that Merton's analysis assumes that the cultural goal of success is in actuality internalized by lower-class individuals."

[17] Robert K. Merton, *op. cit.*, pp. 136–137.

[18] *Ibid.*, p. 170.

tiated values is that "it is a matter of inquiry," [19] which is, in effect, the same statement made by Lockwood with respect to Parsons' assumption of a common value system: it is "a matter for empirical investigation." [20] However, even when we turn to empirical studies the contradictions remain. In a secondary analysis of empirical data on illegitimacy in the Caribbean, Goode concludes that (in at least this area) members of the lower class share the general values of the society,[21] while Hyman, in a secondary analysis of data on educational, income, and occupational aspirations, concludes that the values differ from class to class.[22]

THE LOWER-CLASS VALUE STRETCH

We can illuminate the contradictions, or apparent contradictions, that exist by focusing upon the reactions of the members of the lower class to their deprived circumstances. Even assuming similarly deprived circumstances for members of the lower class, we would not expect an unvarying response to their circumstances because of the known complexity of human behavior. Certain individual responses, such as neurotic or psychotic behavior, may result. Or group responses, such as revolution or the development of religious sects, may result. Walter B. Miller and Albert K. Cohen each discuss three different types of lower-class reactions; [23] Merton, Parsons, and Dubin, respectively discuss four, eight, and fourteen different types of (not necessarily lower-class) deviant reactions.[24] What I intend to do is to discuss an entirely different type of lower-class reaction that has been obliquely hinted at but for the most part overlooked by these writers, and that I believe constitutes the one most important reaction to be found within the lower class. That reaction is what I call the lower-class value stretch, and through a consideration of the lower-class value stretch I believe we can clear up some of the contradictions that have appeared in the literature on the question of a common or a class-differentiated value system.

Merton has called attention to the problem of identifying the social mechanisms that minimize the strains that the (lower-class) person potentially faces—and the value stretch is one such mechanism. By the

[19] *Ibid.*

[20] David Lockwood, "Some Remarks on 'The Social System'," *British Journal of Sociology*, Vol. 7 (June 1956), p. 137.

[21] William J. Goode, *op. cit.*, pp. 21–30.

[22] Herbert H. Hyman, *op. cit.*

[23] Walter B. Miller, "Implications of Urban Lower-Class Culture for Social Work," *Social Service Review*, Vol. 3 (September 1959), p. 231; Albert K. Cohen, *Delinquent Boys* (Glencoe: Free Press, 1955), pp. 128–130.

[24] Robert K. Merton, *op. cit.*, pp. 141–157; Talcott Parsons, *The Social System*, pp. 256–267; Robert Dubin, "Deviant Behavior and Social Structure," *American Sociological Review*, Vol. 24 (April 1959), pp. 147–164.

value stretch I mean that the lower-class person, without abandoning the general values of the society, develops an alternative set of values. Without abandoning the values placed upon success, such as high income and high educational and occupational attainment, he stretches the values so that lesser degrees of success also become desirable. Without abandoning the values of marriage and legitimate childbirth he stretches these values so that a non-legal union and legally illegitimate children are also desirable. The result is that the members of the lower class, in many areas, have a wider range of values than others within the society. They share the general values of the society with members of other classes, but in addition they have stretched these values, or developed alternative values, which help them to adjust to their deprived circumstances.

If I were to deal metaphorically with the development of a wider range of values within the lower class, my analysis, up to a point, would follow the position taken by Albert K. Cohen [25] on the development of a delinquent subculture. Lower-class persons in close interaction with each other and faced with similar problems do not long remain in a state of mutual ignorance. They do not maintain a strong commitment to middle-class values that they cannot attain, and they do not continue to respond to others in a rewarding or punishing way simply on the basis of whether these others are living up to the middle-class values. A change takes place. They come to tolerate and eventually to evaluate favorably certain deviations from the middle-class values. In this way they need not be continually frustrated by their failure to live up to unattainable values. The resultant is a stretched value system with a low degree of commitment to all the values within the range, including the dominant, middle-class values. This is what I suggest as the major lower-class value change, rather than a change in which the middle-class values are abandoned or flouted. [26]

To continue in the metaphorical arena for a moment, I can perhaps clarify what I mean by the lower-class value stretch by referring to the fable of the fox and the grapes. The fox in the fable declared that the unattainable sweet grapes were sour; Merton's "rebellious" fox renounces the prevailing taste for sweet grapes; [27] but the "adaptive"

---

[25] Albert K. Cohen, *op. cit.*, pp. 59–72 *et passim*.

[26] This is obviously only a very sketchy account of the development of the lower-class value stretch. Tracing the historical development of lower-class values is no simple matter, especially since, in Malthus's words, "the histories of mankind that we possess are histories only of the higher classes."

Important clues to the psychological processes that accompany the development of the lower-class value stretch can be found in the literature on learning theory that has come out of the fields of animal experimentation and small group experimentation. For a demonstration of the applicability of such theory see George C. Homans, *Social Behavior: Its Elementary Forms*. See also Allison Davis, *op. cit.*; Genevieve Knupfer, "Portrait of the Underdog," *Public Opinion Quarterly*, Vol. 2 (Spring 1947), pp. 103–114.

[27] Robert K. Merton, *op. cit.*, p. 156.

lower-class fox I am talking about does neither—rather, he acquires a taste for sour grapes.

If I am correct that the predominant lower-class response to its situation is the value stretch, then we can immediately resolve many of the apparent contradictions described earlier. Those who hold that the basic values of the society are common to all classes are correct, because the members of the lower class do share these values with other members of society. Similarly, those who hold that the values differ from class to class are also correct, because the members of the lower class share values unique to themselves, in addition to sharing the general values of the society with others. The theories are "both correct, both incomplete, and complementary to one another." [28]

Values and Levels of Abstraction. Before turning to evidence which can help us to substantiate the existence of the lower-class stretch I want to dwell briefly upon another factor that complicates many discussions about values—the level of abstraction of the values involved. The more concrete a value, the more differentiated a society may appear with respect to it; the more abstract a value, the more integrated a society may appear. Some of the apparent contradictions about a common or class-differentiated value system must therefore be attributed to the confusion that results from the use of different levels of abstraction in talking about values. Clyde Kluckhohn has made the apt comment that

> much of the confusion in discussion about values undoubtedly arises from the fact that one speaker has the general category in mind, another a particular limited type of value, still another a different specific type.[29]

It should therefore be clear that those, like Parsons, who assume the existence of a common value system are talking about values at a high level of abstraction, and they may readily agree that at lower levels of abstraction there can be a great deal of differentiation.[30] Aberle, to cite another example, agrees that "a core of common values is an integrational principle of any viable social system," [31] but he nevertheless also discusses "the diversification of values which in fact exists." [32] Even

---

[28] Homans makes this statement about what he refers to as the "social contract" theory and the "social mold" theory. George C. Homans, *The Human Group*, p. 330. The argument between the egg enthusiasts and the sperm protagonists is another particularly good example of the two warring sides mistaking part of the truth for the whole of it: See N. J. Berrill, *Sex and the Nature of Things* (New York: Pocket Books, 1955), pp. 1–11.

[29] Clyde Kluckhohn, et al., "Values and Value-Orientations in the Theory of Action," in Talcott Parsons and Edward A. Shils, editors, *Toward a General Theory of Action* (Cambridge: Harvard University Press, 1952), p. 412.

[30] Talcott Parsons, "General Theory in Sociology," in Robert K. Merton, Leonard Broom and Leonard S. Cottrell, Jr., editors, *Sociology Today*, p. 8.

[31] David F. Aberle, "Shared Values in Complex Societies," *American Sociological Review*, Vol. 15 (August 1950), p. 502.

[32] *Ibid.*, p. 497.

though Williams outlines a number of major American value-orientations, he nevertheless cautions that in a complex society "a common core of values that could be said to hold for even a plurality of the population would probably be quite thin and abstract." [33] These points are not altogether unlike the distinction that Aristotle makes in his *Ethics* between a "system of rules" and "the exigencies of the particular case." Because of this we can see that it is in theoretical discussions particularly that we may find contradictions about a common or class-differentiated value system that stem from the different levels of abstraction that are under discussion.

When we turn to such specific areas as delinquency and illegitimacy, however, we are presented with more substantial contradictions. Do juvenile delinquents and illegitimate mothers share the conventional values and regard their own acts as deviant? Or do they have values of their own such that delinquency and illegitimacy are normative rather than deviant acts? It is by referring to the lower-class value stretch that we can find the best general answer to these questions.

The Level of Aspiration. Let us now consider very briefly some evidence that can help us to substantiate the existence of the lower-class value stretch. Experimental as well as more qualitative data on the "level of aspiration" within different classes is potentially an important source of evidence. One problem with a great deal of the quantitative data is that the respondent is asked to give a simple, single response, and it is then impossible to tell exactly what the response means. As McClelland points out, it could represent a "level of defense," or a "level of expectation," as well as a "level of aspiration," and probably represents a varying combination of all three.[34] Even assuming that the response does represent a "level of aspiration," if we are interested in testing for the existence of a range of values (or aspirations), and if in fact such a range exists, then by forcing the respondent to give one reply we are in effect forcing him to select a response from within his range of aspirations. This means that such data are limited in their utility, despite the fact that they are quantitative and may cover a wide sample of respondents. For example, Hyman has done a valuable secondary analysis of survey data in which he concludes that there are differences in the level of educational, income, and occupational aspiration of the different classes. Hyman speaks somewhat deprecatingly of qualitative studies done in this area, but it is only by reference to qualitative matters that we can fully appreciate the fact that there are limitations to Hy-

[33] Robin M. Williams, Jr., *American Society* (New York: Knopf, 1951), pp. 388–440; p. 385.

[34] David C. McClelland, *Personality* (New York: William Sloane, 1951), pp. 563–568. Rotter also indicates that some of the earliest workers with the level of aspiration recognized the relevance of these three factors: Julian B. Rotter, "Level of Aspiration as a Method of Studying Personality: I. A Critical Review of Methodology," *Psychological Review*, Vol. 49 (September 1942), pp. 467–468.

man's study beyond those he mentions. On examination of Hyman's study, we find that *in every question from every survey that he uses in his analysis, the respondent was asked for only one response.*[35] It is therefore at least possible to interpret his findings in terms of the lower-class value stretch. That is to say that the lower-class person, having a wider range of aspirations than others, and selecting his response from within that downward-stretched range, would by chance alone appear to have a different and lower level (although in actual fact what he has is a wider range) of values.

A great variety of tasks has been used in level of aspiration experiments, and a great many different measures have been based on these tasks.[36] The task that has been most widely used is the Aspiration Board as described by Rotter,[37] or some minor variation of it.[38] It is an individual task and a single-response task (S is permitted to make only one response when asked for his level of aspiration). Although theoretically it has long been recognized that the level of aspiration is a complex variable, it is only recently that a variety of tests have been formulated which permit or require S to make more than one response.[39] These tests make it easier to isolate the various factors that go into making up a "single" level of aspiration, and they also point the way toward experimental tests of the ideas presented in this paper. Of exceptional interest in this connection I cite the study by Miller and Haller,[40] and even more so, the study by Clark, Teevan, and Ricciuti,[41] and I urge that their methods serve as a model for those experimenting further with the level of aspiration. Perhaps it will not be too much longer before Stouffer's

[35] Herbert H. Hyman, *op. cit.,* pp. 426–442.

[36] For a recent review of level of aspiration experiments see: James Inglis, "Abnormalities of Motivation and 'Ego-Functions'," in H. J. Eysenck, ed., *Handbook of Abnormal Psychology* (New York: Basic Books, 1961), pp. 262–297.

[37] Julian B. Rotter, "Level of Aspiration as a Method of Studying Personality: II. Development and Evaluation of a Controlled Method," *Journal of Experimental Psychology,* Vol. 31 (November 1942), pp. 410–422.

[38] For example, see: Samuel F. Klugman, "Emotional Stability and Level of Aspiration," *Journal of General Psychology,* Vol. 38 (January 1948), pp. 101–118; Norman I. Harway, "Einstellung Effect and Goal-Setting Behavior," *Journal of Abnormal and Social Psychology,* Vol. 50 (May 1955), pp. 339–342; Kenneth C. Jost, "The Level of Aspiration of Schizophrenic and Normal Subjects," *Journal of Abnormal and Social Psychology,* Vol. 50 (May 1955), pp. 315–320; Joseph G. Sheehan and Seymour L. Zelen, "Level of Aspiration in Stutterers and Nonstutterers," *Journal of Abnormal and Social Psychology,* Vol. 51 (July 1955), pp. 83–86.

[39] John R. Hills, "The Measurement of Levels of Aspiration," *Journal of Social Psychology,* Vol. 41 (May 1955), pp. 221–229; Sidney Siegel, "Level of Aspiration and Decision Making," *Psychological Review,* Vol. 64 (July 1957), pp. 253–262.

[40] I. W. Miller and A. O. Haller, "The Measurement of Level of Occupational Aspiration," Paper presented at the meetings of the American Sociological Association, St. Louis, Missouri, September 1961.

[41] Russell A. Clark, Richard Teevan, and Henry N. Ricciuti, "Hope of Success and Fear of Failure as Aspects of Need for Achievement," *Journal of Abnormal and Social Psychology,* Vol. 53 (September 1956), pp. 182–186.

suggestion that a social norm (or an aspiration) not be regarded as a point but as a range will be more widely accepted.[42]

An interesting study that lends support to the idea that there is a lower-class value stretch is presented by Rosen.[43] He studied the occupational aspirations of different ethnic and class groups and showed that certain ethnic groups and also the lower classes are characterized by a lower level of aspiration. This is because he follows the common and in some ways unfortunate habit of reducing his data to single aspiration scores. Nevertheless he correctly points out that "it is misleading to speak of the 'height' of vocational aspirations. For all groups have 'high' aspirations." [44] If we examine his data on ethnic group differences closely, we can see that certain ethnic groups have a wider range of aspirations, and we can safely infer that members of the lower class also have a wider range of aspirations—they express satisfaction rather than dissatisfaction over a wider range of occupational goals. Rosen's study, therefore, in an indirect way, demonstrates the existence of the lower-class value stretch in the area of occupational aspiration.

ILLEGITIMACY IN THE CARIBBEAN

As a final area of evidence to substantiate the existence of the lower-class value stretch I wish to discuss the material on legitimacy and illegitimacy in the Caribbean, and notably Goode's secondary analysis of this data.[45] Goode's article is a tour de force par excellence. In essence, he reviews the writings of about a dozen researchers who have worked in the Caribbean area and who have concluded that legal illegitimacy and a non-legal union are not deviant patterns within the lower class. As a result of this review, Goode contradicts these researchers and supports the position taken by one or two other researchers that these patterns are deviant. He does this by pointing out that although many of the researchers *say* that non-legal unions and illegitimacy are not stigmatized, they nevertheless give a number of illustrations in their writings that indicate that non-legal unions and illegitimacy actually are stigmatized. It would be a simple matter to cite two statements indicating that illegitimacy is not stigmatized to every one statement that Goode cites indicating that it is stigmatized. As a matter of fact, because of the nature of his analysis, Goode himself has carried out half of this task for us, and his analysis serves the very useful purpose of pointing up the contradictory statements made by some authors about the normative state of illegitimacy and the non-legal union. This leaves us with internally inconsistent positions in some of the writings about illegitimacy

[42] Samuel A. Stouffer, "An Analysis of Conflicting Social Norms," *American Sociological Review,* Vol. 14 (December 1949), pp. 707–717.

[43] Bernard C. Rosen, "Race, Ethnicity, and the Achievement Syndrome," *American Sociological Review,* Vol. 24 (February 1959), pp. 47–60.

[44] *Ibid.,* p. 60.

[45] William J. Goode, *op. cit.*

in the Caribbean, as well as with contradictory interpretations of such illegitimacy on the part of different researchers. According to Goode and Blake, illegitimacy is deviant, while according to Henriques, Braithwaite, R. T. Smith, and many others, it is not. Once again, how do we resolve these contradictions?

By a closer examination of a number of writers on the lower-class family in the Caribbean, I believe that we can resolve the contradictions. Both R. T. Smith and Braithwaite have pointed out that within the lower class we can find middle-class values as well as values unique to the lower class. Smith has referred to a "moral system within a moral system" [46] and Braithwaite has referred to "a duality of allegiance to values." [47] In a similar vein, although Kitsuse and Dietrick correctly point out that there is vacillation on this point,[48] Cohen occasionally talks about the simultaneous internalization of a middle-class and a lower-class value system for members of the lower class.[49] In addition, other sociologists writing about delinquency point out that most delinquents "share conventional as well as delinquent aspirations." [50] It should therefore be clear that the ideas I have presented under the rubric of the lower-class value stretch have been stated many times before.[51] What I have done is to highlight these ideas, and to suggest that they represent one useful way of resolving some of the conflicting notions that have been expressed about the lower class as well as a useful way of understanding lower-class behavior. At this point, I submit that it helps us to understand the contradictory statements that Goode has adroitly pointed to in the writings of some researchers on the Caribbean area. These con-

[46] Raymond T. Smith, *The Negro Family in British Guiana* (London: Routledge & Kegan Paul, 1956), p. 149.

[47] Lloyd Braithwaite, "Sociology and Demographic Research in the British Caribbean," *Social and Economic Studies,* Vol. 6 (March 1957), p. 534.

[48] John I. Kitsuse and David C. Dietrick, "Delinquent Boys: A Critique," *American Sociological Review,* Vol. 24 (April 1959), pp. 208–215.

[49] Albert K. Cohen, *op. cit.,* p. 104.

[50] LaMar T. Empey and Jerome Rabow, "The Provo Experiment in Delinquency Rehabilitation," *American Sociological Review,* Vol. 26 (October 1961), p. 683; Kobrin also makes the assumption that "the individual participates simultaneously in both criminal and conventional value systems." Solomon Kobrin, "The Conflict of Values in Delinquency Areas," *American Sociological Review,* Vol. 16 (October 1951), p. 656; McQueen points to "dominant societal values . . . that most persons internalize to some degree as well as lower-class values which do not replace the dominant values, but which exist alongside them." Albert J. McQueen, "Lower-Class Culture, Mobility Aspirations and Juvenile Delinquency: A Functional Analysis," paper given at the meeting of the American Sociological Association, August 1961, p. 10. Cf. Frank E. Hartung, "Common and Discrete Group Values," *Journal of Social Psychology,* Vol. 38 (1953), pp. 3–22.

[51] But to talk about the simultaneous internalization of conventional and delinquent values is not necessarily to talk about the value stretch. All too often those who talk about the duality of values of delinquents place too much emphasis upon the fact that the values are in opposition. The value stretch, however, calls attention to the fact that they are not in opposition for the person holding the values—they are, rather, all part of the range of values the person holds.

tradictory statements reflect the value stretch that has taken place. It is precisely because the members of the lower class value marriage and legitimate children as an ideal, but have also come to value the non-legal union and illegitimate children that Goode is able to pinpoint these contradictions.

I have done research work in a lower-class village (Coconut Village) in Trinidad, and therefore want to amplify the few remarks that Goode singles out of the material written about Trinidad by Braithwaite and the Herskovits's.[52] Most lower-class Coconut Villagers acknowledge that marriage is better than *living* (the Trinidad term for a non-legal union) but they also point out that there are many advantages to *living*.[53] In addition, they have a saying that is clearly the most significant and most widespread saying in the Caribbean area as a whole about family life: "Better a good *livin'* than a bad marriage." They point out that there is no difference between *livin'* and marriage; that only the married woman is entitled to be addressed as Mistress; but they seldom use this form of address for a married woman. A man and woman who are *living* may refer to each other as "my keeper" or as "my husband (wife)." They may insist upon the fact that they intend to marry, but also upon the fact that *living* is as good as marriage and that they have every right to refer to each other as "husband" and "wife." They can tell their priest that they are *living in sin,* but this is a term for the non-legal union that they would never use spontaneously among themselves. Many of the terms they use and many of the behavioral patterns followed are indistinguishable for those who are married and those who are *living*. The researcher who wants to know whether a person who refers to somebody's wife is talking about a couple that is married or *living* must ask, "A married wife?" Given such a mass of "contradictory" data the only interpretation that permits everything to fall into place is that we have here an example of the lower-class value stretch.

DISCUSSION

At the heart of our analysis lies the issue of when old values die and new values develop. It is precisely because old values never die, they only fade away, and because new values only gradually appear, that it may, at times, be difficult to state categorically that a particular value is effectively held by a particular individual, or shared by a particular group. All this is merely to say that people vary in their degree of commitment to a value. Despite the difficulties this poses for us, we can nonetheless see that it is entirely possible for a lower-class person to

[52] William J. Goode, *op. cit.,* p. 23; p. 25.

[53] For additional data on marital relationships see: Hyman Rodman, "Marital Relationships in a Trinidad Village," *Marriage and Family Living,* Vol. 2 (May 1961), pp. 166–170; for an attempt to formulate a general statement of lower-class family relationships and lower-class values see my forthcoming book, tentatively titled *Lower-Class Families: An Empirical, Theoretical, and Practical Approach.*

hold middle-class values only, to abandon middle-class values without developing any new values, or to abandon middle-class values while developing a new set of values.[54] I am certain that these are not merely possible but actual responses of many lower-class people to their deprived situation. But I am equally certain that the dominant response of the lower-class person is the lower-class value stretch. It is because the lower-class person, to a degree, typically shares the middle-class values and also holds values unique to the lower class that he is able to adapt to his circumstances without certain more specific phenomena, such as deviance or revolution, being more evident as actual or attempted responses within the lower class.

Once the lower-class value stretch has been developed the lower-class person is in a better position to adapt to his circumstances because he has a wider range of values with which to operate.[55] Cultural resources, in a sense, come to compensate for his lack of social and economic resources. One aspect of what is involved in the lower-class value stretch is that the lower-class individual with the wider range of values must

[54] The assumption made here, as elsewhere in the discussion of the lower-class value stretch, is that the dominant, conventional, middle-class values have relevance for all members of the society, including its lower-class members. Since many middle-class values, however, are inappropriate to the conditions of lower-class life, the members of the lower class are faced with a problem. Once this value problem has been solved within the lower class—as in the development of the value stretch—then this solution is learned by many in the next generation who therefore do not face the same problem all over again. But a different kind of problem now emerges, and it is perhaps the most serious problem that practitioners in the social welfare, health, educational, and vocational fields face: To what extent are lower-class individuals passing up realistic opportunities for better welfare, health, education, and jobs because of cultural resistances? And to what extent can or should these hard-to-reach lower-class individuals be induced to break away from these cultural resistances? An intriguing answer to these questions that deserves the serious attention of professional practitioners who work with lower-class individuals is given in S. M. Miller and Frank Riessman, "The Working Class Subculture: A New View," *Social Problems*, Vol. 9 (Summer 1961), pp. 86–97.

[55] Members of the middle or upper class would not be under the same degree of environmental stress as lower-class members, and they would therefore not have to stretch their values to the same degree even if they did not adhere strictly to the conventional values. They would have access to resources that would permit them to retain their respectability and a seeming adherence to conventional values even in the face of deviance. Everett C. Hughes, for example, has suggested that any upper middle-class girl can get an abortion by some other name. He points out, in a personal communication, that no canon of behavior is absolutely adhered to, and that there must therefore be "a secondary set of canons of behavior—the rules which govern subsequent behavior after the first canon has been violated." This is an intriguing idea with manifold ramifications. The major comment suggested by a consideration of the lower-class value stretch is that secondary canons of behavior may interact with the primary canons in such a way that the primary canons are stretched.

A similar idea has been expressed by Reinhard Bendix: "Is not indeed every group in some measure engaged in a strategy of argument which seeks to maximize its self-respect in terms of the conventional standards from which behavior is bound to differ to some extent?" (personal communication).

also have less commitment to each of the values within that range.[56] Goode has noted this point with respect to conventional values,[57] but insofar as the lower-class person stretches his values there would be a low degree of commitment to all values he holds. This is perhaps one factor which helps to explain the higher proportion of "don't know" answers to survey questions on aspirations within the lower class. The lower-class person with a low degree of commitment to a wide range of aspirations may find a question asking for his level of aspiration to be inane.[58]

I have already expressed my conviction that the lower-class value stretch is the predominant response of lower-class individuals to their deprived situation, and that it is through an understanding of the lower-class value stretch that we can explain at least some of the apparent contradictions about a common or a class-differentiated value system. The conviction of the reader, of course, must depend upon his own familiarity with lower-class life, as well as upon additional research which seeks to test the existence of the lower-class value stretch.[59] In the mean-

[56] Cf. Albert J. McQueen, *op. cit.*, pp. 10–11.

[57] William J. Goode, *op. cit.*, p. 27.

[58] Speaking generally about the higher proportion of "don't know" responses in the lower class, such factors within the lower class as less knowledge and a feeling that one is less competent to judge undoubtedly account for a good deal of the difference between classes. See Genevieve Knupfer, *op. cit.*, pp. 103–114. On informational questions the factor of less knowledge is especially apparent. But it is interesting to speculate whether on questions of opinion, and especially on questions of level of aspiration, a considerable portion of the difference between the classes can be accounted for by the middle-class interviewer's questions rather than the lower-class respondent's personality. Under skillful questioning it may turn out that many lower-class respondents who "don't know" do know. A beautiful illustration of this point—and it is ironically an even better illustration because it deals with a middle-class sample—is given by Aberle and Naegele. They point out that middle-class fathers always say initially that they have "no plans" for their sons' future occupation. This is clearly a "don't know" response. It turns out, however, that "further questioning always shows that 'no plans' means that any occupation is all right, *if* it is a middle-class occupation." David F. Aberle and Kaspar D. Naegele, "Middle-Class Fathers' Occupational Role and Attitudes toward Children," *American Journal of Orthopsychiatry*, Vol. 22 (April 1952), p. 371. In other words, the middle-class fathers have a wide range of occupational goals for their sons and they therefore reply that they have no plans for their sons' future occupation. But once the interviewers go beyond the initial question and initial "don't know" response they discover that the fathers do know and they are able to elicit from the fathers the range of desirable occupational goals these fathers have for their sons.

[59] In this paper I am adding to the concept of value (whether "dominant" or "basic") the concept of a "value stretch" and a "range of values." It is not the purpose of this paper to relate these concepts to other concepts that have been added to or opposed to the value concept, but I do wish to state, without comment, what some of these additions or oppositions have been. F. Kluckhohn has written about variant values and the range of value orientations to be found in all societies; Redl and Wineman have referred to "ranges" and "stretches" of "value sensitivity and value respect," by which they mean that individuals may show respect for the values of others and modify their behavior on that account; Yinger has referred to

time, I submit that some of the data pertaining to lower-class juvenile gangs and delinquency can be better understood in terms of the lower-class value stretch; I submit that a great deal of the data on lower-class family organization, and specifically illegitimacy in the Caribbean, is incomprehensible unless we assume the existence of the lower-class value stretch; I submit that responses such as mental disorder, juvenile delinquency, and rebellion would occur with greater frequency within the lower class but for the existence of the lower-class value stretch; and finally, I submit that some of the survey and experimental work on the "*level* of aspiration" validates the existence of the lower-class value stretch, and that as greater attention is paid to a "*range* of aspirations" in these surveys and experiments, more data will accumulate to demonstrate the importance of the value stretch as a lower-class phenomenon.

a contra-culture and counter-values, which are opposed to those of the surrounding society; others, like Wrong (and those he quotes), have suggested various ways of conceiving a non-normative situation in dialectic opposition to the concept of value.

See Florence R. Kluckhohn, "Dominant and Variant Value Orientations," in Florence R. Kluckhohn, Fred L. Strodtbeck, et al., *Variations in Value Orientations* (Evanston: Row, Peterson, 1961), pp. 1–48; Fritz Redl and David Wineman, *Children Who Hate*, pp. 203–205; J. Milton Yinger, "Contraculture and Subculture," *American Sociological Review*, Vol. 25 (October 1960), pp. 625–635; Dennis H. Wrong, "The Oversocialized Conception of Man in Modern Sociology," *American Sociological Review*, Vol. 26 (April 1961), pp. 183–193.

FROM **CULTURE AND POVERTY:**
CONCLUSION: ALTERNATIVE VIEWS OF POVERTY AND THE POOR, PRESENT AND FUTURE*

CHARLES A. VALENTINE

CONCEPTIONS FOR THE PRESENT

A number of ideas have been reviewed here, a variety of problems explored, and some suggestions offered for future research. From this discussion there emerge three broad formulations or intellectual models representing varying views of the lower class as a subsociety, its lifeways as a subculture, the sources of subcultural patterns, and associated questions of public policy looking to the future.

These three models emerge from the foregoing discussion in the sense that they are logical alternatives growing out of available knowledge about poverty, society, and culture. While these models can be said to have their roots in different schools of thought, they are not meant to represent positions taken by particular writers.

Model 1: Self-perpetuating Subsociety with a Defective, Unhealthy Subculture
a. The lower-class poor possess a distinct subculture, and in the areas covered by this subculture they do not share the dominant larger culture typified by the middle class.
b. The main distinctiveness of the poverty subculture is that it constitutes a disorganized, pathological, or incomplete version of major aspects of middle-class culture.
c. The poverty subculture is self-generating in the double sense that socialization perpetuates both the cultural patterns of the group and consequent individual psychosocial inadequacies blocking escape from poverty.
d. The poverty subculture must therefore be eliminated, and the poor

* [Editor's note: This is one of the last chapters in *Culture and Poverty* and thus represents Valentine's conclusions based on an extensive review of the literature on poverty. The earlier discussion mentioned has not been reprinted here.]

From *Culture and Poverty* by Charles A. Valentine. Copyright © 1968. Reprinted by permission of the University of Chicago Press and Charles A. Valentine, pp. 141–160.

assimilated to middle-class culture or working-class patterns, before poverty itself can be done away with.

e. These changes may occur through revolution in underdeveloped societies where the poor are the majority; in the West they will be brought about by directed culture change through social work, psychiatry, and education.

Model 2: Externally Oppressed Subsociety with an Imposed, Exploited Subculture

a. The lower-class poor are a structurally distinct subsociety, and their life is therefore situationally distinct from that of all other social strata.

b. Elements of pathology, distortion, and incompleteness in the life of the lower class have their source in the structure and processes of the total system, mediated by denial of cultural resources to the poor.

c. The disadvantaged position of the poor is maintained primarily by the behavior of the higher strata, acting in their own interest as they see it, to preserve their advantages by preventing a redistribution of resources.

d. The structure of the whole society must therefore be radically altered, and the necessary redistribution of resources accomplished, before poverty can be eliminated.

e. Short of a presently unforeseeable willingness of the other subsocieties to share their advantages, these changes can come about only through revolutionary accession to power by representatives of the poor.

Model 3: Heterogeneous Subsociety with Variable, Adaptive Subcultures

a. The lower-class poor possess some distinct subcultural patterns, even though they also subscribe to norms of the middle class or the total system in some of the same areas of life and are quite nondistinctive in other areas; there is variation in each of these dimensions from one ethnic group to another.

b. The distinctive patterns of the poverty subcultures, like those of the other subsocieties, include not only pathogenic traits but also healthy and positive aspects, elements of creative adaptation to conditions of deprivation.

c. The structural position and subcultural patterns of the poor stem from historical and contemporary sources that vary from one ethnic or regional group to another but generally involve a multicausal combination of factors, often including some of those cited above in both 1c and 2c.

d. Innovation serving the interests of the lower class to an optimal degree will therefore require more or less simultaneous, mutually reinforcing changes in three areas: increases in the resources actually available to the poor; alterations of the total social structure; and changes in some subcultural patterns.

e. The most likely source for these changes is one or more social movements for cultural revitalization, drawing original strength necessarily from the poor, but succeeding only if the whole society is affected directly or indirectly.

(1) Such a movement would reinvigorate the poor as it developed, sweeping away subcultural patterns that are merely static adjustments to deprivation.

(2) Particularly where the poor are a numerical minority, such a movement would have to rely significantly on suasion other than physical force to achieve its wider objectives, so that revolution on the classical model would probably not be sufficient.

(3) Social work and education, perhaps even psychiatry, might serve important secondary and supportive functions if they were reoriented in terms of the movement.

(4) The American civil rights movement is perhaps a prototype in some respects, but a successful revitalization movement serving the interests of the poor would have to be much more radical in its aims and command far greater strength.

Among the authors whose works we have reviewed here there are several whose views overlap the boundaries between these formulations.* The three conceptualizations are not by any means altogether mutually exclusive. While there are many important inconsistencies between the first two, one of the intentions behind Model 3 obviously is to reconcile some of these differences by providing a framework to accommodate certain items from both of the other formulations. Thus the third model is, in part, an eclectic synthesis involving the contention that major propositions from the first two may be simultaneously valid.

At the same time, these three outlines do contain the principal theoretical themes touched upon earlier. Model 1 will be recognized as representing the dominant view in most respects. This is the case despite the fact that some of its proponents, notably Oscar Lewis. also subscribe with varying vigor to certain propositions in the other formulations. Model 1 seems to be the prevailing orientation not only among academic poverty experts but also among liberal intellectuals in general, as well as in relevant national policy-making circles. My own view of this model is that the main weight and prevailing direction of available evidence are inconsistent with it, even though most of those reporting the evidence seem to be more or less committed to this interpretation. When it is presented as a total picture of the culture of the lower class, in my considered judgment this portrayal is absurd. In this form it is little more than a middle-class intellectual rationale for blaming poverty on the poor and thus avoiding recognition of the need for radical change in our society.

It seems obvious that Model 1 constitutes the chief conceptual under-

* [Editor's note: The authors mentioned here were discussed in earlier chapters of *Culture and Poverty,* which are not reprinted here.]

pinning for dominant public policy initiatives, preeminently the "war on poverty." In this respect the influence of this conception is profoundly pernicious, unless one adopts the position that the worse relations become between the poor and the rest of society, the more likely it is that constructive change will come about. The basic message of this approach to the poor is that only after they have become conventionally respectable can they hope for a chance to leave poverty behind them. As virtually every good-sized city in the country becomes a battlefield from time to time through the 1960's, it should be apparent that this approach does not work because its intellectual foundation is a woeful distortion. The social-work solution has been given a new rationale in terms of "culture," but the policies have clearly failed and their intellectual justifications could hardly have been more thoroughly discredited.

On the other hand, none of this means that the logic of Propositions 1*a*, 1*b*, and 1*c* is inherently unreasonable or universally invalid. From a theoretical standpoint, there must be few if any cultures or subcultures with *no* dysfunctional or pathogenic elements. More concretely, there is certainly empirical evidence of pathology, incompetence, and other kinds of inadequacy among the people of the ghettos and slums, as there is in the rest of society. There can be no doubt that living in poverty has its own destructive effect on human capacities and that these impairments become part of the whole process perpetuating deprivation. The vital questions are, how important are the internal disabilities of the lower class, and how are they related to significant external factors? An incomplete but important answer seems plain already: subcultural disabilities are definitely not the whole problem and almost certainly not the principal problem. More adequate answers await research not yet done, including the kind of field work suggested earlier.

Model 2 has its roots in scholarship animated by philosophical positions of the radical left. Phrased rather broadly as it is, it is perhaps reasonably consistent with a fairly wide range on this ideological quarter, from the pessimistic orthodox Marxian view of the "lumpenproletariat" to Fanon's more optimistic vision of "the wretched of the earth." These views find no systematic or wholehearted proponents among the authors we have considered in detail. Nevertheless, the general shape of the evidence not infrequently suggests that the propositions of this model must be taken seriously. Moreover, some interpretations in our sources raise intriguing questions in this connection, such as Lewis' suggestion that poverty cultures may have been eliminated in socialist states.

In my opinion, Model 2 is another inadequate formulation, by virtue of incompleteness. That is, it covers part of the available evidence but not all of it. Nevertheless, it seems that, in a general way at least, this theory is consistent with a considerably larger part of the evidence than the first model considered. The broad structural features of Model 2 are difficult to argue against, as are its propositions on the general processes of relationship between subsocieties. The associated strategies for change are more open to question. It seems clear that stratified inequalities in both wealth and power continue to exist in societies that have undergone socialist revolutions, including some where such upheavals occurred decades ago. On the other hand, this does not necessarily mean that either poverty or lower-class subcultures persist in these societies. Again, obviously, more information is needed. On one point, however, general knowledge does seem a sufficient basis for a reasonably secure conclusion. In the United States, and perhaps in other advanced systems of mixed capitalism where the poor are distinctly in the minority, a socialist revolution by violent seizure of power in the interests of the lower class does not appear practicable.

The final model is clearly superior to the others, if it succeeds in its design. It is intended to resolve some of the major difficulties found in the present literature on poverty subcultures, as well as to synthesize the strong points of Models 1 and 2. Most of it is self-explanatory, and supporting arguments for it will be found widely scattered through this entire essay. The predictive propositions dealing with movements for culture change follow logically from the descriptive phases of the model. Nevertheless, one could hardly consider these suggestions anything more than speculative. This remains true partly because existing empirical information is nowhere nearly adequate either to validate convincingly or to discredit fully any of these abstract conceptions. What is most needed is fresh research leading to real ethnographies of the poor.

SCENARIOS FOR THE FUTURE

The suggested research will best achieve its aims if it is oriented and animated by a universalistic concept of culture. Within this conception of panhuman adaptation, each particular culture need not be viewed as an alien mode inimical to one's own lifeways. Each way of life can be seen as a uniquely creative and continually developing synthesis in which human universals and group particularities are inseparable. Similarly, this view will grant a basic human worth and dignity to all subsocieties and to each subculture. This requires a consistent refusal to derogate any subsystem simply because it seems to violate one's own sectional values or to threaten one's own subgroup interests. These are requirements not easily fulfilled, as we have seen.

Anthropologists have succeeded well in living up to these difficult requirements while working with exotic peoples in every faraway part of the world. They also succeeded notably with the American Indians, though it should be remembered that this was achieved mainly after the Indians had ceased to pose any threat to white Americans or their interests. Can we now accomplish the same achievement with our more familiar exotics, the savage underclasses here at home—the potentially predatory nomads who wander with the seasonal cycles of our crops, the pockets of primitive mountain folk still living by a coal-age culture, or the marauding hostile tribes on the frontiers of our inner cities? We have not succeeded as yet in meeting this contemporary challenge to anthropology, though some of us have made valiant attempts. These attempts by the new anthropologists like Oscar Lewis should certainly not be scorned, even if we cannot yet praise them very highly by the older standards. The present challenge of ethnography at home is a far more difficult one than yesterday's fieldwork problems. It is much more difficult here and now to preserve the necessary social distance and creative tension between ourselves and the governors, the missionaries, the purveyors of trade goods, or the labor recruiters. We are much more directly involved in the larger system, which makes it harder to achieve the necessary quality of involvement in certain of the smaller subsystems. More pointedly, we have personal and professional interests that are firmly embedded in the dominant subsociety of this system.

Yet perhaps even this need not disqualify us entirely or make our task impossible. In the old anthropology we had to loosen our intellectual and emotional ties with Western culture considerably, engaging in a sort of professional semialienation to achieve a kind of transcendent viewpoint. The problem of the new anthropology is to achieve sufficient intellectual and emotional independence from the middle class, and from its dominant subculture, so that we can spend substantial time actually living our whole existence with the indigenes on the other side of the tracks, within the black ghetto, or in a public housing project. As in the old pattern, some of us might even go native, slightly and temporarily, though this is certainly a relative matter and an individual problem for each ethnographer. In short, the new problems may not differ so much in kind from the old ones, even though they certainly differ in degree.

If we can really regain the art of living with the natives, it seems reasonable to hope that the rest will flow rather naturally. We should be able to learn to see the world as it is from within the alien subsociety. We should find it possible, by following out the inner logic of the exotic subculture, to discover through direct experience the similarities of the subsystem to others as well as its differences, its order as well as its disorganized facets, its strengths and virtues along with its dysfunctions and pathologies. Gradually we should become less dependent on images of our people communicated to us by outsiders such as policemen or social workers, for we shall know the people ourselves at firsthand. Eventually we will come to regard those outsiders, not as authoritative sources of information, but as objects of study, to be examined in light of our growing experience of and through the subculture. Thus we shall then be investigating relationships between our temporarily chosen subsociety and others. Ultimately we should be able to view the total system with new eyes.

If this point is ever reached, there will be further consequences. The changed vision of the new ethnographer must sooner or later include within its focus the programs of agencies dealing with the subculture, and the policies of governments that rule over the subsociety. We are so far from this point at present that it seems hardly plausible to predict in detail what this reexamination might yield in new understanding or initiative for change. Yet some broad possibilities do appear highly likely. It seems probable that the future ethnographer of the poor will have clear knowledge of what lower-class people want; he will have considerable understanding of what they are willing and able to do, to get what they want. From this viewpoint it will seem obvious that policies and programs to "eliminate poverty" have failed partly because they were designed and launched without any such knowledge or understanding. It will be clear that this lack of success is analogous to the earlier failure of colonial regimes whose knowledge of their subjects was both superficial and distorted. Another obvious conclusion will be that uniform "antipoverty" policies lacking either understanding or respect for ethnic subcultural diversity within the subsociety, based on the shallow simplification of a homogeneous "culture of poverty," could not succeed. Again the historical parallel will be clear: imperial confusion and failure stemming from stereotyped thinking about primitives and savages.

The old arguments about whether the material condition of poverty or its "culture" must be changed first will seem as futile and irrelevant as the still older debates over the question whether subject peoples could be freed before they were "civilized," "modernized," or "prepared." It will be recognized that the many discussions about whether there was anything "worth preserving" in the poverty subcultures, essentially like those other arguments about the viability of non-Western lifeways in the modern world, suffered an irrelevance born of arrogance: they failed to recognize that the answers to these questions would ultimately depend, in significant part, on the people most directly concerned; not on the rulers but on those whom they ruled. From this perspective, the whole strategy of imposing conformity to middle-class manners and codes with the proffered reward of future affluence will have the quality of another historical echo. It will seem no less bankrupt and no less corrupt than the colonial strategy of offering the material comforts of the West to the rest of the world's peoples if only they would accept Western dictates in religion, politics, and economics.

Similarly, the "social-work solution" for the dilemmas of poverty at home will stand revealed as the latter-day equivalent of Christian education and uplift for the faraway heathen, and all the other baggage of the white man's burden. What has been called "maximum feasible participation of the poor" or "working with indigenous leadership" was earlier labeled indirect rule in a different but analogous context. The earlier version, like the later one, was also presented as a civilizing force, but the older policymakers were somewhat more candid about using their appointed chiefs and designated satraps to further the interests of the governors' home constituencies. Perhaps we shall come to see how, even as segregation and discrimination were being officially "prohibited," the newer forms of apartheid and the latter-day bantustans were being established here at home: "compensatory education" as a substitute for integration, whether of races or classes; training those without jobs to do the dirty work still left over after automation; painting and patching the ghetto instead of allowing people to live decently where they choose; "self-examination" and "self-help" by the poor rather than the sharing of wealth and power by the privileged; helping the poor to build "positive identities" and lots of pride—but no prosperity or power —in their slums. Further parallels will abound. Decreeing "equal rights" and "equal opportunities" for people who do not have and are not allowed equality in anything else (e.g., achievement, power) is as empty and hypocritical as the older shibboleths of "dual development" and "separate but equal." "Voting rights" for the poor, when the candidates are chosen and the parties controlled by the rich, are no more meaningful than being a British subject or holding French citizenship is for a South Sea Islander whose homeland is economically, politically, and militarily ruled by a regime of Europeans, by Europeans, for Europeans.

It may be that thinkers of another day will look back with special interest on the spirited and sophisticated debate of the 1960's between the proponents of the "services strategy" and those who favored "income strategies" in the "war against poverty." Like most activities to which the middle class attached real importance and value (seeing them as affecting their own interests), the poor did not play much part in this, even under the doctrine of maximum feasible participation. Nevertheless, it involved a lively division between those who favored winning the war with a lot of social services for the poverty-stricken few, and others who preferred victory by the weapon of a little money for everyone. The income strategists accused their opponents of advocating outmoded approaches that would merely perpetuate the problem by reinforcing the "dependency" universally considered a prime feature of poverty culture. A few even suggested that perhaps some social-service warriors enjoyed fighting poverty (and being depended on), with the implication that subtle motives might therefore prolong the war. The pro-income forces laid great stress on the importance of independence, healthy masculine economic roles, and the therapeutic effect their strategy would have on the sordid sexuality and brutish home life known by all to characterize the depraved lower class.

Moreover, they showed that these benefits would be a bargain for the whole society at only a few billion dollars per year. According to one widely publicized plan, healthy male identities and stable families would flower from Harlem to the Delta if every child in the nation were supported in the style to which public assistance recipients have become accustomed in Mississippi. A handful of reactionaries argued that such income strategies would have bad effects on the incentive to work. This carried little weight, however, for liberals and sophisticates knew that the poor had no motivation anyway, and they had other programs to take care of that problem. So the doctrine of income supports, or "transfer payments," gained supporters from the right as well as the left. Indeed, within a few years even what had previously been generally regarded as a crackpot scheme, the "guaranteed annual income," came to be discussed by congressmen. Perhaps this was partly accountable by the fact that the level of support proposed amounted to guaranteed poverty. Presumably, to some, good morals and healthy home life among the poor began to seem cheap at this price.

Although our future scholars might thus find it easy to discern absurdities by hindsight, it seems possible that they may discern something more important in these income plans and in the general disposition of the 1960's to seek some scheme for minimal relief to the poor. It is possible that these accumulating crumbs may add up to something that those dispensing them are not bargaining for at all. Again there may be a valid analogy with the cumulative effect of minor concessions granted by the colonialists to their subjects in the mistaken belief that token acquiescences would keep the empire secure. It has been widely true that the most severely oppressed peoples and subsocieties have seldom rebelled or risen up effectively. Yet even slight improvements in the level of life and hope have often liberated quite unsuspected strengths, and rising hopes have led, not just to frustration, but to creative forms of action for change. These are commonalities in the history of many revitalization movements, some of which have succeeded in overthrowing old orders and creating new ways of life.

Possibly something like this may be what the confused struggles of the 1960's portend for the poor in America and elsewhere. We must hope that a new anthropology will soon be able to tell us whether this is the case and if so, something about what form it may be expected to take. We must hope also that the beginning of a coming confrontation between the poor and the rest of society has not already so angered and embittered crucial groups that no ethnographer can study them. There is a tragic possibility that the issue is already joined, on battlefields ranging from exploding ghettos to bullet-scarred land claims in the mountains and deserts of the Southwest or to the violently disputed fishing grounds of Pacific Northwest rivers. Our nation, and through its dominion the Western world as a whole, seems little prepared to meet the foreseeable revitalization of the poor with anything other than the reflexes of the cop on the beat in the ghetto, the posse in National Guard uniforms, and the world policeman. Perhaps there will be no new anthropology, no creative resynthesis by the oppressed, but only another long night of blood and pain.

POSTSCRIPT: A PROPOSAL FOR EMPOWERING THE POOR TO REDUCE INEQUALITY

BACKGROUND

The proposal outlined in the following pages springs from the same concerns and is shaped by the same framework of thought as the rest of this book. Yet the plan suggested here goes well beyond the central purposes of the book. Those purposes were to evaluate existing interpretations of poverty; to probe the implications for social policies; and to propose measures for improving our knowledge and understanding of the poor. This may lead to more effective policies in the future. It is all too obvious, however, that our society needs new ways of dealing with the problems of poverty now—not merely at some future point to be determined by progress in research. This postscript proposes a way of meeting this immediate need.

This proposal reflects the urgency of dealing with the national crisis of poverty and related forms of social disadvantage. Such plans must not proceed from any illusion that present knowledge provides a clear guide to foolproof measures. On the contrary, social planners must originate fresh initiatives for change even as they recognize that existing knowledge is extremely imperfect. This will certainly deprive us of any confidence that total answers or certain solutions are at hand. At the same time, however, this recognition should also free us from the limitations of using presently accepted theories of poverty as the only bases for action. One reasonable response to the inadequacy of widely accepted interpretations of poverty is to propose action programs based on alternative interpretations.

A major source of the need for new solutions is the demonstrated failure of existing antipoverty programs and the predictable failure of additional approaches now on the horizon. It is widely agreed that the traditional programs of the welfare establishment have proved inadequate. A principal reason for this is that these programs have not enabled the poor to act in behalf of their own interests, either individually or collectively. Indeed, conventional welfare approaches have often had the opposite effect of perpetuating and reinforcing the dependency and powerlessness of the poor.

The "war on poverty" of the last few years was supposedly designed to overcome these very deficiencies in older approaches. It has neither accomplished this aim nor shown much promise that it will do so. The recent federal antipoverty effort has contributed substantial new resources to old-line social service and welfare agencies. Federal help has typically not required any basic change in agency policies, and thus in effect it has reinforced their traditional orientation. Moreover, it is generally true across the country at the local level, where antipoverty programs are actually carried out, that control over policy lines and action decisions has changed little. By and large this control is firmly held by the traditional power centers of municipalities, counties, and states. This remains true despite the myths of federal intervention and the ornaments of token "participation by the poor."

This means that there has been no significant increase in the power of poor people to act in behalf of their own interests. Under these conditions, there is little or no reason to expect that results from the newer combinations of services, training programs, and "community action" projects will be much different from the older ones. It is equally discouraging that the "war on poverty" is mainly aimed at changing the "culture of poverty" rather than altering the condition of being poor. Not only are the culture patterns of the poor very imperfectly understood, but it is highly doubtful that any "culture of poverty" is the main force perpetuating socioeconomic inequality. As long as the "war on poverty" is focused mainly on changing the supposed customs and values of the poor—rather than on altering the economic and political structure of the nation—it will have little effect on poverty.

The main ideas presently being widely discussed, tried out experimentally here and there, and possibly scheduled for national implementation within the forseeable future are various forms of direct income support for the poor: guaranteed annual income, negative income tax, family allowances. The main contribution of these programs would be to establish an absolute minimum below which no family's or unattached individual's disposable income could fall. Such an approach can be expected to fail because it is based on a misunderstanding of the poverty problem in an affluent society with an ideology of equality. The segments of the poor and their partisans or supporters who are in motion today, creating a national crisis by their outbursts of protest, are not demanding some absolute minimal level of economic security. On the contrary, they are demanding equality—if not total equalization then radically greater equality. This demand applies not merely to economic welfare but to all the material and psychic benefits of membership in our society. This is not to say that a minimum livelihood should not be vouchsafed to all; nor is it implied that this security would not be welcomed by many among the poor. The point is that no measures of minimal income support, whether presented as welfare payments or as guaranteed subsistence, can solve the basic problem of inequality.

With all this in mind, the proposal put forward here is consistent with Model 3, outlined in chapter 6 above [not reprinted here], portraying the poor as a heterogeneous subsociety with variable subcultures. The key to this proposal is to place substantial new economic, social, and political resources under the control of the poor so that they will have the power to act in such a way as to reduce their inequality significantly. Reducing inequality does not mean what has come to be called "equal opportunity." It means equitability of results in the sense of achievement, fulfillment, and enjoyment of the rewards and satisfactions already generally available to citizens outside disadvantaged groups.

THE NEED

It has long been a cherished belief in this country that the poor should overcome poverty themselves. We now know that under modern conditions this has proved impossible for about one quarter of our citizens. Because of historically developed inequalities, equal rights today do not bring about genuinely equal opportunity for these people. Laws that guarantee equal rights cannot create actual equality for those who control only the most inadequate economic, educational, and political resources. We are all paying for this failure of our society. The cruel loss of lives and property in our burning cities makes it imperative that we find new responses to unemployment and powerlessness among the poor. In order to deal with these problems effectively, we must transcend the principle of guaranteed equality even though this principle itself is only barely established in national life. It is necessary to move on immediately to special rights and positive discrimination in favor of the human groups heretofore most disadvantaged.

The program suggested here does not deal with all aspects of poverty. No doubt comprehensive programs will be proposed by others in fields of current interest such as family structure and community organization. The present proposal is focused on the immediate and long-range economic problems of the unemployed, the underemployed, and the unskilled poor. To deal effectively with these problems it is necessary that the program cover the fields of employment and economically valuable training, as well as the related phenomenon of the powerlessness of the poor.

There are three principal reasons for choosing this focus. One is the belief that solutions in the economic realm are both urgent in the sense of great immediate need, and fundamental in the sense that little else seems possible without substantial progress in this area. Second is the hope that a concrete and radical plan in the field of employment may have an immediate appeal to people who suffer economic deprivation every day and who can readily perceive connections between employment difficulties and some of their other problems.

In the third place, germs of a radically new approach already exist in certain employment proposals that have come in the past from civil rights organizations and related sources. One of these germs is the principle of compensatory hiring articulated by Whitney Young of the Urban League. Another is the demand sometimes made by the movement for Negro advancement, that employers who claim qualified workers cannot be found, should hire people whom they consider unqualified and give them the necessary qualifications through on-the-job training.

These ideas clearly go beyond the formulas of equal rights and equal opportunities. The common principal underlying them is that after centuries of severe denial of opportunity the victims of this deprivation cannot possibly catch up through merely equal opportunity. Carried to their logical conclusion, these ideas lead to the demand for a comprehensive national program of positive discrimination in favor of the presently underprivileged. Bayard Rustin has recently pointed out that to win World War II we effectively employed huge numbers of workers without standard qualifications. We must do the same on a larger scale, and with more imagination, to avoid losing today's war of the cities.

THE PROGRAM

Employment. The heart of this proposal is a national commitment to positive discrimination in employment. Present patterns and past trends of employment and job advancement, as reflected in group unemployment rates and median family income, must be reversed to the positive advantage of the unemployed and the poor. The program should cover as many employers as possible, certainly including government agencies at all levels, extending to public utilities under government regulation and private businesses holding government contracts, and ideally encompassing educational institutions receiving government aid and all other employers engaged in interstate commerce.

The ruling consideration should be that all individuals who are unemployed or earn less than an adequate yearly income must be given realistic good-faith opportunities for employment or advancement as soon as possible. This will mean that job opportunities must frequently be opened up regardless of applicants' existing qualifications as traditionally defined. The emphasis should be on full-time work, and all employment under the program should carry reasonable hope of both permanence and advancement. The jobs to be produced should pay no less than an adequate family income for workers who are household heads, and no less than the national minimum wage or union rates, whichever is higher, for other employees.

Hiring under such a program would have to be in accordance with group priorities. The highest priority would be assigned to heads of households who are members of the nonwhite ethnic group which has the highest rate of unemployment in each local area. In practice this would mean that adult Negro males would receive first preference in most but not all areas. The remainder of the priority system could be defined in terms of the measurable relative deprivation of each significant ethnic group in each local area, including of course poor unemployed whites.

An important key to administration of the priority system would be that whenever employers claimed they could not find qualified high-priority applicants for entering positions, they should be required and enabled to establish on-the-job training for such positions. While it should be the responsibility of each employer to find and recruit high-priority applicants for all job openings, a file of such applicants could be maintained by the administering agency for the use of employers in each local area.

. . .

Chapter 7

BLACK AMERICANS IN URBAN GHETTOS

In their thought-provoking analysis of American racial patterns, Stokely Carmichael and Charles Hamilton defined "racism" as the "predication of decisions and policies on considerations of race for the purpose of *subordinating* a racial group and maintaining control over that group." [1] Arguing that such racism has long characterized white actions toward black Americans, they described two types of racism: individual and institutional. Individual racism encompasses overt actions by white individuals to injure persons or destroy property, for example, the bombing of a Negro church; institutional racism is less overt, less dramatic, and more difficult to attribute to specific individuals. Institutional racism resulting in great racial inequalities is constantly manifested in the ordinary operation of the organizations and institutions in the society and stems from the actions of established and "respectable" persons.

While a number of analysts of American society have used terms such as "institutional racism" and "internal colonialism," and while much social science research has been devoted to examining prejudice and stereotyping among whites, few have examined the critical aspects of institutional racism in any depth. An excerpt from one of the relatively few recent books attempting this task is the first selection in this chapter. The author, William K. Tabb, prefaces his analysis as follows:

> The purpose of this work is to describe the economic factors which help explain the origins of the black ghetto, and the mechanisms through which exploitation and deprivation are perpetuated; and to explore strategies for ending them.

In the emotional discussion of race it is too easily forgotten that the same economic laws operate in this area as elsewhere. The systematic racism so often described cannot be effectively fought by merely de-nouncing bigotry and calling for more legislation: the important enemies are not the crude bigots, and there are already too many laws which are not being enforced. Racism is perpetuated by elements of oppression within an economic and political system which must be understood *as a system.*[2]

What are the basic structural features of the ghetto marketplace? Viewing the ghetto's economic system as an indicator of internal co-lonialism, Tabb delineates a number of important structural features of the ghetto marketplace: bait advertising, switch sales, misrepresentative sales contracts, specialized sales and credit techniques, and profiteering in slum housing. Yet the exploitation of the ghetto consumer is not sim-ply the result of the actions of a few disreputable businessmen. Laws and courts tend to favor the businessman over the consumer, even when the consumer has been victimized. Banks and other reputable lending organizations buy up ghetto purchase contracts without questioning how they were obtained, thus playing an important role in keeping black urbanites encapsulated in areas of poor-quality housing.

Following on his analysis of these and other important aspects of the ghetto's economic situation, Tabb explores several strategies for remedying the existing situation—helping individual black businessmen, locating plants owned by white-controlled corporations in black ghettos, and creating community-controlled development corporations. He pro-vides an intriguing analysis of the first two alternatives in terms of the structural situation in ghetto economies and raises serious questions about much of the current emphasis on black capitalism. Policy issues quickly come to the forefront in this discussion, and the community-controlled development corporation is explored as a possible way around the individualistic focus of most prominent black capitalism schemes.

The second selection in this chapter deals with yet another set of im-portant ghetto issues, those relating to the black community. That black Americans are residentially segregated has been documented in nu-merous research studies, but social science analysis has given primary attention to only two determinants of that housing segregation—direct market discrimination and economic inequality. Although Gunnar Myr-dal suggested several decades ago (1941) that a third determinant should be given serious consideration in assessing racial and ethnic seg-regation—the factor of ethnic attachment or voluntary congregation—until recently few researchers would have seriously considered the vol-untary factor as important in the case of black segregation.[3]

Thus, the findings reported in the study by Lewis Watts and his as-sociates, entitled *The Middle-Income Negro Family Faces Urban Re-newal,* may come as a surprise to many readers. Initially, the research-ers themselves expected that the middle-income black residents of the Washington Park area in Boston, Massachusetts, would "embrace any opportunity to escape from their relatively segregated and declining neighborhood." There were certainly compelling reasons to move out, for example, the poor schools in the area. However, this study of 250 middle-income black families, conducted over a sixteen-month period, revealed that in spite of their relatively affluent status, the problems in their area, and the tumult of urban renewal, most did not move from the ghetto area; by the end of the study period only 4 percent had chosen to move to white-dominated suburbs. Even more surprising was the finding that less than 5 percent of the sample had even *explored* the possibility of securing a house or apartment outside the general Roxbury area (the larger ghetto surrounding Washington Park) of Boston.

Why did these relatively well-off black families remain in the ghetto? The answer is doubtless complex, but the research data contain some interesting implications. Since the researchers found that numerous houses outside the ghetto, in the price range of these families, were available on a nondiscriminatory basis, they suggest that other factors than unavailability of housing may explain the lack of mobility. Among the factors touched on are (1) confidence in the outcome of a rehabilitation-oriented urban renewal program (which contrasted with mass "bulldozing" programs), (2) the bargain prices on housing in the ghetto area, (3) the convenience and cosmopolitanism of the central city, (4) strong commitment to the black community, (5) strong identification with being black, and (6) fear of the possibility of white discrimination. Here Myrdal's factor of ethnic attachment or personal choice seems an important factor in the continuing segregation of black families, perhaps especially for middle-income families. Given the importance of community and social networks for black families, one proposal made in the conclusion by Watts and his associates for desegregating central-city areas is both unusual and provocative:

> The alternative, one never honestly faced, is the integrating of the Washington Park community and others like it by stimulating movement from the rest of the metropolitan area. Most of the Negro families we studied do indeed want to live in a community better balanced racially. On the other hand, they are not likely, perhaps are often not psychologically able to move and at any rate are apparently unwilling to do so. *Why not an intensive campaign to attract white families into the community,* breaking the vicious cycle of discrimination and inferiority and, at the same time, bringing in additional leaders and new role models? [4]

NOTES

1. Stokely Carmichael and Charles V. Hamilton, *Black Power* (New York: Vintage, 1967), p. 3.
2. William K. Tabb, *The Political Economy of the Black Ghetto* (New York: Norton, 1970), p. vii.
3. See Gunnar Myrdal, *An American Dilemma,* vol. II (New York: McGraw-Hill, 1964), p. 619.
4. Lewis G. Watts et al., *The Middle-Income Negro Family Faces Urban Renewal* (Waltham, Mass.: Florence Heller Graduate School of Social Welfare, Brandeis University, 1964), p. 108.

FROM THE POLITICAL ECONOMY
OF THE BLACK GHETTO:
BLACK POWER—GREEN POWER

WILLIAM K. TABB

If the ghetto is viewed as an internal colony, it becomes easier to see why white political and corporate leaders are working so hard to convince ghetto dwellers that what they really want is "black capitalism." However, the idea of black capitalism runs counter to an important anti-capitalist strand in the black power ideology.[1]

Black power demands black control over black institutions. This can be achieved in two ways. Individual blacks may own the important resources of the ghetto, or the black community may, in common, own and run its economy. Increasingly blacks are choosing the second course. The "white power structure," on the other hand, prefers individual ownership by blacks, which of necessity will have to be in cooperation with outside white interests. The reason for this choice is apparent. Such an arrangement is amenable to neo-colonial rule, since it guarantees the indirect control of the ghetto economy through a local native class essentially dependent on larger white businesses. The aim is twofold: to win loyalty of an important group of potentially influential local leaders, and to channel protest into less threatening, and incidentally, less useful goals. In this light, increasing the number of ghetto blacks in ownership positions appears to be an important prerequisite for ending ghetto unrest.[2] If blacks are upset because they lack control over the institutions of the ghetto, because they are charged high prices for inferior merchandise, victimized by credit racketeers, and exploited by employers, then perhaps—some would argue—greater black ownership will help end these conditions (or at least lessen anti-white feelings because the local merchants would be black). If the ghetto lacks leadership and a stable middle class, then enlarging the number of black entrepreneurs may provide such leadership and foster stability. If the problem is lack of racial confidence, the success of black capitalists would build pride. If riots are caused by people who have tenuous alle-

Reprinted from *The Political Economy of the Black Ghetto* by William K. Tabb. By permission of W. W. Norton & Company, Inc. Copyright © 1970 by W. W. Norton & Company, Inc., pp. 35–57.

[1] See Raymond S. Franklin, "The Political Economy of Black Power," *Social Problems,* Winter 1969; and Robert Blauner, "Internal Colonialism and Ghetto Revolt," *Social Problems,* Spring 1969.

[2] See, for example, Robert B. McKersie, "Vitalize Black Enterprise," *Harvard Business Review,* September–October 1968.

giance to our system, ownership is the best way to build a commitment to working for change within the system. Increasing the ownership class, in short, is a way to add stability, increase local leadership, lessen the visibility of white domination of the ghetto economy, and funnel ghetto discontent into acceptable channels.

Interest in black capitalism also strikes a responsive chord in the corporate sector. Proposals for black capitalism involve minimal direct government intervention. They provide for subsidies to cooperating private firms. Even though black hostility toward white businesses is increasing, the "Negro market, a market expected to reach $52 billion in 1975," [3] cannot be ignored by even the largest firms. Market penetration is possible through joint corporations partly owned or managed by blacks. Franchising local blacks to distribute products in the ghetto and setting up independently owned but captive suppliers may also be in the corporation's interest. Banks limited by law to city boundaries find that as the black population grows they need to make more loans to minority-group businessmen to maintain their profit position.[4] Labor shortages in a period of rapid growth have sent many firms out to recruit in the ghetto, spurred on by Manpower Development and Training Act (MDTA) funds and a desire to get on better with the increasingly large number of blacks living in the inner city where their plants are located. Thus pushed by the demands of the black community and pulled by societal and corporate interest, government, industry, and black organizations are moving to promote black capitalism.

The purpose of this chapter is to assess the likely success of such efforts and to evaluate the strength and the nature of resistance to black capitalism. Three variations on the theme will be considered: attempts to help individual black small businesses, white corporate involvement in the ghetto, and proposals for community development corporations. Finally, different patterns of ghetto development and their impact on the economic structure of the ghetto will be considered. But it is first necessary to describe the ghetto marketplace itself.

THE GHETTO MERCHANT AND THE CONSUMER

Some economists draw a contrast between how markets work in the ghetto and how they operate elsewhere. There are differences, to be sure, but they should not be allowed to obscure the essential fact that the market mechanism works in the ghetto pretty much in the way traditional theory would lead us to expect. Low-income people, lacking purchasing power and information concerning the quality of available merchandise, and restricted to shopping in ghetto markets, end up with inferior merchandise at higher prices. Seeking to maximize profit, the

[3] "The Soul Market in Black and White," *Sales Management: The Marketing Magazine*, June 1, 1969.

[4] See *Christian Science Monitor*, July 9, 1968.

ghetto merchants adjust their sales practices to the nature of their customers, who are characterized as having low incomes and comparatively limited education.

Shady business practices are often reported in ghetto areas: use of bait advertising of goods which are "sold out" when the customer arrives; the switch sale, where the customer comes in to look at specials and is told that the special is not of good quality and what he really wants is some more expensive item; the refusal to return deposits; the misrepresentative sales contract; the used furniture sold as new; the coercive pressures on buyers; the attempts to collect non-existent debts. All these practices so frequently complained of have their roots in the powerlessness and the lack of educational and financial resources of the urban poor. Deliberation in buying durable goods, surveys find, is more highly correlated with education than with income.[5] Judging quality in consumer durables takes some skill, and understanding credit arrangements is not easy. With a low income, one naturally is on the lookout for a "good deal."

A specialized sales network has developed to deal with low-income people. The friendly smooth-talking dealer who makes the uneducated, poorly-dressed customer feel at home, gaining his confidence, offering generous credit terms impossible to obtain elsewhere—and all this right in his own neighborhood—is much easier to deal with than a hostile downtown department store salesman. However, the prices paid reflect this special service. A recent Federal Trade Commission (FTC) report concludes:

> The low-income market is a very expensive place to buy durable goods. On television sets (most of which are the popular 19-inch black and white portables), the general market retailer price is about $130. In the low-income market a customer can pay up to $250 for similar sets. Other comparisons include a dryer selling for $149.95 from a general market retailer and for $299.95 from a low-income market retailer; and a vacuum cleaner selling for $59.95 in the general market and $79.95 in the low-income market.[6]

The same FTC study found investment credit used more extensively by retailers selling in low-income neighborhoods than by retailers selling to consumers elsewhere.[7] Further, given the greater risks involved, much higher carrying charges are exacted in ghetto stores than on the general market.

Speaking of the reluctance of the poor to seek legal aid even when they have clearly been victimized, Mary Gardiner Jones, an FTC com-

[5] See Louise G. Richards, "Consumer Practices of the Poor," in *The Ghetto as Marketplace*, ed. Frank D. Sturdivant (New York: The Free Press, 1969), p. 51.

[6] Federal Trade Commission, "Economic Report on Installment Credit and Retail Sales Practices of District of Columbia Retailers," in Sturdivant, *The Ghetto as Marketplace*, p. 101.

[7] *Ibid.*, p. 77.

missioner, says the problem is not only that the poor lack financial resources to get legal assistance:

> With the poor, this reluctance is aggravated by their unfortunately realistic
> fears of retaliation by the merchant or credit agency on whom they are so
> dependent, by their inabilities to express themselves in the language of the
> Establishment and by their sense of inferiority, hopelessness and general
> mistrust of any government authority, which they regard not as the pro-
> tector of their rights, but as the body which puts them into jail, evicts them
> from their apartment or garnishes their salary.[8]

This sort of explanation is not sufficient. The legal system does favor
the businessman over the ghetto resident. Garnishing of salaries for
nonpayment of debt is relatively easy, even when the debts were con-
tracted in ignorance and the contract obtained by fraud. The small print
on installment contracts, unread by the buyer, allows for easy repos-
session. The city marshals, paid by the taxpayer to act as collection
agents, earn a commission for their services. The entire legal system is
set up to protect property and ensure contracts. Nor is the Better Business Bureau of much help to the low-income consumer. Not only has it
no legal enforcement power, but it serves as a lightning rod, absorbing
anger while protecting both the image and the profits of business.

> Its claims notwithstanding, the Better Business Bureau is little more than
> a businessman's protective association often syphoning off consumer com-
> plaints that would be better directed to other agencies. That it has less than
> the consumer's interest at heart is indicated by the fact that in many states
> it has lobbied against consumer representation in government on the
> false premise that the Bureau is already doing the job of protecting the cus-
> tomers.[9]

David Caplovitz, whose studies of consumer practices of low-income
families brought the unscrupulous dealings of ghetto merchants to the
attention of the general public, has suggested that he may have "unwittingly created the impression . . . that these problems exist only
because of a small class of disreputable sellers." [10] Caplovitz points out
that the sellers could not exist without the banks and finance companies
which buy up dishonestly obtained contracts. The finance companies
know what they are doing, as do the highly respected banks who lend
to the finance companies.[11] The involvement of the financial community
in the exploitation of the poor is similar here to the role it plays in perpetuating housing segregation.

Again, as in the case of the slum landlord, the typical ghetto merchant
does not appear to be making high profits. The market, with a large
number of buyers and sellers and ease of entry and exit, assures that

[8] Mary Gardiner Jones, "Deception in the Marketplace of the Poor: The Role of the
Federal Trade Commission," in Sturdivant, *The Ghetto as Marketplace*, p. 252.

[9] David Caplovitz, *The Poor Pay More: Consumer Practices of Low Income Families*
(New York: The Free Press, 1967), p. xxiii.

[10] *Ibid.*, p. xvii.

[11] *Ibid.*, p. xvi.

only normal profits are earned in the long run. In addition, the major studies in this area all show that marketing goods to low-income consumers is costly. Insurance premiums are high, pilfering and robbery are major problems, and the use of salesmen who canvass on a house-to-house basis, make home demonstrations, and collect debts is expensive. Summarizing a study of durable goods merchants, the FTC reports: "Practically all of the substantially higher gross margins of the low-income market retailers were offset by higher expenses and did not result in markedly higher net profits as a percentage of sales." [12]

It seems doubtful that exchanging black merchants for white in ghetto stores would make much of a difference, given the realities of doing business in the ghetto. The discussion of black capitalism which follows must be seen in the light of these economic realities.

BLACK CAPITALISTS

The small size of the black business class has generally been explained in two ways. First, there are barriers to an individual's advancement in business because he is black. Second, the nature of segregation and the economic relations between the black ghetto and the white society preclude, for the most part, the possibility of successful black businesses. Stressing one of these approaches over the other has major policy consequences; if blacks have not been successful because of discrimination, then classic civil rights strategies of groups like the Urban League and the NAACP should be followed. If the ghetto is viewed as an internal colony requiring collective liberation, then other strategies are called for.

Many scholars have pointed out the conspicuous absence of blacks in managerial and proprietary positions.[13] It has been argued that this situation exists because blacks are arriving in the cities at a time when opportunities for the establishment of small businesses are on the decline.[14] This may well be true, but the black man's failure to achieve success as a businessman must certainly be attributed more centrally to racism. As Eugene Foley has written, "The culture has simultaneously unduly emphasized achievement in business as the primary symbol of success and has blindly developed or imposed an all-pervading racism that denied the Negro the necessary opportunities for achieving this success." [15]

The only area in which black businessmen were able to gain entry

[12] Federal Trade Commission, "Economic Report on Installment Credit," p. 104.

[13] See, for example, Nathan Glazer and Daniel Patrick Moynihan, *Beyond the Melting Pot* (Cambridge, Mass.: The M.I.T. Press and Harvard University Press, 1963), pp. 31–32; and Daniel Patrick Moynihan, "Employment, Income, and the Ordeal of the Negro Family," in *The Negro American*, ed. Talcott Parsons and Kenneth B. Clark (Boston: Beacon Press, 1967), p. 143.

[14] Glazer and Moynihan, *Beyond the Melting Pot*, p. 143.

[15] Eugene P. Foley, "The Negro Businessman: In Search of a Tradition," in Parsons and Clark, *The Negro American*, p. 572.

was within their own segregated communities. In this regard the closing off of the ghetto may have helped black businessmen as a group. But even in the ghetto other groups often have the most prosperous businesses. In many cities Jews are more heavily represented in retail businesses than other groups as a result of past European restrictions on Jews which forced a disproportionate number to become traders and merchants because other professions were closed to them. Of the immigrant groups to come to America the Jews were as a result the group whose members went heavily into trade. In many ghettos anti-white feeling against merchants has taken on strong anti-semitic tones. However, a study of New Orleans, where the black ghetto businesses are heavily owned by Italians, showed the presence of strong anti-Italian feeling. In all cases hatred is aimed at the group which economically dominates the ghetto.[16]

In getting started in business the European immigrants had three major advantages over the blacks. First, the immigrants usually had a sense of clannishness. Glazer and Moynihan point out that because of such group solidarity, funds were more readily available. "Those who had advanced themselves created little pools for ethnic businessmen and professionals to tap." [17] This has not been as true of blacks, until the present decade, when a sense of identity and group pride has developed among a sizable number of blacks. Second, there is the legacy of slavery. Blacks have not only the "badge of color but also the ingrained burden of generations of cultural and economic deprivation." [18]

> The plantation system offered the Negro no experience with money, no incentive to save, no conception of time or progress—none of the basic experience to prepare him for the urban money economy. Instead, it indoctrinated him to believe in his own inferiority, to be resigned, while it held him in a folk culture dominated by a spiritual, other-worldly, escapist outlook. . . .[19]

This is a limited view of the effects of slavery. It ignores the "calculated cruelty . . . designed to crush the spirit," the malice and the hatred which blacks endured under slavery. Nor does such a view speak to the continuing record.

"When slavery ended and large scale physical abuse was discontinued, it was supplanted by different but equally damaging abuse. The cruelty continued unabated in thoughts, feelings, intimidation and occasional lynching. Black people were consigned to a place outside the human family and the whip of the plantation was replaced by the boundaries of the ghetto." [20]

[16] St. Clair Drake and Horace R. Clayton, *Black Metropolis*, vol. II (second edition; New York: Harcourt, Brace and World, 1962), p. 432.

[17] Glazer and Moynihan, *Beyond the Melting Pot*, p. 33.

[18] Jeanne R. Lowe, *Cities in a Race with Time* (New York: Vintage, 1967), p. 283.

[19] *Ibid.*, p. 283.

[20] [William H.] Grier and [Price M.] Cobbs, *Black Rage* [(New York: Bantam, 1968)], p. 20.

Whether one blames the dominance of folk culture or at a more fundamental level the limits slavery placed on black development, it may be concluded that blacks do lack "managerial skills and attitudes. Negroes as a race have been little exposed to business operations and lack technical experience and entrepreneurial values that are necessary for succeeding in business." [21]

In the 1920s and 1930s West Indian-born blacks coming to this country did very well as a group, going into business and proving quite successful. They had drive and determination to succeed, and did so in surprisingly large numbers. Sociologists have attributed their success to the Jamaican social structure, where in spite of British colonial administration rule, there was upward mobility for blacks. Coming to this country, West Indians had separate customs and accents and an identity distinct from the masses of black descendants of American slaves. The Jamaicans showed the same self-confidence and motivation as did other immigrant groups. [22] While this experience is not conclusive evidence, certainly enough has been written about the debilitating effect of the slavery experience that it must be counted high as a cause of the lack of black entrepreneurship. It is also of interest to note that the race pride and self-help ethic preached by the Black Muslims may well be responsible for their success in numerous ghetto-based business operations.

A third and last factor, also difficult to assess, is the importance of an economic base in some occupation or trade in which the group has a special advantage—a phenomenon not found among the black population.

> Thus the Chinese in America, a small group who never dreamed until World War II of getting jobs in the general American community, had an economic base in laundries and restaurants—a peculiar base, but one that gave economic security and the wherewithal to send children to college. It has been estimated that the income of Chinese from Chinese-owned business is, in proportion to their numbers, *forty-five* times as great as the income of Negroes from Negro-owned business. [23]

The lack of a business tradition may in and of itself be a handicap of some significance. The businessman is an important customer for other businessmen, and Italian bakeries are more likely to hire Italian truckers, suppliers, and so on. [24] Such ties are both natural and important. This is why black groups use their buying power to force white-owned businesses to hire black sales personnel. Black ownership could lead to the informal formation of "black" forward and backward linkages in procurement and sales patterns.

[21] McKersie, "Vitalize Black Enterprise," p. 90.

[22] Glazer and Moynihan, *Beyond the Melting Pot,* p. 34.

[23] *Ibid.,* p. 37.

[24] *Ibid.,* p. 31.

Another disadvantage the black businessman has is that he is limited to the ghetto as a place of business. This means that his customers have lower incomes than those of businessmen located elsewhere; his insurance rates, if indeed he can get insurance at all, tend to be much higher than elsewhere; [25] his customers are worse credit risks; loss rates from theft are higher; and so on. Further, when the black businessman goes to get bank loans, all of these disadvantages are thrown back at him. A commercial loan is "based on the proven management ability of the borrower in a stable industry and a stable locality." [26] Black businesses are for the most part marginal, unstable, and very poor credit risks. They also tend to be almost exclusively in retail and service trades. If "there exists, among Negroes, a rather low image of the significance and possibilities of business endeavors," [27] this feeling seems justified. The evidence available suggests a low rate of return for black entrepreneurs.

There are black businessmen who have grown quite wealthy and others who are modestly well-to-do who have built up sizable businesses in the black communities of Atlanta, Durham, Chicago, and New York, but they have done so by overcoming extensive obstacles. The argument here is twofold. First, black business is much smaller and less profitable than white business. Further, small business—white or black—will not do well and is not what the ghetto needs.

In a 1964 study of the Philadelphia black ghetto it was found that "[p]ersonal services were the most numerous, hairdressing and barbering comprising 24 percent and 11 percent, respectively, of the total number of Negroes in business. Luncheonettes and restaurants comprised 11.5 percent of the total. Many of the businesses would be submarginal if free family labor were not available. For example, median sales for a sample of Negro-owned beauty shops were $2,500, for Negro-owned luncheonettes, $6,800, and for barber shops, $4,400." [28] It seems safe to say that the 1970s will not be the decade of the small businessman. The number of black-owned businesses decreased by more than a fifth between 1950 and 1960, faster than the also declining rate for white-owned small businesses.[29] In spite of the relatively unimportant

[25] See The President's National Advisory Panel on Insurance in Riot-Affected Areas, *Meeting the Insurance Crisis of Our Cities* (Washington, D.C.: Government Printing Office, 1968). Also, *Hearings before The President's National Advisory Panel on Insurance in Riot-Affected Areas, November 8 and 9, 1967* (Washington, D.C.: Government Printing Office, 1968).

[26] Foley, "The Negro Businessman: In Search of a Tradition," p. 560.

[27] See National Conference on Small Business, *Problems and Opportunities Confronting Negroes in the Field of Business*, ed. H. Naylor Fitzhugh (Washington, D.C.: Government Printing Office, 1962), p. 8.

[28] Foley, "The Negro Businessman: In Search of a Tradition," p. 561. For more recent evidence see James Heilbrun, "Jobs in Harlem: A Statistical Analysis," *Regional Science Association Papers*, 1970.

[29] Eugene P. Foley, "Negroes as Entepreneurs," in *The American Negro Reference Book*, ed. John P. Davis (Englewood Cliffs, N.J.: Prentice-Hall, 1966), p. 294.

and declining role of small businesses in the economy, blacks are being encouraged to open such businesses.

Restraining potential violence seems to be the major reason for the push for black ownership. One reporter making the ghetto tour in the spring of 1969 found:

> Despite the ruins and other physical deterioration, black leaders say there is a new spirit of restraint, and perhaps a little more hope, among the people. "A community that sees itself coming into ownership of businesses and other property," said Thomas I. Atkins, Negro member of the Boston City Council, "is not anxious to destroy that which it will own." [30]

A great effort is therefore being made to give more blacks "a piece of the action."

HELPING INDIVIDUAL BLACK BUSINESSMEN

One of the major differences in the ways white middle-class communities and black ghettos are organized is in the nature of formal and informal communication and decision-making. In white communities one of the most important groups on school boards, in charity fund raising, and in other commercial undertakings is the business community. The lack of black businessmen in the ghetto deprives the community of the important contribution such groups make elsewhere. A second disadvantage in this regard is absentee ownership. As James Q. Wilson has pointed out, "Communal social controls tend to break down when persons with an interest in, and the competence for, maintaining a community no longer live in the area. . . ." [31] Resident businessmen, it is believed, add stability to their community.

The desirability of fostering the growth of small businesses has been recognized and accepted by the federal government for a long time. The Small Business Administration (SBA) makes loans to aid struggling businessmen. The extent of such aid going to blacks before the middle 1960s was minimal. A study of the ten and a half years of operation of the Philadelphia office of the SBA showed that out of 432 loans made through the fall of 1964, only seven had been to black businessmen. [32] Attempting to remedy this situation, the SBA set up a program on an experimental basis in Philadelphia to reach the "very" small businessmen, especially Negro businessmen, who operate a large segment of the very small business sector. The program involved loans up to $6,000 for six years (hence the name "6 × 6" Pilot Loan and Management Program). The SBA also offered individual training and counseling.

[30] John Herbers, "Mood of the Cities: New Stakes for Blacks May Cool Things Off," *The New York Times,* April 27, 1969, Section 4, p. 8e. See also Jacob Javits, "Remarks to the 56th Annual Meeting of the U.S. Chamber of Commerce," in U.S. *Congressional Record,* 90th Cong., 2nd Sess., May 7, 1968, p. S5053.

[31] James Q. Wilson, "The Urban Unease: Community vs. City," *The Public Interest,* Summer 1968, p. 34.

[32] Foley, "The Negro Businessman: In Search of a Tradition," pp. 574–575.

The program was judged successful in overcoming traditional barriers faced by black businessmen, and, to the surprise of some old-time SBA people, the delinquency rate was very low.[33]

In the late 1960s the SBA accelerated its search for qualified black borrowers, instituting special outreach programs, lowering equity requirements (which in 1968 could be less than 15 percent), guaranteeing up to 90 percent of bank loans, and developing counseling programs in cooperation with volunteer groups such as the Service Corps of Retired Executives (SCORE) and Minority Advisors for Minority Entrepreneurs (MAME).[34] In fiscal 1968 the SBA aided 2,300 minority-owned businesses with various services and promised to increase this number in years to come.[35] One thousand six hundred seventy-six minority loans were approved in fiscal 1968, about 13 percent of total SBA loans, and five percent of the total value of loans made.[36]

Unfortunately, the rapid increase in the number of loans made to minority businesses was dramatically matched with climbing loss and default rates. In fiscal 1966 the loss rate was 3.6 percent. The next year it was 8.9 percent, and in fiscal 1968 the loss rate was nearly 12 percent of loan disbursement.[37] It was hinted in the spring of 1969 that the climbing rate of losses on loans might lead to cutbacks in the SBA program.[38] Once the best prospects were helped, the economies of the more typical ghetto business had become evident. Merchants with limited capital and markets purchase on a small scale and so must charge higher prices, creating customer resentment.

One way to minimize the failure rate of new businesses is through franchising, which utilizes a "proven" product, service, and marketing technique. The franchisor usually provides location analysis, helps negotiate a lease, obtains a loan, initiates training for the personnel, helps design and equip the store, and offers economies of centralized purchasing and advertising.[39] Franchising is also a safe way for white firms to enter the ghetto market. Franchising and the SBA programs are subject to the same criticism: small retail businesses are on the decline, and certainly to rely on small business as a way to promote black advancement in competition with white capitalism "is little more than a hoax." [40]

[33] *Ibid.*, p. 575.

[34] Small Business Administration, *Fact Sheet: Project Own* (Washington, D.C.: Small Business Administration, n.d. [received April 1969]).

[35] Allen T. Demaree, "Business Picks up the Urban Challenge," *Fortune*, April 1969, p. 176.

[36] Small Business Administration, Office of Reports, *Management Information Summary* (Washington, D.C.: Small Business Administration, May 1969), p. 25.

[37] *The New York Times*, April 21, 1969, p. 27.

[38] *Ibid.*

[39] See U.S. Department of Commerce, *Franchise Company Data for Equal Opportunity in Business* (Washington, D.C.: Government Printing Office, 1966), especially p. 4.

[40] W. Arthur Lewis, "The Road to the Top Is through Higher Education—Not Black Studies," *The New York Times Magazine*, May 11, 1969.

An equally important criticism of attempts to create a greater number of black businessmen is that the economics of the ghetto may itself force the black capitalist to shortchange his "brothers," selling inferior merchandise at high prices just as other ghetto merchants do. For these reasons two other strategies seem more relevant to the economic development of the ghetto—the involvement of big business in partnership with the local community and local development corporations owned and operated by neighborhood residents.

THE WHITE CORPORATION IN THE BLACK GHETTO

The latter part of the 1960s witnessed the growing awareness on the part of the business community that it should become more "involved" in urban problems. Writing as a mayor of a large city with a background in business, Alfonso Cervantes stated in the fall of 1967 in the *Harvard Business Review* that before Watts he believed "businessmen should commit themselves to making money, politicians to saving the cities, do-gooders to saving the disadvantaged, and preachers to saving souls. . . . Observing the riots of Watts (and now Newark, Detroit, and other Harlems throughout the country) has converted me to an updated social orthodoxy. As a public administrator I have discovered that the economic credos of a few years ago no longer suffice; I now believe the profit motive is compatible with social rehabilitation." [41]

In a similar vein a group of corporation executives at the close of a Columbia University School of Business meeting devoted to "The Negro Challenge to the Business Community" spoke not only of the moral responsibility of business to take action, but of its self-interest in doing so. The report said, in part:

> Business cannot tolerate such disturbances. Business could be brought to a virtual standstill in such an atmosphere, as indeed it has in many parts of the world . . . the political realities are such that restrictions, legislation, and the direction of business could bring an end to what we call free enterprise.[42]

While involvement would unquestionably be of benefit to corporations as a whole, unless there is a profitable return to individual firms they will not participate.[43] The problem for government is to insure profitability through subsidies and tax incentives without allowing un-

[41] Alfonso J. Cervantes, "To Prevent a Chain of Super Watts," *Harvard Business Review*, September–October 1967, pp. 55–56.

[42] The Conference Group, "Reports of Corporate Action," in *The Negro Challenge to the Business Community*, ed. Eli Ginzberg (New York: McGraw-Hill, 1964), p. 87.

[43] Robin Marris, "Business Economics and Society," in *Social Innovation in the City: New Enterprises for Community Development*, ed. Richard S. Rosenbloom and Robin Marris (Cambridge, Mass.: Harvard University Program on Technology and Science, 1969), p. 30.

earned windfall gains. As the Nixon Administration found out when it
tried to make good on campaign promises, this [is] a difficult balance to
achieve.[44]

The pattern of support that has emerged in the late Johnson and early
Nixon years is that an independent corporation with a name like "Opportunity Unlimited" or "Economic Resources Corporation" is set up
with a predominantly black board of directors, funded by Economic Development Administration grants and loans, Labor Department training
funds, and perhaps an Office of Economic Opportunity grant and
Department of Housing and Urban Development assistance.[45] The key
ingredient is an ongoing relation between the newly established corporation and a large established firm which supplies know-how and a
long-term contract for the independent firm's output. Thus, in one well-
publicized case a black group, FIGHT, in Rochester, New York, was
assisted by Xerox in getting started. The extent of dependency in such
a relationship has been described as follows:

> FIGHT's venture would have been a pipedream without the unstinting
> support of Xerox Corporation—from planning to production. Xerox helped
> to define FIGHT's product-line—metal stampings and electrical transform-
> ers. The office-copier giant will lend FIGHT two key management advisors,
> conduct technical training, and open the doors to bank financing. Even
> more important, Xerox has guaranteed to buy $1.2 million of the firm's
> output over a two year period.[46]

In discussing the role of Xerox in getting the Rochester firm started,
another writer stated:

> Here lies one of the principal strengths of the program: a corporation often
> initiates a company, guarantees it a market, helps set up the business,
> furnishes the training, and helps iron out any start-up problems. Indeed,
> all the manufacturing enterprises have been established so far at the
> instigation of potential corporate customers.[47]

The encouragement of black entrepreneurship not only raises the
income of blacks who manage the new businesses, but changes or reinforces their attitudes towards the proper methods of achieving social
change. One counselor who evidently learned "a good deal from his experience" in helping a black man enter the business world, describes in
the following terms the enlightened attitude of his pupil toward Negro
development:

> As a leading Negro, Howard has not been fully able to accept the rebel-
> lious nature of the present civil rights movement. Certainly, he resents the
> forces that have limited the Negroes' development, but in many ways he
> rises above this. He sees himself not only as a Negro but as a member of
> the society of man. As the movement advances and Negroes become more

[44] *The New York Times*, May 11, 1969, p. 1.

[45] *The New York Times*, February 27, 1969, p. 1.

[46] *Christian Science Monitor*, July 26, 1968.

[47] McKersie, "Vitalize Black Enterprise," p. 98.

educated, Howard's values may be accepted. As he says, "Education without civilization is a disaster." He expresses his indebtedness to society when he says, "Let me be recognized, let me contribute." [48]

"Howard" would be described by some militants as an Oreo (black on the outside, white on the inside) or simply as a Tom. The achievement of such black men only reinforces the idea that blacks must struggle as individuals to escape their poverty. What is needed is not the salvation of a few but the redemption of all. This, militants argue, can be done only if all ghetto dwellers cooperatively own the economic resources of the ghetto and use these resources for the common good.

THE COMMUNITY DEVELOPMENT CORPORATION

The contrast between those who favor aiding individual blacks or encouraging white corporations to become involved in the ghetto and those who want independent black development is not always very distinct. Current proposals being put forward in the Congress have in fact adopted the rhetoric of militancy and the trappings of the radicals' own analysis. For example, Senator Jacob Javits, addressing the U.S. Chamber of Commerce in late 1968, compared the ghetto to an emerging nation which rejects foreign domination of its economy. He suggested:

> American business has found that it must develop host country management and new forms of joint ownership in establishing plants in the fiercely nationalistic less-developed countries, [and so too] this same kind of enlightened partnership will produce the best results in the slums of our own country.[49]

In 1968 Javits along with others (including conservative Senator John Tower) proposed a bill which would establish community self-determination corporations to aid the people of urban (and rural) communities in, among other goals, "achieving the ownership and control of the resources of their community, expanding opportunity, stability, and self-determination." [50] The proposed "Community Self-Determination Act" had the support of some militant Black Power groups such as the Congress on Racial Equality (CORE) because it promised self-respect and independence through ownership by blacks and community control of its own development. The bill set as an important aim the restoration to the residents of local communities of the power to participate directly and meaningfully in the making of public policy decisions on issues which affect their everyday lives. "Such programs should," the bill stated, "aim to free local communities from excessive interference and

[48] *Ibid.*, p. 96.

[49] Javits, "Remarks to the Fifty-sixth Annual Meeting of the U.S. Chamber of Commerce," p. 5053.

[50] U.S. Congress, Senate, *Hearings on S. 3876*, 90th Cong., 2d Sess., July 24, 1968, p. S9284.

control by centralized governments in which they have little or no effective voice." While the proposal was not enacted into law, it gives some indication of the type of thinking being done by influential groups and individuals. It has also directed attention to the community development concept.

Most schemes for community development corporations (CDC's) propose (1) expanding economic and educational opportunities through the purchase and management of properties and businesses; (2) improving the health, safety, and living conditions through CDC-sponsored health centers, housing projects, and so on; (3) enhancing personal dignity and independence through the expansion of opportunities for meaningful decision-making and self-determination; and (4) at the discretion of the corporation, using its profits to pay a "community dividend" rather than a return to stockholders.[51] The relation between CDC-sponsored businesses and privately owned ones is hard to delineate satisfactorily.

Some proposals suggest that the CDC should also be a development bank to make loans and grants to local businesses in order to encourage ownership. Others suggest CDC's should bond black contractors and act as a broker between ghetto residents and outside groups for government grants, franchising, and subcontracting. Such an organization would be something on the order of a central planning agency, making cost-benefit studies of business potential in different lines, keeping track of vacancies, and conducting inventories of locally available skills.[52] One study in Harlem has made "feasibility analyses," detailed cost-benefit "profiles," for different industries which might be developed in the ghetto. These involve a consideration of employment and income-generating potential as well as any externalities not reflected in private profit calculations.[53] After detailing the best development plan (developed by technical analysis, subject to community approval under some suitable organizational form), a development planning group would make two final measures. First, an estimate would be made of the *efficiency gaps* (the expected differences in unit operating costs between Harlem projects' activities and similar businesses already operating outside the ghetto). "These gaps will suggest the magnitude of the public subsidies necessary to complement private capital in the implementation of the plan." [54] Second, estimates would be made of needed infrastructural requirements which would "permit the Project businesses to function efficiently. This bill of requirements will then be presented

[51] *Ibid.*, pp. S927–S929.

[52] *Ibid.*, Section 110; Richard S. Rosenbloom, "Corporations for Urban Development," in Rosenbloom and Marris, *Social Innovation in the City;* and Frederick D. Sturdivant, "The Limits of Black Capitalism," *Harvard Business Review,* January–February 1969.

[53] Bennett Harrison, "A Pilot Project in Economic Development Planning for American Urban Slums," *International Development Review,* March 1968, p. 26.

[54] *Ibid.*, p. 27.

to local government officials," [55] or funded by a well-financed CDC. Under such a plan the CDC would provide social infrastructure and funds but eschew an ownership role.

Such a development bank and planning agency approach would encourage black entrepreneurship through low-cost loans and technical help. It downplays mechanisms for community control while stressing neighborhood involvement in an individual entrepreneurial role, rather than community cooperation.

The CDC schemes are expected to be financed either through stocks and bonds sold in the local community or through funding by federal agencies. Some suggest that in addition to the Neighborhood CDC's there should be a national Urban Development Corporation (UDC). The UDC, it is suggested, would not engage in development projects but could give financial and technical advice to the CDC's. The UDC would sponsor experiments and demonstration projects. A UDC could "be a source of knowledge, as well as assistance, generating new ideas for community ventures. It would develop, test, and disseminate knowledge of new means for organizing and implementing projects for creating housing, nurturing new businesses, training the unskilled, and so forth." [56] By selective distribution of resources, based on performance measures, the UDC could increase the scale of operations of the more "effective" CDC's.[57] In this view, the CDC would be limited for funding to what it could earn and what the UDC allocated to it as a "reward for social effectiveness." Profit in the usual sense would not be the measure of efficiency.

The power relations here are subject to much debate. The idea behind the CDC is to give an organizational tool for ghetto development. The extent of control by any group outside the ghetto would in all likelihood be fought by the local leadership. Rosenbloom argues that a UDC would be needed as a "surrogate" for the market, since many CDC undertakings (day care centers, a community newspaper, health services, and so on) might not be run as profit-making ventures but are important programs worthy of financing. Through financial rewards, the UDC would recognize enterprises which improve community conditions. The danger that such controls might lead to covert or overt "manipulation" and the charges of "same old paternalism" have been recognized, but it is also pointed out that there must be an overseeing of public funds through audits and some sort of supervision.

Conflicts might also arise between CDC and powerful local interests. CDC housing rehabilitation programs might not get very much cooperation from local slumowners; buyers' cooperative stores might find local merchants using their influence to fight them; the community-run schools might have trouble reaching agreements with the city-wide board of education, the teachers' union, and so on. On the other hand,

[55] *Ibid.*, p. 28.

[56] *Ibid.*, p. 29.

[57] Rosenbloom, "Corporations for Urban Development."

the inclusion of (white) businessmen in advisory capacities to take advantage of local expertise might be rejected by the community. The demand by the mayor and city council that they be given veto power over projects or that all money should be channeled through them would also be resisted vigorously. If poverty program experiences are indicative, militant local CDC's would find their funds cut off as political pressures of the vested interests made their power felt. The Model Cities Program has been carefully channeled through the local governments, and the ghetto has usually lost the battle for community control. Some of the problems involved, from the city council point of view, are shown in the vigorous resistance to giving neighborhood boards real power under Model Cities legislation.[58] This occurs partly because mayors and councilors do not like to "play second fiddle" to locally elected boards. There is a feeling that special consideration is unfair and that all parts of the city should be treated equally, and the argument that "fairness" requires restitution for past misallocation are rarely accepted by residents of the wealthier white neighborhoods. The narrow-mindedness of most local white electorates indicates that clashes between local autonomy and federal priorities may prove to be one of the more important conflicts in intergovernmental relations in the coming years.[59] Distinguishing among proposals which will encourage local control by black communities while not allowing racist policies in white neighborhoods which democratically vote to be racist is a problem that can be overcome through the application of the U.S. Constitution. It is not as difficult a task as some suggest; in fact, the suggestion that local control strengthens white bigotry, while real enough, is often stressed by those who do not want to see black communities gain real power. The inner-city blacks are asking only for the same degree of autonomy as is already enjoyed by the suburban whites who do run their police, school boards, etc. Each small town in suburbia duplicates facilities, some of which might on economic grounds be run on an area-wide basis. They do so to retain local control, even at the expense of the added financial burden.

BLACK COOPERATION

Corporations have been criticized by some for not going far enough in terms of ghetto autonomy. Others suggest that such proposals, by going too far towards ghetto autonomy, encourage black separatism.

The limits of black capitalism have been well stated by James Sundquist:

Federal credit and technical assistance should be extended, and discrimination against Negro enterprises in such matters as surety bonds

[58] *Ibid.*

[59] See Mahlon Apgar IV, and S. Michael Dean, "Combining Action and Research: Two Cases," in Rosenbloom and Marris, *Social Innovation in the City*, especially pp. 194–96.

and other forms of insurance should be dealt with—if necessary, through federal legislation. Much can be said for a federal program to support and assist ghetto-based community development corporations that will have power to operate or finance commercial and industrial enterprises. But even with all these kinds of encouragement, to suggest that Negro entrepreneurship can produce much more than a token number of new jobs for the hard-core unemployed, at least for a long time to come, is pure romanticism. Ghetto anarchy is impossible. Even if the ghetto markets could be walled off, in effect, through appeals to Negroes to "buy black," the market is not big enough to support significant manufacturing, and the number of white employees who could be replaced by black workers in retail and service establishments is limited.[60]

For the ghetto to develop a strong "export" sector would take a great deal of expertise and capital. Both would have to be imported from outside, and for this to happen, long-standing flow patterns would have to be reversed. There are three ways this could happen.

First, private funds could be guaranteed against "expropriation" and special tax treatment given to assure profitability. The difficulty here would be that given foreign ownership, decisions would be made externally and profits could be repatriated.

Second are the proposals usually offered to help any underdeveloped nation badly in need of capital: better terms of trade and technical assistance. Foreign aid could be used to build up social overhead capital, to make investment in human capital, and to give loans to local entrepreneurs. The ghetto's one major export, unskilled labor, could be aided through a continuing national commitment to full employment. Technical assistance would include economic consultants, the establishment of research facilities to study potentially profitable lines of ghetto development, and a financial commitment to pursue such avenues.

Third, if the problem is viewed as one of underdevelopment, efforts could be made to retain profits and wages of ghetto-based enterprises by demanding that those who work in the area live there. Those who hold jobs as policemen, teachers, postal employees, clerks, or small businessmen would have a greater interest in "their" community if they lived in it. Cooperative forms of ownership would also lead to greater community control and to a greater retention of capital in the ghetto.

· · ·

[60] James L. Sundquist, "Jobs, Training, and Welfare for the Underclass," in *Agenda for the Nation,* ed. Kermit Gordon (Washington, D.C.: The Brookings Institution, 1968), p. 58.

FROM THE MIDDLE-INCOME NEGRO FAMILY FACES URBAN RENEWAL

LEWIS G. WATTS ET AL.

SUMMARY

Families in Washington Park, a section of Boston with a heavy concentration of Negroes, are involved in the City's most massive urban planning effort. In Washington Park, several hundred Negro families of middle income ($5,000 a year or over) because of urban rehabilitation and renewal are being brought face to face with the problem of choosing housing and of deciding whether or not to move. Each family in the renewal area has to decide whether it wishes to remain where it lives, find another dwelling in thè same neighborhood or a contiguous section, or leave Washington Park and find a new home elsewhere in Boston or one of its white suburbs. What follows is a report of an inquiry into their wishes as to housing and how they changed as renewal progressed, as well as into the moves some families actually made and how they fared.

Unlike previous urban renewal in Boston and most programs throughout the country, the Washington Park program is predicated upon the rehabilitation of existing housing stock rather than upon extensive demolition. Many of the residents of the Washington Park community, both Negro and white, are of low economic status; the Negro families of middle income who live among them are a small but critical aggregation. It is the intent of the renewal program not only to improve the local physical conditions but to develop a more organized and "respectable" community and these families are important as leaders and role models for Washington Park residents in less fortunate economic circumstances. Further, they constitute a group whose presence may help attract into the area other middle-income families, be they Negro or white.

On the other hand, these families are important to the many civil rights groups and policy-makers interested in integrating Negro families into predominantly white neighborhoods. Unlike most families in the community, those we studied have the economic means to move into

From *The Middle-Income Negro Family Faces Urban Renewal* by Lewis G. Watts, Howard E. Freeman, Helen M. Hughes, Robert Morris, and Thomas F. Pettigrew (Waltham, Mass.: Brandeis University Research Center of the Florence Heller Graduate School for Advanced Studies in Social Welfare, 1964). Reprinted by permission, pp. 7–11, 90–98.

201

the suburbs and the more prosperous parts of Boston. The study was designed to arrive at a description of their residential mobility, both actual and merely planned, in the first phases of the urban renewal program.

The sample consists of 250 families with incomes of at least $5,000 most of whom have children. Our report is based upon two structured interviews (the first in the spring of 1962, the second ten months later) with the wives in these families, information on their places of residence ten and sixteen months after the first interview, and lengthy, informal interviews with wives and husbands in selected families among them. All the interviewing was undertaken by Negroes trained in social work.

We began the study in the belief that Roxbury's Negroes would rush to embrace any opportunity to escape from their relatively segregated and declining neighborhood. Integration is in the air and the longed-for appears at last to have become the possible. Of course, one of the issues we considered was the availability of housing outside Washington Park to middle-income Negro families. Could they move out, if they wished? We checked the availability of housing at a number of sources including families who had previously successfully integrated into the suburbs —these we call "self-integrators."

We can conclude firmly on the basis of the materials collected that, while there is not completely free choice, there is considerable housing for sale without discrimination in and around Boston. Rental housing is less likely to be available to the Negro family and informal discriminatory practices do prevail in the rental market outside of Roxbury. Although many of these houses and apartments would require the expenditure of a greater proportion of income than the families we studied typically are paying and could afford for their current place of residence, most of them could obtain housing outside, particularly if they chose to buy. To our minds everything pointed to an exodus from the ghetto into the till-now white parts of Boston.

In the first interview, we attempted to obtain information from the 250 families on their inclination to move in the face of urban renewal, their views of the urban renewal as they were experiencing it and their reasons for wanting to stay or leave the Washington Park area. We found that at the beginning of urban renewal less than half the families definitely planned to move out or even thought there was a 50-50 chance that they were not going to be living in Washington Park some ten months later. Virtually all the families were favorable to urban renewal as an effective instrument of local improvement. Their househunting,—what there was of it—was on the whole not extensive and not even very serious. Thus we began to expect that relatively few families would be leaving Washington Park and to question our original view.

We attempted to distinguish those families who reported they planned to move and those who planned to stay. In large part, the characteristics of the middle-income family most likely to move, or who at least expressed much intention, are similar to those found in comparable studies of white families. Age, in particular, appears to be strongly associated with the wish to move, the youngest families being most so inclined. We also found that families who complain about community conditions in Washington Park, especially the schools, are most inclined to move, as also are those who have had wider experience in the white world. The families who state they plan to stay in Washington Park are the older ones, those families who attend Negro churches, who own their own homes, and who have lived the longest time in Roxbury. And, as has been found in other studies, those most satisfied with their current housing arrangements are least likely to move. Furthermore, the families with the highest incomes, with the greatest prestige in the community, are the least likely to spearhead the movement of middle-income families out of Washington Park into areas predominantly white at present.

Ten months after we first interviewed our sample of 250 families in Roxbury and learned of their plans we went back to talk again with the female head of each household. The findings on their mobility surprised us. We obtained information on the place of residence of all but one of the 250 families and found that in the ten months between the two interviews only 13 percent of the 250 families moved at all. Of the 33 that did move, ten relocated in other parts of Washington Park, two outside it but still in Roxbury, and eleven in contiguous parts of adjacent Dorchester. At most nine families could be considered as having left the Negro community during the ten months. Some 96 percent of the families we studied were still living in Negro areas after ten months, despite a climate favorable to selling if not to the renting of homes to Negroes in various parts of the metropolitan area.

Indeed, we were so surprised at the low proportion of families who had moved to a less segregated area that we wondered whether or not we had allowed sufficient time to elapse between the initiation of the renewal program and our second wave of interviews. Therefore, some six months later, 16 months from the time we began to study these middle-income Negro families, we again ascertained where they resided. A few more did move, of course, in that six months, but the pattern remained unchanged. In 16 months less than four percent had chosen to live among white families in predominantly white communities.

Not only was there a low rate of actual mobility but indeed there was very little effort to find new places to live. Less than five percent of the families in a ten-month period actually inspected a dwelling outside of Roxbury and the families used public and voluntary bodies very little to assist them in hunting outside of the Washington Park community or its contiguous neighborhoods.

We attempted, of course, to try to understand the unanticipated fact that few families had moved or even tried to find housing outside the area. We have pointed out they would find that the cost of living outside the area would be markedly higher than in Roxbury and in many cases the bargain they are enjoying there in housing is obviously a major ground for their persisting attachment to the community. Coupled with the economic advantage is their continued, if not increasing, confidence that the Boston Redevelopment Authority's program will make Roxbury a more satisfactory place to live in. Also, it must be kept in mind that there are advantages in living in so central a location, one served well by public transportation and expressways. Moreover there is no doubt they are afraid of being treated prejudicially because of race when trying to acquire dwellings. Of the 70-odd families that reported they looked for living quarters during the ten months, 50 percent felt they had trouble because of being Negroes and 20 percent claimed that on grounds of race they were not even allowed to inspect premises. Their experiences may account for the very limited search for housing outside Washington Park. Families who actually sought housing outside the area suffered or at least felt they were subjected to discrimination and humiliation and indeed these feelings were probably transmitted to other Negroes of similar income level living in Washington Park. The few families that did move tend to have the same characteristics as those that reported they were most likely to leave the area, namely, they are the younger and the most dissatisfied with community conditions. Their number is very small, however, and this is perhaps the most important finding.

In the conclusion of our report, we depart from the data collected and seek to indicate some of the implications of our study for policy-making. It is quite clear that contradictory values are entailed in this effort at urban renewal. From the point of view of the local redevelopment, the limited mobility can be looked upon as an index of success and of an optimistic appraisal of the future. On the other hand, it is quite clear that if the group of families continues to integrate to such a limited extent, the possibility of more residential heterogeneity in the Boston area is most limited, in spite of the considerable efforts of many civic organizations to develop racially mixed communities. From this point of view, an implication of our study is that the cause of integration in housing may best be served by private and public organizations, actively encouraging the moving of white families into such communities as Washington Park, in addition to striving to bring Negroes freer access to housing.

Finally, in this last section of the report, we wish again to emphasize that the middle-income Negro family sees itself as having a personal stake in Washington Park. It must be borne in mind that *non-discrimination is not the same thing as integration.* Often—and this is true of the Washington Park program—the two are confused. The family willing to support the Negro rights organizations in striving for wider choice in housing may perhaps be personally committed to life in Washington Park, at the same time regarding it as a social responsibility to fight for the opportunity *not* to live there. One must recognize that the individual Negro family must and will decide for itself the right and the wrong and the appropriateness or unsuitability of moving out, the same decision as other ethnic groups in the city must make.

[Editor's note: The next section is taken from a later part of the research report by Watts and his associates. Here we have a discussion of the housing experiences of middle-income blacks, drawing heavily on actual interviews with 250 families. The omitted sections deal with a diverse assortment of issues, ranging from the income levels of the families to life styles and housing plans.]

But from our interviews, we know that these families do receive rebuffs and probably as well sometimes interpret routine house-hunting problems as to be explained by race. Whether psychological or not, whether all or partly imaginary, the possibility of discrimination undoubtedly limits the effort they devote to house-hunting and their interest in relocating. Most of the group studied, we believe, would be most surprised by this report from one of the few families who moved, given us by the young wife, a college graduate, whose husband earns $10,000 a year:

"Despite a change of life styles, as it were, most Negroes in Roxbury can move to white neighborhoods if the husband is in the higher income bracket. I had no difficulty purchasing a house outside of Roxbury and never experienced racial discrimination. I saw a 'for sale' announcement in the daily press and called the real estate broker. I never identified myself as Negro and was never asked by the broker. But because I lived in Roxbury, the broker knew I was Negro. He permitted me to examine three houses in my price range. After I made a selection, the broker called three banks to arrange for financing. All three banks agreed to finance my house on an FHA or GI loan. In my presence, my race was never discussed."

Looking for a New Place to Live. Let us look at the experience in house-hunting reported by some among the 250 families in the ten months between the two interviews:

Some of the 234 families we interviewed a second time did say they looked for living quarters in the previous ten months. As before, many of them were obviously not serious about moving. Of the 70, seven never actually inspected a place and 23, one third of them, looked only at one. Moreover, even if they actually moved, many still were not leaving the community at all: only a third limited their apartment or housing-seeking to a white area; an equal proportion looked solely within Roxbury or the contiguous neighborhood of Dorchester. *Less than five percent of the families during the ten months actually inspected a dwelling outside the part of Roxbury where they now live.* These data strongly indicate that house-seeking in the ten months was not at all predicated upon leaving the community. Only eleven families actually tried to use Fair Housing Incorporated or similar services and three made the effort to contact the Massachusetts Commission Against Discrimination.

The families used public and voluntary bodies very little in the ten months. In addition to the three who reported to the Massachusetts Commission Against Discrimination, only 26 or approximately 11 percent requested advice from the Boston Redevelopment Authority and few had any contact at all with community agencies and resources of

Washington Park despite the activity there. Only fifteen percent had any contact with the information center located in Washington Park's Freedom House, although the latter is a very active independent voluntary group and an organization to which many of the families belonged. Moreover, only one family requested advice or assistance from the United Community Services of Boston, although it, too, is ready to help the public and is concerned with the urban renewal program.

Not only was there little contact with the various groups interested in renewal and with Negro rights, but few of the requests for advice or assistance were even related to moving from Washington Park. Only nine requested any information or assistance regarding buying outside of Roxbury and an additional five requested it about renting. The remainder of the requests, if they were connected with housing at all, concerned mortgages for houses purchased in Washington Park or elsewhere in Roxbury, loans for the improvement of current dwellings, the local enforcement codes, how to induce landlords to improve their property and what type of housing will be built locally by the Boston Redevelopment Authority.

All this is evidence that there will be little movement of the middle-income Negroes out of the area. Current research on housing has usually been concerned with why families move; in our case, the question is "why don't families move?"

Why Don't Families Move? Our second wave of interviewing with the large sample provided support for the conclusion that many families will prolong their economically advantageous position by remaining in Washington Park. This is particularly so for renters, who had seemed somewhat more willing at least to leave the area. Apartments large enough for families of four and five persons would as we have noted undoubtedly cost considerably more elsewhere than they do in Roxbury. Furthermore, they would cost more than these families are willing to pay; and, of course, this is compounded with the discrimination against those renting, which is much greater than against those buying.

These families are for the most part unwilling and unlikely to increase markedly their costs of housing and this would be incurred if they moved away. One finds many families paying rents of $100 a month or less, which is so low a proportion of their income as to reconcile them to what they complain of as Roxbury's drawbacks. Their bargain in housing obviously is a major ground for their stubborn attachment to the community and a deterrent to moving away. Coupled with the economic advantage is their continued confidence that the Boston Redevelopment Authority's program will make the area a more and more satisfactory place to live in. And, as we have noted before, there are also advantages in living in so central a situation, so well served by public transportation and expressways.

Thus the wife of a professional man whose earnings exceed $15,000 annually explains:

"I believe the convenient, cheap, rapid transit system which makes it possible to commute to downtown department stores in five minutes compensates for drawbacks; and my husband prefers to remain in Roxbury where he is within walking distance of his office and near his clients."

And the wife in a family who had been living before in a white neighborhood and who knew whereof she spoke, pointed out:

"It is more economical to live in Roxbury. The cost would be much more in Newton, Arlington, or Lexington. Moreover, I am eight minutes from work. I am happy with my housing arrangement in Roxbury. I don't have to be concerned with driving my children into Roxbury so that they will have a social life as other suburban Negro families have to do."

As also has been emphasized, without doubt, they are afraid of being discriminated against when trying to acquire dwellings. Of the 70-odd families who reported they looked for living quarters during the ten months, half felt that they had trouble because of being Negro, and a substantial number claimed that on grounds of race they were not even allowed to inspect premises. Their fears and feelings may account for the very limited search for housing outside Washington Park. Thus, of this number of families who actually sought housing outside the area, many suffered or felt they had been subjected to discouragement and humiliation.

Likewise, despite what appears to be a reasonable acceptance by their white neighbors of the nine families who moved into white suburbs and despite comparable experiences told us in our protracted interviews with the few families who moved during the ten months, many living in Washington Park are fearful of the treatment white neighbors may visit upon them and, even more feared, upon their children. Much of this may be due to the fact that they hear in detail of the unfortunate experiences of a few Negroes who have moved back into Roxbury after living in predominantly white neighborhoods; they are less likely to hear about the (more typical) successes, whose ties with Roxbury grow thin. And so the fears and doubts accumulate.

"One of the things that people do think of is that you're cutting the teen-agers off from the roots right at the time that they should be socializing. But children move around much more than we do. . . . You can get out to Sudbury in 45 minutes or an hour and out to Natick and they can come in. There are maybe two cars in the family and the mother has access to one or the youngsters themselves are driving. So there's that type of, well, apprehension—I don't know if you can call it fear—that we think of in connection with teenagers taken from Roxbury or from a predominantly Negro community. Then there's this other type that would involve the primary school children. . . . There would be little neighborhood birthday parties. But would my child be invited? You can explain some of this to an older child but what can you tell a five-year-old if he isn't invited?"

Most of the 250 families, we are reasonably certain, do know about the active program of Fair Housing Incorporated, although they do not make use of it. These are not uninformed, isolated families, unaware of what Boston can do for them: a fifth of them, for example, reported they attended Boston Pops Concerts in the past year, almost half had been to concerts of the Boston Symphony, and 40 percent to the Museum of Science. Can they really be uninformed about their housing opportunities? Many have white families as friends and most have white associates at work. These very families who are disposed to stay on in Roxbury have been most active in seeking to remedy the school system. They have stood in picket lines, signed petitions, and voted for candidates who want to improve Washington Park schools. They read the Boston newspapers and are keenly aware of the general changes in the community and the possibilities, at least in theory, of leaving it.

It is important to recognize that the very autonomy of these families, their place at or near the top of the Negro community, their respectable and well-ordered lives, render them unresponsive to many of the social efforts directed at integration. Unlike many of their neighbors, they have little contact with the world of health and welfare agencies, appear only infrequently to seek counsel on matters in their personal lives —as witness their limited use of the services of the urban renewal project—and thus represent a determined group who appear to have thrown their lot into changing Washington Park, not leaving it.

"We sort of held our breath because there was some talk about someone with a nursing home coming here. But by and large, the owners on this street have a feeling for the street and we have no formal block association; but it's a funny thing, we have an informal arrangement. We get out while we are raking leaves and pass the word around. So I imagine something like that probably wouldn't happen unless say, someone got strapped for money; and that happens any place. We have the same problems as they have in white neighborhoods—which takes it a little out of the racial world.

As long as the present owners live here and the owners are people who maintain certain standards, I think that will protect this street and I think that it could protect any street where there aren't apartments and not absentee owners. I think that you will find this in almost any area. A lower-class family couldn't buy here because well, take this house; when we were going to sell it a year ago, we were going to get $25,000 for it and two weeks ago, a man whose house is going to be taken in the area and did not know that our house was no longer for sale offered us $28,000. So he feels that it is going to improve. But you can't get a house on this street under $18,000."

For the most part, they are identified with being Negro and, on their side, identify themselves as such and this militates against their leaving. For example, over sixty percent of the families believe that Negroes should give their business to other Negroes as much as possible, other things equal; less than 40 percent feel that skin color should not enter into one's choice in buying goods or services. Virtually all—96 percent —of the families believe that Negroes should continue to have special newspapers and magazines, such as *Ebony*. Their strong identification with Negroes permits and, indeed, stimulates them to fight and to engage in community activities to abolish discrimination and all the barriers of segregation: but they appear not to be the ones who are willing and desirous to commit themselves *personally* to integration. Thus a civil rights leader in Roxbury who has participated in protest meetings against *de facto* segregation in Boston public schools stated: "I feel that a strong Negro community located in Roxbury has more political and economic power."

We asked all the families where they would feel most comfortable: Living in a neighborhood where there were mostly whites? About half Negroes and half whites? Or mostly Negroes? Less than five percent of the 234 felt that they could be most comfortable living in a white community and our informal interview material pointed to a similar division of sentiment. A wife under 35, a university graduate, whose family did move during the ten months, put it this way:

> "Negroes do not move, because they feel more comfortable with other Negroes. This is to be expected: most people feel more comfortable with their own kind. For example, I am more guarded in a white group. Since I am living in a white community, I realize that I am representing Negroes."

However, a professional man who moved back into Roxbury from a white suburb thinks personal feeling is changing with the times:

> "Until two years ago I had a feeling of low status when I would be in a group of people who were playing one of the old middle-class games, you know, of 'where do you live?' And in this sort of competition, if you are living in Roxbury, you come in for comments: 'why don't you move?' and who wants to justify why they are living in a place or even be faced with the question when quite reasonably I could respond with the same sort of question, 'Well, why do *you* live where you live?' However, in the last couple of years I have not had this feeling; . . . In the last year when people talked about Negroes I listened with discomfort because it was not a question for open exchange; but this year it has become an open subject and I think that I no longer feel any discomfort on this score."

As though in corroboration of the sentiment of attachment to one's own kind the housewives, judged by their impressions of the racial organizations, support a relatively conservative view of personal commitment to integration: when asked to rank a number of organizations with respect to their programs to increase the supply of acceptable housing for Negroes in Boston, they mentioned first organizations which are committed to the improvement of Washington Park and chose them rather than those focused upon integration. CORE, for example, was chosen by only six of the families as the leader in improving the housing situation. In general, these families tend not to join and to rate most unfavorably CORE, which might be described as the most radical of the three major Negro organizations; the NAACP in their eyes comes before the Urban League, which, in turn, they put before CORE.

Thus, while Negroes who go outside of Washington Park to seek housing suffer discrimination, although certainly less than we anticipated, it is not a simple matter of being afraid of searching and of moving into white areas. Rather, they have many motives for remaining in Washington Park; for example, merely the fact of being comfortable with those of their own skin color or perhaps just sheer apathy in a plight in which in many ways they are quite secure. And, in addition to the economic advantages already discussed, continued residence in Roxbury is, as some families see their particular situation, an economic imperative:

"We have thought about moving to a white neighborhood. I think that if my husband were able to continue his professional relationship, if he could still be available, then there wouldn't be too much objection: But then there is always some, for one reason or another, and it would not be the real reason but they could latch on to this and say, "I'll drop you." I think that seeing my husband is a physician, he has a different type of relationship with his patients than what pertains to someone who is working in some other profession or field. Traditionally, the family doctor lives in the community. They want to know where the doctor lives. They may not come here to the house, but it's knowing where you live or that you're here. I imagine that someone else might come in here and take that role from him. On the other hand, one would suppose that if everything else was equal he could conceivably develop a practice wherever he is."

Thus one suspects that the fear of discrimination which is the ground given for the largely self-imposed limits upon their own mobility may in some part be a convenient and face-saving rationalization. If integration is to be promoted, then the tactics are not solely to provide signed statements from white families that they will sell or rent without discrimination; most of the families we studied are unlikely to move to white areas, given even five or ten or twenty times the number of available houses.

Which Families Move? The number of families that moved into white parts of the inner city or to white suburbs is too small to justify generalizations about differences between them and the families that have stayed or moved to other parts of Roxbury and Dorchester. Nevertheless, we did closely scrutinize the five families who moved into white areas in or around Boston between the two waves of interviewing and certain characteristics that they exhibited permit us to offer some very *tentative* observations:

Consistent with our data about mobility, the families that are likely to integrate tend to be younger: the wives in four out of the five who moved are under 35 years of age, in contrast to only one-third of the wives in the total study group.[1] Further, and again consistent with our attitudinal data, four out of the five wives had gone to college: two of

[1] It will be remembered that in these families, wives are close to husbands in age; hence we describe as young the family in which the wife is young.

them achieved the baccalaureate and one had undertaken post-graduate professional studies. Likewise, their families are smaller than the average in the 234 we studied; two that moved had no children and the others had one, two and three, respectively. Certainly, from among small and relatively well-educated families come the integrators, although again one must remember with caution that the numbers are very small. All five had previously reported to us that they intended to move or that there was a 50-50 chance of their doing so. Clearly, then, there is some link between the hope of moving into an integrated area and the realization of it, although only a minute fraction do execute their intentions. Likewise, four out of five families were renting their dwellings at the time they moved, a proportion of renters that was greater than the proportion renting among the families who stayed.

All of them reported at the time of the first interview that they were willing to pay more for their dwelling and four out of the five reported that they would probably buy their next residence—which indeed they did. Again, four out of five were among a group of 77 who reported that they had hunted outside Roxbury. Describing their Roxbury situation, four of the five complained of too little open space, two, of street noises and four, of the amount of room; three of the neighbors; and three of the schools.

Thus they appear to have been more dissatisfied than the rest of the families with general conditions in the community and somewhat less satisfied with their personal situations.

Another point, made by one of the wives whose family stayed:

"I think that it is unfortunate that you have to move out of Roxbury to get a certain type of housing. I don't think that race enters into this thing as we think it does. A lot of people for particular reasons tied in with their working patterns and what-not want to live in an area close to town. I would like a modern one-storey house—I have a two-storey house—with the amount of space I have here but all on one floor. I have to have one floor because of my son. I would like to feel that there would be a house like this available. My husband's practice is here and it makes sense to me that he is within a half-hour's drive of any patient; and when he comes in at night, if he *does* have to go out again he doesn't have to drive an hour each way to make a call. He is a general practitioner, so it makes sense to me to be here regardless of what kind of people are here. I think that I can get a certain type of house in this area. Moving out, people are thinking in terms of certain types of houses. That is one of the things that they are looking for. The fact that these are in areas that are predominantly white areas, you see, brings in the racial angle. I don't think that too many people start out by saying, 'I want to move into a white neighborhood.' They want to move to a neighborhood that has modern housing, good schools, that has close shopping centers, that has a plot of grass around it; where people don't go through the street and drop paper; they want something clean. The fact that it is not here means that they *have* to look elsewhere and then the racial angle comes in because that's where it is. Now this may be in support of this 'Golden Ghetto'; but it really isn't, because I think it should be a permissive thing. I think that you should live in a place that best fits the need of your particular family. If this happens to be in the suburbs, and it is convenient then I think that you should move there. But if you live in a certain area and you are Negro and this is where you *have* to live, then I think that this is wrong. And I think that people should know that it can be done—that you can move out of here without fear of reprisal because of your race."

The movers varied considerably as to income. Of the three families who moved to other parts of Boston, two were in the highest of our income categories with earnings over $10,000 a year; of the two that went to the suburbs, one, a family with an income of six thousand dollars a year, moved away to a very modest suburb. The other was quite well off. All had been attending integrated churches while living in Roxbury and there is some hint that they were more in contact with white persons than the rest of the sample, at least during their adult lives.

. . .

Chapter 8

THE STRUGGLE FOR POWER IN AMERICAN CITIES

A major weakness in many assessments of urban issues is the failure to link the phenomena being discussed to the political process. An understanding of the urban political process is critical to an adequate interpretation of such issues as diverse as poverty, the increase in prominence of teacher unions, and racial conflict. In order to better see the relationship between the political process and urban problems, in this chapter we will focus on the serious problem of urban racial conflict.

Charles Tilly is one of the new breed of social scientists who have accentuated the critical political circumstances surrounding the development of collective violence in Western countries. He comments:

> As comforting as it is for civilized people to think of barbarians as violent and of violence as barbarian, Western civilization and various forms of collective violence have always been close partners. We do not need a stifled universal instinct of aggression to account for outbreaks of violent conflicts in our past, or in our present. Nor need we go to the opposite extreme and search for pathological moments and sick men in order to explain collective acts of protest and destruction. Historically, collective violence has flowed regularly out of the central political processes of Western countries. Men seeking to seize, hold, or realign the levers of power have continually engaged in collective violence as part of their struggles.[1]

Operating in the same intellectual tradition as Charles Tilly, Richard E. Rubenstein directs his analysis toward American society in the first excerpt reprinted here. A central theme of *Rebels in Eden* is that the collective violence of many dissident groups can be directly linked to the character and operation of the American political process—to the inequality of wealth and power. While the focus in the selection reprinted here is primarily on recent collective actions by blacks in American cities, and on the political response to those actions, elsewhere in his book Rubenstein makes it clear that blacks are by no means the first group to use collective violence in trying to acquire increased power and wealth. Historically, American society has seen a procession of dissident groups utilizing violence for their own ends, including the attack by Appalachian debtor farmers on the agents of East Coast exploitation in the 1700s, the rebellion of white Southerners against Northerners in the 1860s, the riots of white Anglo-Saxon Protestant Americans against a variety of other white immigrant groups, and union-management warfare in the decades between the 1870s and the 1930s. Indeed, one can argue convincingly that the fundamental dilemma of urban politics in America has been—and continues to be—how to transfer power and wealth nonviolently from existing power-holding groups to challengers.

Assessing reactions to the urban violence engaged in by black Americans in the 1960s, Rubenstein suggests that Richard Nixon's victory in the 1968 presidential election signaled a shift from a conservative-liberal debate over urban issues to what he terms a liberal-radical debate. He describes a *conservative* perspective as one that typically views the causes of collective violence in terms of riffraff and agitators and the cure in terms of amplifying police-control measures and slowing the reform process. The *liberal* perspective, however, perceives the causes as discrimination and deprivation and the cure as more effective police-control measures coupled with at least a plea for large-scale reform. In contrast, the emerging *radical* perspective sees the causes of collective violence not primarily in lawlessness, deviance, or poverty but in the "system of interlocking elites operating at the local level through the machinery of urban government to keep blacks in a state of quasi-colonial subjection." Consequently, the radical solution places primary emphasis on community control and self-determination for dissenting groups. In proposing policy directed at a resolution of the urban racial crisis, Rubenstein seems inclined to this radical point of view and suggests that the future health of American cities hinges on a resolution of the debate in terms of political decentralization.

In the second selection, the concluding chapter to a book entitled *Community Control,* Alan Altshuler also examines the community-control approach to resolving urban racial problems, but he argues that this is a *practical* rather than a radical solution. Unlike alternative solutions, granting a substantial measure of community control to ghetto residents might well be the least serious threat for the majority of white urbanites, who in fact have no direct stake in who rules the ghettos. More and more white Americans are coming to recognize that minorities can severely disrupt a complex technological society; and most whites now seem to prefer peace based on reconciliation to a "peace" based on conquest. Thus, Altshuler presents the reader with a policy-oriented set of arguments; by responding seriously to black demands for community control, whites can persuade blacks that they will make reasonable progress within the existing framework, thus averting continuing warfare in American cities. In this sense, then, racial inequality is *every* urbanite's problem.

In pursuit of his argument for black self-determination Altshuler explores additional questions of some importance: (1) "Would community control be conducive to racial peace?" and (2) "Would community control be conducive to the development of black skills and incomes, and to the improvement of other conditions in the ghettos?" In the process of answering both in the affirmative, he develops intriguing ideas relating equality and self-determination to the legitimacy of political institutions. From serious concessions to community control might come not only a general shift in black confidence in American institutions and an increase in overall black political experience but also concrete improvements in such specific areas as ghetto housing, the ghetto economy, and ghetto policing. Thus this proposal for community control is in effect a call for a pragmatic compromise on the part of white Americans.

Moreover, the policy-oriented arguments made by Rubenstein and Altshuler have important implications in regard to the situations of minorities other than black Americans. Some of their basic arguments, with modest alterations, might be applied to the subordinate situations of other relatively powerless groups in urban areas, such as Mexican Americans, Puerto Ricans, and Native Americans. Readers who find these analyses suggestive should consider the relevance of the arguments to the broader issue of transferring power from white groups to a *variety* of nonwhite groups in American cities.

NOTES

1. Charles Tilly, "Collective Violence in European Perspective," in *Violence in America: Historical and Comparative Perspectives*, Hugh D. Graham and Ted R. Gurr, eds. (New York: Bantam, 1969), p. 4.

FROM REBELS IN EDEN:
CENTRALISM VS. DECENTRALISM:
THE DEEPENING DEBATE

RICHARD E. RUBENSTEIN

The real significance of the election in 1968, as several commentators
have noted, lay less in Richard Nixon's narrow victory over Hubert
Humphrey than in their joint victory—a triumph of what Louis Hartz
called "the liberal tradition in America"—over George Wallace. In an
election year plagued by civil disorder and assassination the two parties
of the Center performed the extraordinary feat of holding the challenges
from both Right and Left to less than fifteen percent of the total vote
cast. Paradoxically, despite the political divisions created by accelerating social change, Mr. Nixon's victory represented a mandate for
continuity rather than for change.

Nixon the campaigner had moved to silence protest from the Right
by paying rhetorical obeisance to the theme of "law and order." But with
extreme conservatives eliminated (however temporarily) as a politically
potent national political force, Nixon the President acted to consolidate
the liberal Center, pledging to continue federal efforts aimed at the "big
three" urban problem areas—jobs, housing and education. His appointment of Daniel P. Moynihan as chief White House Adviser on Urban
Affairs was the clearest indication that what might be called "establishment liberalism" was to become the policy of the new administration, at
least in the field of domestic policy. A certain subtle shift of emphasis
away from the blatant centralism of New Deal Democracy was also
apparent in Nixon's announcement of his intention to rely more on
private enterprise, in his appointment of Robert Finch to reorganize the
Department of Health, Education and Welfare, and in his private ne-
gotiations with certain black militants. In fact, the keynote of the new
administration might well have been sounded by Moynihan's former
colleague at the Harvard-M.I.T. Joint Center of Urban Studies, James
Q. Wilson, who suggested that urban police departments should be
functionally rather than politically decentralized.[1] Functional decentralization—the devolution of discretionary power downward within an
otherwise unchanged central power structure—seemed a likely tack for
the new administration to take.

Richard Nixon's victory marked the ending of the first phase in the
great debate over urban violence and the beginning of a second. To sum
it up rather crudely, the liberal-conservative debate, having been won by

the liberals, was now to be succeeded by a liberal-radical struggle whose outcome, as this chapter was written, was very much in doubt. It is important to trace the development of this controversy, for upon its result may hinge the future of America's cities.

The *conservative* position, summarily stated, held that ghetto riots were produced by a combination of explosive material—the black mob or "underclass" consisting of the unemployed, those with criminal records or tendencies and lawless youth—and a spark, the rhetoric of local gang leaders or outside agitators. Reactionaries like George Wallace of Alabama stressed the role of the agitators, seeking to explain their activities as part of a sinister, conspiratorial design to disrupt American society. More sophisticated conservatives emphasized those characteristics of the mob which made them vulnerable to demagoguery and "acting .out." For example, the McCone Commission report on the Watts uprising underlined the impatience and "nothing to lose" recklessness of those without a stake in society;[2] other commentators blamed the mass frustration engendered by failure to deliver on liberal promises, or the absence of social controls within the black community produced by centuries of slavery and social disorganization. The common element which justifies labeling these diverse views "conservative" was the assumption that the causes of the violence lay ultimately in the group itself—that ghetto rioting could be attributed to characteristics indigenous and peculiar to certain segments of the urban black community.

The short-term strategies dictated by conservative views were the immediate suppression of actual riots or revolts by the use of *force majeure,* and the avoidance or limitation of potential uprisings by means of police counterinsurgency techniques: surveillance or jailing of agitators, infiltration of gangs and community organizations, the training of specialized riot squads and equipping them with sophisticated antiriot weapons, adoption of preventive detention and high-bail policies intended to keep certain persons off the streets during periods of tension, and so forth. The assumption underlying the strategy of *force majeure* was that black violence, however started, was at bottom expressive rather than instrumental, and that rioters or potential rioters would respond to superior force on the basis of a fairly simple pleasure-pain calculus.

Long-term conservative strategy, however, was more complex. Whether the lumpenproletariat constituted a small minority of the urban black community (as many conservatives believed) or not, its existence as a cause of civil disorder dictated the adoption of economic and political measures designed to eliminate it. One way in which this could be done was to give the rascals a stake in society by providing them with jobs, housing and education. On the other hand, since unfulfilled promises tended to inflame the mob, and since many of the lumpenproles were probably beyond salvation (confirmed criminals, inveterate shirkers, etc.) it was necessary to slow down rather than to accelerate the pace of reform. The dilemma was very much like that faced by counterinsurgency practitioners in Vietnam in their attempt to change South Vietnamese society rapidly enough to provide an alternative to communism while keeping popular expectations "realistically" low. Precisely as in Vietnam, a clear short-term military strategy tended to dominate a vague long-term political strategy. In Chicago as in Saigon, counterinsurgency outweighed reform in the municipal budget for the "hot" season.

Immediately after the Watts uprising, the *liberal* view of urban violence, soon to become the quasi-official governmental interpretation, was also given voice. Critiques of the McCone Commission Report by respected scholars, as well as fresh analysis of later uprisings in other cities, undermined the view that the rioter was a lumpenprole stirred up by lawless despair or outside agitation, emphasizing instead the instrumental nature of civil disorder.[3] The liberal masterwork, the report of the National Advisory Commission on Civil Disorders, found that the rioters were not "criminal types, overactive social deviants, or riffraff" but ordinary blacks born in the city in which the riot took place, economically on a par with their nonrioting neighbors and generally better educated and more politically aware than nonrioters.[4] (Subsequent studies found not only that rioters were "representative" of ghetto communities but that nonrioting members of the community often responded positively to outbreaks of violence in which they did not participate.[5])

The Kerner Report viewed the 1967 outbreaks primarily as a form of protest against the rejection of blacks by American society. It laid very heavy emphasis on patterns of discrimination which kept blacks out of better paying jobs, higher quality housing and competent educational institutions. Noting that, relative to whites, the position of blacks in terms of income, health, education and job employment was worsening rather than improving, it explicitly linked the termination of urban violence to the integration of blacks into the white working and middle classes and elimination of the barriers separating the "two societies." Finally, the report recognized that violence was engendered, in part, by the unresponsiveness of local, white-dominated institutions to black demands for redress of grievances, and offered several suggestions aimed at improving communications between blacks and local governmental agencies.

With respect to short-term solutions to the problem of racial violence, the report's recommendations, like the liberal position in general, varied only slightly from that of the conservatives. It emphasized more effective riot-control training, stricter discipline and command of police and troops in the field, and better planning to avoid disorders or to cut them short after an initial outbreak. The principal departures from the conservative view involved recommending alternatives to deadly force, and the use of community assistance in crisis situations as a way of avoiding escalation of riots. In addition, the report recommended the establishment of intermediary institutions which would open channels of communication between city governments and ghetto residents, for example, neighborhood action task forces, better grievance-response mechanisms, expanded legal services to the poor, and so forth. The combination of short-term recommendations has been described, not inaptly, as a restatement of the philosophy of Theodore Roosevelt: open channels of communication, but carry a big stick.

On a longer-term basis, the liberal strategy for the city, aimed as it was at terminating the "two societies" postulated by the Kerner Report, dictated massive federal efforts to improve the status of blacks relative to whites in the field of jobs, housing and education. This represented a rededication to—rather than an alteration of—political principles espoused by every United States President since Franklin Roosevelt: to wit, that the federal government should take primary responsibility for improving the standard of living of the poor, and ending racial discrimination. The twin principles of governmental centralism and racial integration, which dominated subsequent liberal proposals for reconstruction of the ghetto, shaped the commission's recommendations as well. While advocating large-scale federal programs to solve the unemployment, housing and education problems, the report was vague in recommending measures to increase the collective power of urban blacks at the expense of existing white economic and political interest groups. It therefore contained within itself the seeds of an explosive controversy between centralists and decentralists, integrationists and advocates of black power.

As the first phase in the debate over urban violence and urban strategies was ending in the humiliation of George Wallace, a second phase began. Plans to decentralize the New York school system ended in near bloodshed, a crippling Teachers' Union strike, and the estrangement of New York's Negro and Jewish communities. Indeed, it seemed to some that the consequences of attempted school decentralization verified entirely the principles of strategy defended in Daniel P. Moynihan's *Maximum Feasible Misunderstanding*.[6] There Moynihan had excoriated intellectuals and radicals whose concern for the exercise of political power by the poor—"maximum feasible participation"—had provoked political reprisals causing serious cutbacks in the Democrats' poverty program. Nevertheless, a new and growing school of thought insisted upon the proposition that urban peace could only be achieved, in the long run, by maximizing the power of ghetto dwellers to govern themselves—to control their own schools, police forces, businesses, unions and their own institutions of local government. Like the conservative and liberal strategies, the radical approach reflected a particular view of urban violence—one which emphasized the powerlessness rather than poverty of rioters, and analogized the ghetto uprisings to struggles for national liberation being waged in the Third World. In this view, the chief villain of the piece was not lawlessness, poverty, ignorance or poor housing but a system of interlocking elites operating at the local level through the machinery of urban government to keep blacks in a state of quasi-colonial subjection. The reader is by now familiar with this view. It is time to consider the practical and theoretical objections which have been expressed by liberals in this second phase of debate, and to return again to the question raised in Chapter 4 [not reprinted here]: how, other than by revolution, can an oppressed group accumulate power in a centralized state?

Long-term radical strategy for the city proposes that the ghettos be treated, in certain respects, as cities in themselves: that business enterprises and real property within be turned over to black ownership (preferably by community organizations), that control over ghetto schools be vested in school boards representing ghetto parents, that police forces operating in black territory be made directly responsible to those inhabiting that territory, that the stranglehold of white-dominated political machines over ghetto political life be broken, and that local housing, health, education and welfare programs be administered, whenever possible, by blacks. Each of these proposals, it is recognized, will require serious shifts in the distribution of power in urban areas. Slumlords will be compelled to give up valuable property and businessmen profitable businesses. Urban political machines allied with racketeers will have to abandon a rich vein of political power and graft. An army of welfare workers will be forced to seek other employment and unionized schoolteachers will become responsible to local boards rather than to more acquiescent central authorities. (Little wonder that the Kerner Commission, with its panel of seven politicians, the presidents of a union and a business, a chief of police and a civil rights lawyer, avoided these issues!)

At the same time, radicals believe, federal and state governments must increase their efforts to end poverty, to upgrade schools and housing, to improve urban social services and to end racial discrimination. The apparent inconsistency between this position and the advocacy of black power strategies (which roused the criticism of Mr. Moynihan in *Maximum Feasible Misunderstanding*) deserves comment. Theoretically, the inconsistencies vanish when one recognizes that communities, like nations, may retain their independence while receiving "foreign aid," provided that the aid is consistent with their own development plans. There is no reason why federal aid cannot be given to a community-controlled school or to a community-controlled police force. Similarly, there is no reason—in theory—why the central government should not attempt to create jobs in the ghetto by luring in industry, provided that the relevant unions are entirely open to blacks, and that the industrial development plan has community support. (To increase white power in the ghetto under the guise of reform without simultaneously increasing black power is, as we have seen, an invitation to disaster.) On the other hand, the *political* inconsistency between demands for local autonomy and governmental aid remains. How can one drive white landlords out of black communities and then ask the landlords to pay increased taxes to improve ghetto housing? How can one expect white industrialists to locate in areas possessing powerful, black-dominated labor unions, when the same industrialists are moving south in droves to escape strong *white*-dominated unions?

These difficulties cannot be wished away. Urban renewal, which has been a bonanza for white construction industries and unions, may lose their powerful support if black demands for control over urban renewal planning and for a "piece of the action" (through black construction companies and building trades unions) are met. Federal aid to education has had the strong backing of local, state and national teachers' organizations, few of which would be inclined, say, to fight for Rhody McCoy in the Ocean Hill–Brownsville school district of New York. Despite their reported demise, urban political machines proved healthy enough to block the implementation of "maximum feasible participation" by local communities in poverty programs; presumably they are healthy enough to control the local administration of federal aid to the ghettos in 1969–1970. And what of the Average White American? Will he be inclined to foot the tax bill to support black independence in a newly divided city?

No—political reality cannot be wished away. Unfortunately for liberal optimists, however, neither can the desire of the powerless for power and of the dependent for self-rule, which is also a political reality. One is thus confronted with an inescapable strategic choice: to fight for black liberation at the risk of alienating white support for social welfare programs, or to fight for welfare programs at the risk of increasing relative deprivation and further alienating blacks. The radical position is to place primary emphasis on increasing black power at the local level while attempting simultaneously to educate the white public to the need for "foreign aid" to the ghetto. More important, radicals are working to create new political linkways between blacks and other oppressed groups (workers, women, students, and so on) in the hope of creating a coalition which will replace the crumbling liberal alliance in the cities. We explore this in greater detail in the following chapters.

Perhaps the best example of the liberal attack against radical decentralization is a book about the police, *Varieties of Police Behavior*, by Professor James Q. Wilson of Harvard.[7] The following quotations reveal the core of the argument:

> For one thing, a central city cannot be fully suburbanized however much we may want to—it is, by definition, *central*, which means that many people from all over the metropolitan area use it for work, governing and recreation and that, as a result, competing life styles and competing sets of community norms come into frequent and important contact. Necessarily, this generates political pressures to maintain order at the highest level expected by groups who use the city. . . . (p. 288)
>
> Giving central city neighborhoods, many bitterly apprehensive of and hostile toward adjoining neighborhoods, control over their own neighborhood police would be to risk making the police power an instrument for interneighborhood conflict. Proposals for communal police often are based on the tacit assumption that, somehow, only Negroes, and poor Negroes at that, would get control of the police. In fact, legislation that would give the police to Negroes would, out of political necessity, give it to others as well. . . . (pp. 288–89)

. . . if the unit of government becomes the neighborhood . . . the opportunities for a small, self-serving minority to seize control of the police or the schools will become very great indeed. (p. 290)

When the community is deeply divided and emotionally aroused, the proper governmental policy is not to arm the disputants and let them settle matters among themselves; it is, rather, to raise the level at which decisions will be made to a point sufficiently high so that neither side can prevail by *force majeure* but low enough so that responsible authorities must still listen to both sides. (p. 290)

Some advocates of communal law enforcement seem inclined to defend the model precisely on the grounds that it avoids the "middle class bias" of the legal code and the moral order. If by "middle class bias" is meant a concern for the security of person and property and a desire to avoid intrusions into one's privacy and disturbances of one's peace, it is not clear why such concern is a "bias" at all. . . . (p. 295)

Wilson himself recognizes, by mentioning in the same phrase "control of the police or the schools," that the same arguments might be directed against any proposal to treat the ghetto as a political unit, whether for electoral, law-enforcement, educational or other purposes. It is important to understand, therefore, that they are based on a series of fallacies which inevitably arise when one attempts to apply the political philosophy of the New Deal to the facts of urban life in the 1960's.

The first among these I would call the *fallacy of objective order:* the doctrine which assumes that since all major economic classes and ethnic groups in America share certain values—such as "a concern for the security of person and property and a desire to avoid intrusions into one's privacy and disturbances of one's peace"—there is a "highest level" of order which may be enforced by a neutral central government. However accurately this consensus theory may describe the various groups which the New Deal attempted to conciliate and order in the 1930's, as applied to the divisions between ghetto dwellers and middle-class whites in present-day cities it is simply untenable. Of course the poor and the rich share certain values, like the desire not to be robbed and murdered. But the existence of such a commonality, in which Fiji Islanders and Albanians also participate, hardly proves the existence of an objective order enforceable in all these communities. Given the necessity of establishing priorities in order to make use of scarce order-maintenance resources, the fact is that black communities and white have different priorities, and therefore different concepts of order.

Like many liberals, Wilson refuses to recognize value differences between domestic groups serious enough to warrant political expression. Those intergroup differences which are acknowledged are treated as evanescent in light of the inevitability of lower-class groups becoming middle class: "Throughout history the urban poor have disliked and distrusted the police, and the feeling has been reciprocated; the situation will not change until the poor become middle class, or at least working class. . . ."[8] This sounds plausible, but it is not. The Irish poor, for instance, rioted in New York in the 1860's when they had not achieved control over the police or the machinery of city government; a few years later, not much richer, they began to take over both the police department and Tammany Hall, and the "wild Irishman" was no more. Cincinnati's Germans followed the same pattern between 1884 and 1900. Many other domestic groups, as previously noted, resorted to violence in order to gain or protect their control over local government, and to build their particular notions of "law and order" into the legal system, after which violence declined or ceased. Throughout our history, groups seeking embodiment of their group values in governmental form have been compelled to improvise new institutions to do so—the political party, the political machine, the farmers' cooperative, the labor union, the suburb. There is no reason to believe that blacks labor under a necessity any less pressing, or that the existing political system is any more capable of accommodating their demands now than in the past.

Wilson's warning against "making the police power an instrument for interneighborhood conflict" suggests a second fallacy, which I would call *the consensus model of the city.* The warning assumes that the urban police are not now such an instrument, and that through central city government, decisions may be made at "a point sufficiently high so that neither side can prevail by *force majeure* but low enough so that responsible authorities must still listen to both sides." This model describes the operation of no major American city past or present; in fact, it is not even a sensible utopia.

When a city contains within its jurisdiction, as ours have always done, groups differing radically in wealth, power, and degree of political development, the chief purpose served by "raising" the level of decision making is to permit ruling groups to govern through the impersonal machinery of legal bureaucracy—to disguise the exercise of power. As practiced under such circumstances, "coalition government" (including balanced tickets, patronage sharing among groups, etc.) is part of the masquerade, since the representatives appointed for or elected by weak, poverty-stricken, politically unawakened groups are almost inevitably led to serve the interests of the more powerful (or where they do not, they meet the fate of Vito Marcantonio). In short, the interneighborhood conflict which moderates so fear is part and parcel of American urban life. By "raising" the level of decision making to the level, say, of Mayor Yorty's office, or Mayor Daley's, one neighborhood, or set of neighborhoods, is permitted to dominate another so completely that conflict does not seem to exist at all.

As a matter of fact, the fear of conflict runs like a somber thread throughout the work of many urban affairs experts and city planners. Strangely, they seem to prefer the present type of urban government, in which conflict is ignored or "managed" in totalitarian fashion, to one in which very real differences between large racial and economic groups would be embodied in systematic form. I say "strangely" because institutionalization of political differences seems a likely way to lessen rather than to increase violent conflict. For example, if governmental power were to devolve downward to the black, Spanish-American or

Appalachian ghettos, meaningful bargaining and coalition government would then become a possibility, since only then would the poor have something to bargain with. Similarly, although "making the police power an instrument for interneighborhood conflict" may seem a frightening prospect to some, to the residents of various ghettos the police are already the principal instrument of interneighborhood conflict (disguised as a conflict between law enforcers and lawbreakers). It is for this reason that they feel constrained to support the activities of antipolice neighborhood organizations, citizens patrols and political organizations like the Black Panther party.

In this respect, it is particularly important to emphasize that blacks seeking local power want what whites, whether in urban or suburban areas, already possess. Wilson's third fallacy is *the false black-white analogy*—the notion that the present structure of urban government seriously limits white power, and that the extension of community control principles to the white community will therefore lead to weakening the position of minorities. ("In fact, legislation that would give the police to Negroes would, out of political necessity, give it to others as well. . . .") In the first place, a downward devolution of power *within* the majority community need not occur if whites are satisfied with the extent to which the institutions of local government now respond to their demands and desires. For example, it is perfectly possible to imagine Harlem or Bedford-Stuyvesant with its own police force (or, for that matter, with its own mayor) without the Bronx feeling it necessary to secede from Queens or Staten Island. This is because those middle-class groups which have sought community control of local institutions have obtained it, or can obtain it on demand.

When white parents remove their children from urban public schools and send them to private and parochial schools, this is not called "community control" and produces little conflict. When whites move to the suburbs, whose governmental institutions are responsive not only to demands but to whims, this does not create great political issues or generate strikes. And although urban groups like the Jews of New York, the Poles of Chicago, the Irish of Boston, and the WASPs of Dallas clearly control not just their own schools or police forces but segments of industry and the professions, labor unions, churches, networks of fraternal and voluntary organizations, rackets and political organizations, these groups have all successfully opposed community power for others. It would be difficult to show how the present structure of urban government constrains such groups or limits their power locally. Nevertheless, in those cases in which whites do not enjoy self-government it is hardly proper to subject them to oppression on the grounds that they might misuse their power, or that they are "racist." Community control is not intended to repeal the United States Constitution.

The final fallacy which deserves comment is contained in the statement that, with community control a reality, "the opportunities for a small, self-serving minority to seize control of the police or the schools will become very great indeed. . . ." This is a familiar colonialist argument—the same, in fact, which was directed by Great Britain against the independence of the American colonies and India, by France against the independence of Algeria and her other colonies, and by the American South against the independence of the slaves. As applied to local government in the United States, it is based on an outmoded reading of history which assumes that "that government is best which governs most," and that the worst thing one can do is to permit the government to get too close to the people. For example, Wilson states: "If the study of urban politics has taught us anything, it is that, except on referenda, and perhaps not even then, 'the people' do not govern—organizations, parties, factions, politicians, and groups govern. . . ." [9]

Is it so easy to destroy all distinction between elitism and democracy? In the real world, I would have thought, one could attempt in a rough way to rank various governmental types and arrangements along a continuum leading, let us say, from the relative elitism of Saudi Arabia to the relative democracy of Sweden. However, the quoted statement simply begs the question. If indeed "groups govern," the question remains whether it is possible and advisable for specific groups to govern themselves, or to be governed by indigenous rather than exogenous subgroups. And the question suggests an answer: it is the state of political development of the group governed as much as the form of government which decides the extent to which "the people" govern, either directly or indirectly. In practice this means that one simply cannot "prefer" central governmental power to local power, or vice versa, as a matter of principle for all time. Under some circumstances, maximizing human freedom may require that the central government assume vast new powers in order to counterbalance increased private power; in others it will require that oppressed and alienated communities become self-determining. The argument between Hamilton and Jefferson is unending precisely because the source of unfreedom shifts over time. At the moment its focus lies in the coalition of white interests dominating urban governments.

The fear of the small, pernicious minority which will take power in a communal government in order to oppress the community is a phobia generated by certain specific traumas. In the last century the chief advocates of strong local government were either southerners, to whom "states' rights" meant white rights, or industrialists, to whom "freedom of persons" meant freedom of corporations to ride roughshod over workers and consumers. From 1880 to 1930 "strong city government" meant rule by machine bosses and their myrmidons over the hapless, malleable immigrant masses. Strong local government under conditions of political somnolence means that power will be grabbed by those piratical enough to grab it and utilized by those ruthless enough to utilize it. However, under conditions in which the governed are awakening to their collective identity, history, suffering and rights, the situation is reversed, and the traumatic precedents mentioned above do not bind. Others, more relevant to the case at hand, come to mind: local government after the Jeffersonian revolution, when state legislatures and

town meetings struck down property qualifications for voting and religious tests, established state universities and began, for the first time, to
reflect the demands of the "little man"; state legislatures in the South
under Reconstruction, which pioneered in social legislation and racial
reform; state and local legislatures under Populist rule, which sixty
years before the New Deal attempted to regulate industry and to control
the quality of food sold to the public; cities under Socialist or Progressive mayors early in the present century, which initiated modern city
planning and "good government," and certain state legislatures in the
1920's and 1930's which attempted to secure the rights of labor and to
legislate for the poor.

The argument against political decentralization and community control, therefore, seems to me to rest on a series of fallacies—elaborate
rationalizations, really, for preserving the status quo and the hegemony
of the Center. This leaves us, however, with the dilemma described earlier and restated by Moynihan's argument from political infeasibility:
with power both at local and federal levels in the hands of the same
interlocking elites, how can an outgroup gain sufficient collective power
to enter into the bargaining process? . . .

NOTES

1. James Q. Wilson, *Varieties of Police Behavior* [Harvard University Press],
   1968.
2. California Governor's Commission on the Los Angeles Riots, *Violence in the
   City—An End or a Beginning?* (McCone Report), 1965.
3. See Robert M. Fogelson, "White on Black: A Critique of the McCone Com-
   mission Report on the Los Angeles Riots," *Political Science Quarterly,*
   September 1967; Bayard Rustin, "The Watts Manifesto and the McCone
   Report," *Commentary,* March 1966; Robert Blauner, "Whitewash Over
   Watts," *Transaction,* March–April 1966; Stanley Lieberson and Arnold
   Silverman, "The Precipitants and Underlying Conditions of Race Riots,"
   American Sociological Review, December 1965.
4. *Report of the National Advisory Commission on Civil Disorders* (Kerner
   Report), pp. 128–135.
5. See works cited in ch. 1, note 4.
6. Daniel P. Moynihan, *Maximum Feasible Misunderstanding: Community
   Action in the War on Poverty,* 1969.
7. Wilson, *op. cit.* (see note 1).
8. *Ibid.,* p. 297.
9. *Ibid.,* p. 290.

FROM **COMMUNITY CONTROL:**
A PERSONAL STATEMENT

ALAN A. ALTSHULER

Social science tends toward the static view. It is helpful in explaining how things got the way they are, but its understanding is too crude to support forecasts of where they will go from here. This is least so where trends are measurable and steady, but these qualifiers have little bearing on the present subject.

American social science, reflecting the stability of this country's social and political patterns, has tended to make of its limits an ideology. Its primary concern has been how to explain "fundamental" (i.e., stable) rather than transient phenomena or the process of change itself. Thus, it has been preoccupied (a) with the obstacles to change, (b) with the basic satisfaction of the American people, on which these obstacles have rested, (c) with the benefits of social peace and gradualism. It has tended till recently both to ignore the study of revolution and to deprecate the possibility of bringing about rapid change by illegal means.

I have been unable to surmount the basic limits of my calling, but, along with many of my colleagues, I have been alerted by recent events to the possibilities of rapid change and disorder, and to the acute dissatisfaction of at least some Americans. My concern has been with the options before us rather than with the obstacles to any change at all. I need hardly add, however, that the force of white resistance has been ever in my mind, shaping my view of which options were even worth discussing.

I have eschewed precise blueprints, judging that the needs at this point (and in a general volume of this nature) were rather for broad indications of direction, flexible approaches, and a great deal of experimentation. I would add the caveat, however, that designers of particular experiments will do well to specify rights and procedures with the most painstaking care. As S. M. Miller and Martin Rein have noted, ambiguity can be invaluable in getting a plan accepted initially. This benefit will normally be more than offset, however, by the battles born of misunderstanding which subsequently occur.[1] The tension between clarity and flexibility can hardly be exaggerated, but it is far from unique. It is rather similar, in fact, to that between liberty and law.

In the remainder of this chapter, I propose to set out the main judgments to which I have been led in preparing this volume. I trust that they do not strain the evidence presented in Chapters One through Four [not reprinted here]. Quite clearly, however, they draw upon it in highly selective fashion. The purpose of those chapters was to review a wide variety of relevant propositions with supporting evidence for each, not to build a case. So I make no pretense that the judgments which follow are the only ones to which a careful reading might lead. They are simply my own, at the moment of completing this interim report.

The central issues, I would argue, are social peace and political legitimacy, not abstract justice or efficiency. No society adopts fundamental change because its dominant groups have suddenly acquired virtue or become horrified by waste. This is not to deny that some individuals act from idealistic motives, or that some societies are less rigid and brutal in their defense of established privilege than others. But it is to state predominant truths first.

White America has tolerated racial injustice on a grand scale for three centuries, and it has quite regularly placed other values before efficiency in its politics. Its resistance to housing and school integration, and to large-scale redistributive programs, remains overwhelming. The efficiency experts who call for metropolitan government continue to be ignored. For most Americans, ours is a society of abundance, not scarcity. We purchase things (such as small-scale suburban government) because they please us and their cost seems tolerable. We recognize that "efficiency" is a word with little meaning where values are problematic.*

Here is the crux of the problem. Whites (especially those who live in homogeneous jurisdictions) take the basic values of local government for granted. Blacks do not. Whites disagree on precise spending priorities, and they grouse about tax increases; but they do not question the system itself. Blacks do. Whites chuckle over bureaucratic inefficiency, but they assume that the objectives being sought are proper. Blacks do not. Whites are fundamentally satisfied because they sense that the institutions of American government have been shaped by men like them, for men like them. Blacks are not, because they do not. As Stokely Carmichael has observed, no one talks about white power because it goes without saying that power in America is white.

For Negroes, the issue is indeed justice—not abstract justice, justice for others, but justice for themselves. They are a small and isolated minority, however. Most whites are little moved by their moral claims. If they played entirely by the rules of the democratic game, they would get little attention, let alone satisfaction. But ours is a highly interdependent society. Small, even tiny, minorities can disrupt a great deal.

---

* I confess that I do not believe any important political group cares much about efficiency. Many care about it a little, but almost no one cares about it a great deal. It has ever been so. The Progressive reform movement of the early twentieth century may seem an exception, but its primary value was democracy, and its appeal rested largely on its hostility to malefactors of great wealth and power. On the local scene, its main vote-getting theme was to "throw the rascals out."

The riots have brought this lesson home, and raised black demands to the top of the national political agenda. At the same time, the riots have stirred white anger; they could lead the majority to seek peace by brutal repression.

Most whites, I believe, would prefer a peace of reconciliation to one of conquest. They—or rather, we—are a decent people; there are certain kinds of horrors we do not want in our midst; we have guilty consciences about the nation's racial record; we imagine that a peace based on compromise will be cheaper than one which permanently alienates one-ninth of the nation; and we fear that a sufficiently ruthless policy to bring peace would stamp out liberty for us all.

It makes quite good sense, of course, for a society to allocate its resources in accord with the "squeaky wheel" principle. Most people are instinctively opposed to social change; they dislike paying taxes; what privileges they have, they are loath to give up; they are full of self-serving rationales about the justice of their own claims and interests. In other words, resources are scarce, claims abundant; people are selfish, the consensus on priorities weak. This is not to say that the public lacks any sense of what is right and proper, or that this sense can be ignored. It is merely to say that this sense is extremely general, and is itself largely an indirect and lagged product of power relationships. It does not dictate an across-the-board attack on injustice. Its role is rather to help determine which of the passionate claimants deserve serious hearings, and to help define the range of plausible solutions. At every point, it interacts with power. The mix between morality and pragmatism in specific political settlements can never be fully sorted out.

The "squeaky wheel" principle works best when few people know about it, when general satisfaction is high, and when power relationships are stable. It is by no means costless to exploit. A group must expend enormous energy to attract notice, and its activity is likely to spur opposing groups to do likewise. The more extreme the means employed, the greater the risk of boomerang.

In urban America, however, the word seems now to have reached nearly everyone—a development for which the civil rights movement can probably take substantial credit. A great many people are angry. And power relationships (primarily because of the rapidity of techno-economic change) are anything but stable. At times in the largest American cities it seems that we are on the verge of universal war: the war, that is, of all against all.

For this whites are inclined to blame blacks, calling on them to abide by the traditional rules of American political conflict. The trouble is that many young blacks are so angry that they are prepared to take enormous risks, and that they view the white demand for "law and order" as sheerest hypocrisy. The law itself, they argue, is an expression of power—the power of wealth and whiteness. The majority is content to see military force applied in support of American interests around the world, and it is indifferent to police brutality at home. Public employee strikes are increasingly common, despite laws forbidding them, and punishment is rare. Those who most loudly cry "law and order" are typically the most vociferous critics of the Supreme Court's efforts to protect the rights of accused criminals. Some of them have called for outright defiance of the Court's decisions on integration, reapportionment, and school prayers. But usually they are spared the embarrassment of having to challenge the law, because it is on their side.

It seems to most rebellious blacks that the majority demand is for black acquiescence in the status quo rather than rapid, orderly change. Looking around the world, they conclude that fundamental change rarely occurs except as the product of revolutionary pressure. Many cannot express this entire rationale, but they have absorbed key slogans which express its essence: that "power speaks through the mouth of a gun" and that "violence is as American as cherry pie." They are aware, of course, of how little capacity to match white violence they have. This intensifies their frustration, but also keeps most of them searching for ways to make small gains. Just as the black mass desire for integration persists, so does the black activist recognition of the necessity for compromise. The public record often suggests otherwise, but it should not be overemphasized—any more than the rhetoric of white politicians. All over the country black activists are struggling patiently, against enormous odds, to develop ghetto wealth and political power by legal means.

I address myself to fellow whites who believe that this nation's highest priority must be to achieve a peace of reconciliation. The question for us is more than one of peace; it is one of legitimacy. It is first: how can we sustain the interest of blacks in peaceful compromise—in sharing laws, institutions, even a common nationality with the white majority? And it is second: how can we pursue this aim effectively within the American political system?

Blacks have a great many grievances, and they are making a great many demands. The need, I suggest, is for substantial positive responses to at least some of these. Permit me to draw an analogy. In a fascinating paper, based on a survey conducted in Watts following the 1965 riot, H. Edward Ransford has maintained that the willingness to use violence to correct racial injustice is a function of cumulative other factors. Highly educated* Negroes in his sample, whatever their other characteristics, were indisposed to use violence (though other studies have found them much *more* disposed toward participation in the organized civil rights movement). Among those with low degrees of education, however, three subjective conditions appeared to have a great impact: high dissatisfaction with their treatment as Negroes, a high sense of powerlessness, and a low degree of status-equal contact with whites. *The effect of combining these factors was much more than simply additive.* Isolation from status-equal contact with whites, for example, did

* The cutoff point was some college education. Respondents with a high school education or less were lumped together in the low education category.

not increase the propensity to use violence among those who were satisfied and had a high sense of efficacy. But it had a very substantial impact when combined with high dissatisfaction and powerlessness. More generally, among respondents with one or two of the subjective characteristics deemed conducive to violence, the actual willingness to use violence was only 24 per cent (vs. 12 per cent for those who had none of these characteristics). Among respondents with all three, however, 65 per cent expressed a willingness to use violence.*[2]

It is certainly true that concessions today will be followed by new demands tomorrow. But that is not the point. The aim must be to persuade Negroes that playing by the rules can produce some meaningful gains. If this involves revising the rules, so be it. The hope must be that we can domesticate American racial conflict as we have done with labor-management conflict. Labor makes new demands at every opportunity, but it is far from a revolutionary force.

How important is the participation issue in this context? How necessary is it to revise the political rules? I would judge that the answers depend more on white preferences than black. Blacks, to repeat, want many things. They want more and better jobs. They want massive redistributive public programs. They want integration. They want to own property. They want to be treated with respect by civil servants, employers, and merchants. They want to see their own kind in positions of power, prestige, and wealth. They want credit, insurance, and decent merchandise at prices comparable to those paid by whites. And, of course, many of them want community control.

There is almost surely a good deal of substitutability among these wants. The tradeoffs cannot be specified with quantitative precision; but at some level, higher relative incomes would probably alleviate the intensity of black anger as effectively as integration. More responsive substantive policies could do as well as participatory reform. And even within the participatory realm, jobs, contracts, and elaborate consultation could doubtless reduce (even if not eliminate) the pressure for transfers of authority to the neighborhood level.

Why, then, give serious consideration to community control, in view of the powerful arguments that have been raised against it? The answer, I submit, is that for all the obstacles to it, it is probably the most feasible major demand that blacks are now making. White resistance to community control, by contrast, is centered in the big city public bureaucracies. Many other whites are hostile—out of family, ethnic, or racial solidarity—but they really have no stake in who governs the ghettos.

A little progress can be made without massive redistribution and a

---

* Other studies have shown that those most likely to take part in riots are young unmarried males who have been raised in northern cities and who live in segregated neighborhoods. Income and employment status do not seem to have much independent effect. More conventional civil rights protestors tend to be middle class, among the better educated, northern and urban by upbringing, young, male, and socially mobile.[3]

willingness of whites to integrate, but only a very little. In the early sixties reducing unemployment was an alternative path to progress, but its potential has been exhausted now for several years. The current direction of policy, in response to inflation, is just the reverse. In any event, prosperity itself has little effect on relative incomes, and it is inequality (rather than absolute poverty) that is at the root of black unrest.*

The outlook for grand national reform, then, is bleak. What can be done at the local level? Certainly not much about segregation and inequality. Central city whites are already in massive flight to the suburbs; vigorous efforts to promote integration simply hasten their exodus. The cities also lack resources to engage in much redistribution; and efforts to soak the affluent (again) just accelerate their pace of departure.

That leaves participatory reform. At the citywide level, a mayor can engage in elaborate consultation with black leaders, appoint some of them to citywide office, encourage black recruitment and rapid promotion by the career bureaucracies, seek to transform the bureaucratic subcultures, insist that Negroes secure employment on government contracts, and so on. Except where citywide Negro majorities exist, however, his efforts are likely to have a minor impact at best. He will find that he can consult, but he cannot pass ordinances, appropriate funds, make more than a few appointments, or dominate the civil service bureaucracies. In fact, he will normally find that the bureaucracies have far greater political strength in their respective spheres than he. They are much more likely to defeat him for reelection than he is to alter their subcultures. He may be a racial "statesman," but he will find that few members of the councils, boards, and commissions with which he must deal share his outlook. They will be more typical working through middle-class whites. They will be determined not to give blacks any "special preference."

A single mayoral administration, of course, may surmount these obstacles enough to achieve a fair rate of progress. In doing so, however (if the record to date is any indication), the mayor will stir widespread and bitter white antagonism. With his defeat or decision to retire, the pattern of city government will return to normal. Blacks may be left

---

* As is frequently pointed out, American Negroes are quite well off by world and historic standards. They think of themselves as Americans, however, and thus it is against contemporary American norms that they evaluate their lot.

It should be noted, parenthetically, that the relative incomes of the poor do improve during the upswing from a recession to high employment. Another way of putting this is to say that the poor bear a disproportionate share of the cost of recessions. In particular, they are the ones who get laid off as employment contracts.

After high employment is achieved, its maintenance (at any given level) has no further tendency to alleviate inequality. As incomes rise, the same degree of inequality (to repeat: a relative concept) involves larger and larger absolute differentials. In the most advanced modern economies, moreover, those at the bottom of the income pyramid have become liberated from peasant traditionalism and consumers of the mass media. Thus, they are intensely conscious of their poverty—and they question it.

more bitter than ever, because they will have had their hopes raised and then dashed.

The hope of community control is that it might provide a base for long-term reform. It would provide an arena in which blacks might engage their energies and experience power. It would provide a mechanism for transforming the bureaucratic subcultures (by changing their basic lines of political dependence). It would provide a focus for black political organization. It might help to build black skills and self-respect. But most important, it would give blacks a tangible stake in the American political system. By giving them systems they considered their own, it would—hopefully—enhance the legitimacy of the whole system in their eyes.

What is to be said of the white liberal argument that community control would be a step toward increased separatism? Although I have made clear . . . that I do not think neighborhoods should be defined on racial lines, I accept the force of this argument. Small jurisdictions in large urban areas do have a tendency toward homogeneity, and the drive toward racial homogeneity within social units in our society is particularly strong. Were this not so, we could have small-scale local government and integration, too. As it is, we have extremely few integrated neighborhoods even within large jurisdictions. And the forced political mix in big city government appears on balance to be a force for increased friction rather than reconciliation.

The primary reason for this is white prejudice. The black desire for integration is well documented and overwhelming. Thus, liberals are faced with a bitter dilemma. They desire a peace of reconciliation and they also desire integration. They would like to pursue the former by implementing the latter. But they are a tiny minority within the white majority. (I am speaking now of the few who are truly prepared for massive desegregation—and in their own lives, not just those of the less affluent folk.) Thus, they cannot deliver integration. At least, they cannot deliver it at a rate that is nearly rapid enough.

Having long envisioned complementarity, they are unwilling to contemplate the possibility that their two primary values may have to be traded off. This is especially so because the facts are ambiguous. A plausible case can be made that community control will heighten, rather than alleviate, racial antagonism. And then there is the long history of liberal battle with the racist proponents of "states' rights." It is imperative, nonetheless, for white liberals to face the possibility that a tradeoff price exists. If it does, the reason is that most whites do not subscribe to liberal values, and thus would not consider the transaction in question a tradeoff at all. What liberals contemplate as a cost (setback for integration), they are more likely to contemplate as a benefit.

Let one point be absolutely clear. I have said that a tradeoff price in terms of liberal values *may* exist, not that it does. This is not to call for an immediate wholesale revamping of our local government structure to provide community control; but it *is* to call for a vigorous program of experimentation looking toward that possibility. Such a program might well include the use of federal incentives to bring about a total restructuring of local government in one or a few cities (and/or metropolitan areas).

On the very limited evidence to date, what might one expect the main products of community control to be? In particular: (1) Would it be conducive to racial peace? (2) Would it be conducive to the development of black skills and incomes, and to the improvement of other conditions (health, housing, security from crime, etc.) in the ghettos?

WOULD COMMUNITY CONTROL BE CONDUCIVE TO RACIAL PEACE?

My own view is that, where properly designed and after an initial shakedown period, it would tend to be. This is not to say that it would be in every case, or to deny that great political battles will be necessary to achieve it (if it can be achieved at all). But it is to suggest a direction of probabilities, and to recall that every great transition involves a period of crisis and apparent chaos. The best such transitions, like the American Revolution and the acceptance of the labor movement into the American political mainstream, enhance tranquility within a few years even if not overnight.

The primary considerations on which I base this view are the following:

(a) The keys to legitimacy in the modern world are equality and self-determination.

There are many dimensions of equality, but of these the most important are equality of opportunity and equality before the law. With respect to the former, community control would open up a good many local, highly visible, opportunities to just those blacks who are the most articulate and skilled at organization.* The primary impact of community control, however, would be on the latter. On the day-to-day level, it would go far toward persuading blacks that governmental be-

---

* David Cohen has recently written of the special interest that black school professionals have in community control as follows: "Even in itself integration is a difficult path: it promises strain, tension, and unfamiliarity to black and white administrators and teachers equally, and hence it has never inspired real enthusiasm except among a few Community control, on the other hand, avoids these pitfalls. It offers concrete gains long overdue—jobs and promotion to administrative and supervisory positions, without the accompanying discomfort of venturing into foreign schools and neighborhoods—under the ideological aegis of assisting in the development of one's own community. A more perfect coincidence of ideology and self-interest can hardly be imagined.

"The coming-of-age of the black professional class, a potent aspect of the struggle for community control, may turn out in the end to be the most important element in the battle over the schools, more significant than the substitution of parent for citywide boards, or community for bureaucratic control." [4] Community control would also, of course, extend numerous opportunities to black politicians, whether highly educated or not.

havior toward them was not based on racial discrimination. More generally, blacks consider the existing situation a blatant denial of equality. The vast majority of whites enjoy small-scale, essentially neighborhood (by big city standards), local government. The black heritage is one of extreme oppression in the rural South, and more recently of exclusion from the northern suburbs. It seems to them that their permanent minority status is not simply a product of accident. Wherever it seems that equal application of the rules might permit them to enjoy local majority status, the rules are applied unequally. The last several years have witnessed a few exceptions—in long-established northern cities and southern towns where Negroes have won political control—but in general that's the way it is.

The current white policy is not in fact so consciously discriminatory. The problem is rather the incredible force of inertia. *It is possible neither to consolidate the suburbs nor to break up the central cities.* Add to this that blacks are confined to the central cities. Add also that the one central city in the nation with a Negro voting majority (Washington, D.C.) is also the one that lacks self-government. And it becomes readily comprehensible why many blacks view the present structure of American urban government as a barefaced gerrymander.*

The primary need, then, is for parity between black and white "neighborhoods" in each urban area. My own preference would be for a two-tier pattern, on the model of metropolitan London.[5] The bottom tier authorities in such a system—today's suburbs and central city neighborhoods—would have less power than the suburbs now do. In particular, they would have less power to practice racial exclusion, to veto programs of great metropolitan interest, and to engage in tax competition for commercial and industrial investment. With respect to the last, taxation of commercial and industrial property would be a metropolitan function, so that tax rates might cease to be a factor in business location decisions (at least, within each urban region), and so that these decisions might become uncoupled from the distribution of public services.

But my preferences, quite clearly, are of little importance. The critical issue is what it will take to persuade blacks that the system is fair. To

---

* My stress here on the force of inertia is not meant to deny the critical role of prejudice in sustaining the status quo. It is undeniable, for example, that while Congressional rule of Washington, D.C. predates the Negro majority, the hostility of Southern Congressmen to that majority has been the decisive obstacle to home rule in recent years.

What I am denying is that the white determination to maintain racial superiority is today sufficient to revise the structure simply because it permits blacks to achieve some power. At certain extremes it may well be, but not in the ranges we can currently observe.

The problem, rather, is that our system is one of minority vetoes. It takes very large majorities to change the status quo in any fundamental way. Blacks, together with fair-minded whites (a category which includes many others in addition to hard-core liberals) seem to have reached the point where they can veto fundamental changes. But as a deprived group they want much more. And one heritage of the past is that the existing structure, on balance, is radically biased against them.

that end, some dramatic move toward parity would seem essential, whatever the precise nature of the design.*

If equality is one key to legitimacy in the modern world, the other is self-determination. Not every group, of course, desires or can have independent nationhood. We are fortunate that the vast majority of blacks are not yet making this demand. (But we had better keep an eye on its rate of growth.) What they *are* demanding is that they sometimes, at the lowest tier of American government, be permitted the experience of majority status.

To endorse this demand is not to say that every group which comes forward with a similar demand in future should be accorded the same privilege. The fact is that race is the most critical variable in American politics. To be a Negro is to have the fact of race pervade all of one's other roles. It is also to face constant exclusion and hostility. As the saying goes: we are faced with a condition, not a theory. The Constitution may be color-blind, but Americans are not. To be a Negro in white America is to be *always* in the minority. It is rather difficult to have much sense of self-determination in such a situation. This is especially so if one is poor, and cannot even exercise much choice in the marketplace. It is not significantly less so because the system is democratic. Where race is concerned, majority tyranny is much like any other.

To endorse this demand is also not to suggest that opportunities for integration should be curtailed, or that neighborhood boundaries should be drawn on racial lines. My own position is that the battle to extend integration opportunities for those who want them must be pressed more vigorously than ever, and that neighborhood boundaries should be drawn (and periodically reapportioned) like legislative districts. The aim must be not to promote separatism—though an incidental effect of community control may be to increase the present, almost total degree of segregation. It must rather be to provide blacks with the chance in some circumstances (and when they care enough) to experience majority status. Suburban-neighborhood parity would accomplish this aim. If the boundaries were drawn in color-blind fashion (e.g., for compactness and equal population), many members of each race would find themselves in neighborhood minorities. But there would be no racial bias to the system, and those who cared enough could move to neighborhoods that were predominantly of their own race.

(b) The bureaucratic subcultures, which produce behavior that so infuriates young blacks today, are unlikely to be transformed by any reform short of community control. At the citywide level in most cities (the exceptions are those few with Negro-white liberal voting majorities), the bureaucracies can count on majority support from the electorate and nearly all policy-making bodies. Even where they cannot,

---

* It is perhaps worth adding that one move toward parity (fortunately, the least likely) might actually exacerbate black anger. That would be to consolidate a city and its suburbs into a one-tier metropolitan gargantua. This would look like a transparent ploy to dilute black influence in the central city without offering anything in return.

their power to veto and delay is generally sufficient to block fundamental change. Community control would not change them everywhere, but it would change them where it counted most—in the ghettos. Not only would it change them in fact, but it would change them very obviously. Blacks would be much less likely to see slurs where none were intended when dealing with employees of governments they considered their own.

(c) There is no reason to believe that neighborhood power would tend to increase black radicalism. Indeed, precisely the reverse hypothesis is more plausible.

The evidence suggests that elections would produce more moderate black leaders than the current process of screening for newsworthiness and support among the activists alone. Community control would give authority, resources, and newsworthiness to those who could win elections. It would also set them astride the channels of liaison with units of the larger society. They would be the logical and legitimate leaders for outsiders to deal with. This would both simplify matters for the outsiders and render the conclusion of bargains more feasible. (Consider the "exclusive bargaining agent" mechanism in labor-management relations.)

There is every reason to believe, moreover, that the possession of property and the exercise of responsibility are both "conservatizing" experiences. Power is a form of property; it gives its holders a great psychic stake in the system. Home and business ownership would probably be even more effective moderating influences on ghetto politics; it should be recalled that they are important parts of the full community control demand package. The exercise of responsibility would be a vital educational experience for black leaders. They would be forced to go beyond slogans, to grapple with ghetto problems in all their dull complexity. This would lead them to press higher levels of government for greater resources (as just about all city officials now do), but it would also decrease their confidence in simple, radical panaceas.

Community control might or might not facilitate ghetto political organization. The reason it might not is that, in removing the "enemy" from immediate proximity, it would reduce the incentive to mobilize. On the other hand, it would provide a clear-cut set of rewards for successful mobilization. Let us assume for the moment, therefore, that the effect on balance would be to increase ghetto organization.

The critical point to keep in mind is that greater organization does not necessarily mean heightened black-white conflict. For one thing, a great deal of the increased black organization would be competitive. Alternative groups would be vying for power. For another, the most successful organizational leaders would probably be among the more moderate (for the reasons noted above). For a third, heightened organization in itself is generally a force for peace. The rioters, it will be recalled, have been drawn predominantly from the young, the unmarried, the politically inactive—i.e., those least integrated into stable social organizations. Those most involved in organized protest and political activity have been among the least likely to riot. Indeed, they have been the most likely to act as counterrioters when disorders have occurred. If one's aim is a peace without black political activism, then one's method must be ruthless repression. But if one's aim is a peace of reconciliation, the sensible thing is to concentrate on replacing violent disorder with nonviolent political and protest activity. That is the kind in which the labor movement engages. The best resolution of the current racial crisis for which we can hope is that the labor precedent will be emulated.

Finally, there is no reason to equate even separatism with heightened antagonism. Less contact has often in history meant less conflict. When the quality of contact is negative, the option of reducing its quantity is not to be sneezed at. Once again, this is not to oppose integration. It is just to deal with the facts as they are. When two parties both passionately insist on separation, who am I to refuse it? But of course the situation is really less extreme, so let me put it another way. Blacks have been an oppressed minority. I have championed their right to integration, and I still do. But I can recognize why they might want something of their own while they wait; and I can see that having it might make the wait less infuriating.

WOULD COMMUNITY CONTROL BE CONDUCIVE TO THE DEVELOPMENT OF BLACK SKILLS AND INCOMES, AND TO THE IMPROVEMENT OF OTHER CONDITIONS IN THE GHETTOS?

This seems to me a more relevant way to put the question than to ask whether neighborhood governments would be as "efficient" as city-wide governments?

There are tremendous disagreements over what the specific objectives of public policy in the ghettos should be. Thus, there is no basis for achieving consensus on what is efficient. But there is substantial agreement on what black aspirations are. So let us speak of outcomes, and arrangements that might be conducive to them, rather than of government efficiency.

Let us dwell on this point a moment longer. It is possible for a remarkably "efficient" government to produce disastrously negative results. Its objectives may be irrelevant, perverse, or self-defeating. Or it may simply be so overwhelming in its competence that it destroys the capacity of its clients to help themselves.

When spokesmen for the civil service bureaucracies speak of "efficiency," they typically refer to process rather than outcome variables—just as when they speak of "merit," they typically refer to degrees and test scores rather than on-the-job accomplishment. For example, they speak of police response times reduced, not crime rates. They speak of smaller classes and "better qualified" teachers, not student acquisition of skills and self-respect. They speak of ironclad guarantees against

ALAN A. ALTSHULER 239

corruption, not the reduction of inequality, segregation, or racial bitterness.

It has long been a central tenet of the American tradition that the best government is often no government, or at least government which confines itself to arranging environments rather than tending to every detail. Thus, we leave most economic decisions (other than the very largest) to the marketplace. This leaves a great many decisions to be made by extremely unsophisticated actors; but most Americans believe that it is highly conducive to "efficiency" on balance.

Similarly, Americans have always left the bulk of governmental decision making (national security affairs excluded) to state and local authorities. They have done so despite a widespread belief that state and local officials are less competent, less innovative, and more corrupt than those of the federal government. Why have they done so? They have judged that decentralization would produce a finer tuning of government to varied local tastes. By insisting on no more uniformity than was necessary, satisfaction with union would be maximized.* They have considered widespread participation in government a value in itself, noting its utility as an instrument of democratic education and socialization. They have believed that distributing responsibility widely would spread competence throughout the society (even though the most competent might still gravitate toward the center). Those with a taste for the classics have frequently noted Tocqueville's observation that the American system was very wasteful but also incredibly vigorous, and that these were two sides of the same coin: decentralization.**

* They have also recalled the wisdom of the framers, who recognized that no union would be possible at all without numerous concessions to state separatist sentiment.

** The flavor of Tocqueville's moving defense of American localism may be gathered from the following key passages: ". . . Centralized administration . . . may insure a victory in the hour of strife, but it gradually relaxes the sinews of strength. . . .

"Centralization imparts without difficulty an admirable regularity to the routine of business . . . maintains society in a status quo alike secure from improvement and decline; and perpetuates a drowsy regularity in the conduct of affairs, which the heads of the administration are wont to call good order and public tranquility. . . . Its force deserts it when society is to be profoundly moved or accelerated in its courses; and if once the cooperation of private citizens is necessary to the furtherance of its measures, the secret of its impotence is disclosed.

"Even whilst the centralized power, in its despair, invokes the assistance of the citizens, it says to them: 'You should act just as I please, and in the direction which I please. You are to take charge of the details, without aspiring to guide the system; you are to work in darkness; and afterwards you may judge my work by its results.' These are not the conditions on which the alliance of the human will is to be obtained. . . .

"In America, the power which conducts the administration is far less regular, less enlightened, and less skillful, but a hundred-fold greater, than in Europe. In no country in the world do the citizens make such exertions for the common weal. I know of no people who have established schools so numerous and efficacious, places of public worship better suited to the wants of the inhabitants, or roads kept in better repair. Uniformity or permanence of design, the minute arrangement

Finally, students of colonialism have frequently noted that people who do not have self-government somehow never seem ready for it. In part this is a prejudice of the colonialists, but in part it is true. Countries new to self-government are rarely very good at it. Unfortunately, there does not seem to be any other way to learn than by practice. The colonialists might have done well to transfer power gradually, but they rarely moved at all until confronted by revolution. Sound familiar?

What should we expect, then, of neighborhood government in the ghettos? Clearly, we should not expect high efficiency "in the small." [7] We should not expect the quality of political debate to be highly logical or the test scores of civil service candidates to improve. We should not expect more innovative programs or cleaner streets. We should probably not even expect lower crime rates or higher pupil reading scores.

We may hope, however, that community control will help cement the American union by providing an adequate outlet for racial pluralism. We may hope that it will help build black confidence in, and understanding of, our political institutions. We may hope that over time it will provide a mechanism for increasing competence throughout the black community.

There is substantial reason as well to hope for more specific benefits. A great many black problems are due to pathologies of the ghetto spirit —or rather, more accurately, to behavior patterns that are adaptive to the ghetto as it is, but which constitute severe obstacles to improving it.[8] These problems are the products of black self-hatred, despair, fatalism, and alienation from authority much more than of poverty itself. (Many other groups have been poor, and still are, around the world, without experiencing the social disorganization of the American ghetto.) These characteristics have been fostered primarily by oppression, but

---

of details, and the perfection of administrative system, must not be sought for in the United States: what we find there is the presence of a power which, if it is somewhat wild, is at least robust; and an existence checkered with accidents, indeed, but full of animation and effort. . . .

"There are countries in Europe where the natives consider themselves as a kind of settlers, indifferent to the fate of the spot which they inhabit. The greatest changes are effected there without concurrence, and (unless chance may have apprised them of the event) without their knowledge; nay, more, the condition of his village, the police of his street, the repairs of the church or the parsonage, do not concern him; for he looks upon all these things as unconnected with himself, and as the property of a powerful stranger whom he calls the government. . . .

"When a nation has arrived at this state, it must either change its customs and its laws, or perish; for the source of public virtues is dried up; and though it may contain subjects, it has no citizens. . . .

". . . A democracy without provincial institutions has no security against [disorder and despotism]. How can a populace, unaccustomed to freedom in small concerns, learn to use it temperately in great affairs? What resistance can be offered to tyranny in a country where each individual is weak, and where the citizens are not united by any common interest? Those who dread the license of the mob, and those who fear absolute power, ought alike to desire the gradual development of provincial liberties." [6]

also by paternalism. The active oppression is decreasing rapidly, but the legacy of the past will be spinning out its consequences for a long while to come.

There is almost surely a greater potential for improving the ghettos by transforming their spirit than by inundating them with paternalistic programs. This is not to deny that resources are essential. Quite obviously, rapid change will be impossible without massive infusions of outside aid. But it is to maintain that resources are not enough. It seems quite obvious that the existing system is not getting any mileage at all (except perhaps in reverse) from its expenditures of resources in terms of transforming the ghetto spirit. Self-determination might not produce any better results. But a great many people, including just about all the nation's black leaders, believe that it would. It would certainly seem to merit serious trial.

Let us be more specific. How might self-determination lead to improved outcomes in specific policy arenas, even if it operated with less qualified personnel by existing civil service standards?

George Sternlieb has shown that by far the most impressive way to improve ghetto housing is to replace absentee ownership with resident ownership. He has based his argument not on conjecture, but on painstaking analysis of the histories of large numbers of specific properties.[9] Home and tenement ownership also builds management skills, and it provides a powerful incentive to become active in neighborhood improvement efforts. Thus, it is likely to produce leadership as well as more narrow business skills, and to channel energies into sober, constructive political efforts. Sternlieb notes that a public policy which encouraged resident ownership would have precedents dating to the Homestead Act and beyond.* Note that such a policy would not require a large bureaucracy, nor would it give the recipients of aid any sense of being on the dole. The beneficial outcomes which ensued would be viewed as more the products of free enterprise in action than "efficient" government.

Theodore Cross has recently noted that black lending institutions can operate much more effectively in the ghettos than white. The reason is simple. To break even in the ghettos, let alone make a profit, it is necessary to charge higher interest rates than elsewhere. The reasons: high bad debt rates, very small average loans, the need for intensive counseling of customers, a resource base of very small and highly active accounts, the need to devote a great deal of effort to community improvement activities. White banks are afraid to charge higher interest rates in the ghettos, recognizing their vulnerability to charges of racial discrimination. Thus, they have tended to stay out of the ghettos entirely, except for token money-losing operations undertaken for public relations purposes.

* The owners studied by Sternlieb, of course, were far from typical ghetto residents. Without unusual drive and skill, most of them would never have become owners. But their number has been growing, and Sternlieb argues convincingly that the process could be accelerated to a very marked degree without a serious dilution of benefits.

The result has been to make credit virtually unavailable in the ghettos, except from loan sharks, small loan companies, and individual merchants. In part, the answer to this problem should be subsidies to enable private banks to make profits lending in the ghettos on the same terms as elsewhere. Realistically, however, the subsidies will not be sufficient to meet the demand for a long time to come (if ever). Thus, a very sensible alternative, to which some large white financial institutions have already turned, is to channel resources for ghetto lending through black banks. This at least can make bank-style credit available, and at rates only 1.5 or 2 percentage points higher than elsewhere, instead of 30, 50 or 1,000.* [10] Cross notes, incidentally, that the same phenomenon operates in retailing. The large white-owned chains avoid the ghettos, and brand names tend to be unavailable because their manufacturers refuse to permit them to be sold at higher than list prices. The primary results: ghetto residents buy shoddy, nonname brand merchandise from small and frequently shady merchants.[11] Community-owned black retailing operations would have a much better chance to secure permission from the brand-name manufacturers to charge what they had to; they would also have a better chance to secure subsidies (perhaps from government, perhaps from the manufacturers themselves) to enable them to break even while charging list prices.

Christopher Jencks has recently noted that, although most of the debate on ghetto education focuses on specific skills, there is little evidence that these skills have much bearing on earning capacity:

> If you ask employers why they won't hire dropouts . . . they seldom complain that dropouts can't read. Instead, they complain that dropouts don't get to work on time, can't be counted on to do a careful job, don't get along with others in the plant or office, can't be trusted to keep their hands out of the till, and so on. Nor do the available survey data suggest that the adult success of people from disadvantaged backgrounds depends primarily on their intellectual skills. If you compare black men who do well on the Armed Forces Qualifications Test to those who do badly, for example, you find that a black man who scores as high as the average white still earns only about two-thirds as much as the average white earns. Not only that, he hardly earns more than the average black. *Even for whites, the mental abilities measured by the AFQ account for less than a tenth of the variation in earnings.*[12]

If Jencks's reading of the evidence is correct—and I believe it is— black poverty and unemployment are much more products of poor socialization (by the standards of the job market) than of poor reading and arithmetic skills.** The likelihood that the current citywide educational bureaucracies will be able to alter the socialization patterns of

---

* Credit from loan sharks typically comes at prices ranging from 5 per cent a week to $1.00 a week for each $5.00 borrowed. The former works out at 260 per cent a year, the latter at 1,000 per cent a year.

** They are also, doubtless in very large part, products of discrimination, but that is outside the scope of the present discussion.

ghetto youth is nil. The problem is not one of qualifications. It is one of trust and rapport. It is essentially political, not technical. Black-controlled educational systems might fail to do any better, but they could hardly do worse. In all honesty, it is hard to believe that they would not do better.

If unemployment is a product of socialization, how much more obviously so are crime and disorder.* So long as it is *de rigueur* for all black leaders to view the police as armies of occupation, no one is likely to have much success in altering the socialization patterns involved. Nearly all students of police work agree, moreover, that the most important variable determining effectiveness is community cooperation.** Existing citywide police forces are the least likely agencies to secure such cooperation. They even have great difficulty using their black personnel effectively, because black police are widely perceived by ghetto residents as having "sold out." Critics of the black participation movement frequently speak as if this showed the unimportance of black police recruitment. Actually, what it suggests is the need to link black recruitment with political reform to enhance the legitimacy of the whole police system.

So far as civil disorder is concerned, the police have often been less than ineffective. They have themselves been a major source of disturbance.

As Burton Levy notes, nearly every recent disorder has begun with a police incident. The police have often not been particularly blameworthy in these incidents (and, in any event, every organization contains some rotten apples). But that is not the point. What matters is that such particular events have been able, because of the context of hostility within which they occurred, to trigger such general disorder. To quote Levy: "Whatever the factual reality is—as contrasted to the belief systems—clearly the cops serve as the 'flash point' for black anger, mob formation, and civil disorder." [14]

Once again, then, the problem appears to be primarily political (though it could doubtless be stamped out with sufficient force). For those of us bent on a peace of reconciliation, the overwhelming need is not for better equipment but for rapprochement. With respect to personnel policy, it suggests less emphasis on academic degrees, test scores, and seniority, and much more on relationships of trust with the community.

* This is not to judge the ultimate responsibility of institutions vs. individuals, but simply to point out that the institutions have failed to inculcate behavior patterns conducive to their peaceful survival, and to persuade the individuals of their legitimacy.

** For example, James Q. Wilson—an opponent of community control on other grounds . . . writes as follows: "The police can do relatively little about preventing most crimes, and those they can help prevent—street crimes—are precisely the ones that require the greatest knowledge of local conditions and the greatest support, in terms of a willingness to report offenses and give information, from the populace." [13]

Would community control increase efficiency? The issue, it seems, is less clear-cut than it sounds. The answer will largely turn on whose conceptions of problem and purpose one adopts. From a somewhat different perspective, it is likely to depend on whether one interprets the question to be about efficiency "in the small" or "in the large."

It goes without saying that we can foresee very little. One of the more useful research efforts that might be undertaken in the next few years would be a series of case studies examining the record of Community Action, Model Neighborhood, and community control designers in forecasting even the very short-run consequences of their actions. One need have little doubt that these will be, from the standpoint of would-be social planners, quite discouraging tales.

But like sailors in a hurricane, we can ill afford to drift. We must estimate our bearings, on the meager information we have, and act. We may have a little time for experimentation. If so, we would do well to exploit it vigorously. But we probably will not. Societies are transformed by revolution and inadvertence, but they rarely conduct experiments to improve political forecasting. In the end, if community control becomes reality, it will probably do so little more because of experimental findings than white altruism. It will be a product of protest and pragmatic compromise.

NOTES

1. S. M. Miller and Martin Rein, "Participation, Poverty, and Administration," *Public Administration Review*, January–February 1969, pp. 15–25. . . .
2. H. Edward Ransford, "Isolation, Powerlessness, and Violence: A Study of Attitudes and Participation in the Watts Riot," *American Journal of Sociology*, January 1968, pp. 581–591. Unfortunately, Ransford did not adjust for education in his analysis of the cumulative effect of the three factors. Presumably, however, doing so would not have altered the finding of a combination effect. All it might have done was to show that low education plus two of the other three variables sufficed to bring it into operation.
3. Cf. [Louis H.] Bowen and [Donald R.] Masotti, eds., *Riots and Rebellion* [(Beverly Hills: Saye, 1968)], articles by Jay Schulman, E. S. Evans, and T. M. Tomlinson; Robert M. Fogelson and Robert B. Hill, "Who Riots? A Study of Participation in the 1967 Riots," in *Supplemental Studies for the National Advisory Commission on Civil Disorders*, pp. 221–248; Gary T. Marx, *Protest and Prejudice* (Harper & Row, 1967), ch. 2; and John M. Orbell, "Protest Among Southern Negro College Students," *American Political Science Review*, June 1967, pp. 446–456.
4. [David] Cohen, "The Price of Community Control," [*Commentary*, July 1969], pp. 23–32. The quotation is from p. 30.
5. Cf. Frank Smallwood, *Greater London: The Politics of Metropolitan Reform* (Bobbs-Merrill, 1965).
6. Alexis de Tocqueville, *Democracy in America* (Mentor Edition, 1956; first published in 1835), pp. 64–71.

7. My usage of this phrase follows that of [Edward C.] Banfield and [James Q.] Wilson in their book, *City Politics* [(Harvard University Press, 1963)]. See esp. pp. 18–22.

8. For an elaboration of this theme, see Lee Rainwater, "Crucible of Identity: The Negro Lower-Class Family," in Talcott Parsons, ed., *The Negro American* (Beacon, 1966), pp. 160–204.

9. Cf. George Sternlieb, *The Tenement Landlord* (Rutgers, 1966), and George Sternlieb, "Slum Housing: A Functional Analysis," *Law and Contemporary Problems*, Spring 1967, pp. 349–356.

10. [Theodore L.] Cross, [*Black Capitalism: Strategy for Business in the Ghetto* (Atheneum, 1969)], pp. 45–55, 168, 214–219.

11. *Ibid.*, pp. 33–34.

12. Christopher Jencks, "A Reappraisal of the Most Controversial Educational Document of Our Time [the Coleman Report]," *New York Times Magazine*, August 10, 1969, pp. 12 ff. The quotation is from p. 44. Cf. also Peter Blau and Otis Dudley Duncan, *The American Occupational Structure* (Wiley, 1967), ch. 6; and Michael J. Piore, "Public and Private Responsibilities in On-the-Job Training of Disadvantaged Workers," Department of Economics, Massachusetts Institute of Technology, Working Paper No. 23, June 1968.

13. [James Q.] Wilson, *Varieties of Police Behavior*, [(Harvard University Press, 1968)], p. 295. Cf. also The President's Commission on Law Enforcement and Administration of Justice, *The Challenge of Crime in a Free Society* (USGPO, 1967), pp. 99–103.

14. [Burton] Levy, ["Cops in the Ghetto: A Problem of the Police System"], in Masotti and Bowen, *op. cit.*, p. 349.

Chapter 9

THE FUTURE OF URBAN SOCIETY

In numerous social science books on the city, surprisingly, the future of America's urban places receives remarkably little attention, at least beyond concern with projected demographic growth and the short-range urban planning process. Neither the possible shapes that the urban socioeconomic and political future might take nor the possibility and character of a long-range urban planning process have undergone much systematic analysis. In the excerpt from *Future Shock* that is presented in this concluding chapter, Alvin Toffler grapples with some of these extraordinarily important issues.

The basic argument of *Future Shock* is that modern American society, unless its members learn to adapt quickly and adopt radical new planning procedures, is headed for a massive breakdown—the result of bombardment by a myriad of profound social changes. "Future shock" is the phrase used to "describe the shattering stress and disorientation that we induce in individuals by subjecting them to too much change in too short a time." [1] Yet individuals are not the only ones who seem unable to cope with too much change. Governments, too, often appear incapable not only of developing mechanisms and policies to deal with the problems created by societal change, but also of clearly determining the long-range goals toward which the society should be directed.

Rejecting the procedures of technocratic planning, as well as the "hang loose" philosophy of some among the New Left, Toffler argues for a revolutionary new approach which he terms "social futurism"—a strategy which he sees as more farsighted, humanized, and democratic than most strategies of the past. One aspect of this social futurism

247

would be the development and periodic review of social indicators, which could be used to determine what is actually happening over time in this society. An established system for evaluating social and cultural indicators is deemed essential by Toffler to the technical equipment of a society before "it can successfully reach the next stage of eco-technological development." Indeed, this would be the first step in the direction of humanizing the entire urban-planning process.

In defending the need for long-term, future-oriented planning, Toffler presses hard against those whom he sees as basically conservative, those who argue that the future is unknowable and not predictable, those who see Americans as helpless in the face of rapid social and cultural change. Indeed, a limited amount of scientific effort directed at predicting the future has already begun. Dramatic expansion of these experimental efforts is advocated by Toffler, together with the development in a variety of existing organizations and institutions of what he calls "imaginetic centers"—"think tanks" where people with wide-ranging imaginations and probing minds can speculate freely about possible and probable developments in such areas as race relations, urban transportation, education, and pollution. In addition, these "imagineers" might explore possibilities and probabilities for the future of modern urban society as a whole, dissecting and laying out the various utopias that reflect different values and perspectives.

Social futurism as a strategy should not be limited to think tanks and the development of institutions to assess social indicators; social futurism has implications for the political arena as well. Answers to a number of basic questions about the future come up hard against government and economic arrangements currently grounded in a leadership structure characterized by elitism. Critical questions arise about *who* will determine the values, possible futures, and goals to be pursued by a society. In most scenarios focusing on the near future, traditionally prominent elites have been seen—or have seen themselves—as controlling the planning process. Yet with regard to social futurism and long-range planning this will not suffice. Toffler argues for a new, democratic approach to the setting of societal goals and the shaping of America's future. Elitist processes of goal determination are no longer efficient in rapidly changing postindustrial or superindustrial societies. Greatly increased democratic participation in information gathering and decision making is critical, not just for idealistic but for practical reasons. Popular democracy is more efficient, he argues, because it allows for greater feedback than other arrangements in rapidly changing, complex urban societies: "As the number of social components grows and change makes the whole system less stable, it becomes less and less possible to ignore the demands of political minorities—hippies, blacks, lower-middle-class Wallacites, school teachers, or the proverbial little old ladies in tennis shoes."

Stressing goals of determining national priorities and extending democratic participation, Toffler proposes the convening of social-future assemblies that will represent all geographical and demographic groups.

Although he is aware of the difficulties in involving previously isolated persons in politics, he still considers this the critical political objective of the next few decades. Throughout *Future Shock* Toffler is following his own admonitions, for in fact he is playing the role of imagineer. Although his conception of social-future assemblies on a national or global basis may seem farfetched or naïve to many readers, Toffler argues that greater naïveté can be found among those who argue that business-as-usual arrangements can continue indefinitely in a hard-pressed American political and economic system.

NOTES

1. Alvin Toffler, *Future Shock* (New York: Random House, 1970), p. 4.

FROM **FUTURE SHOCK:**
THE STRATEGY
OF SOCIAL FUTURISM

ALVIN TOFFLER

Can one live in a society that is out of control? That is the question posed for us by the concept of future shock. For that is the situation we find ourselves in. If it were technology alone that had broken loose, our problems would be serious enough. The deadly fact is, however, that many other social processes have also begun to run free, oscillating wildly, resisting our best efforts to guide them.

Urbanization, ethnic conflict, migration, population, crime—a thousand examples spring to mind of fields in which our efforts to shape change seem increasingly inept and futile. Some of these are strongly related to the breakaway of technology; others partially independent of it. The uneven, rocketing rates of change, the shifts and jerks in direction, compel us to ask whether the techno-societies, even comparatively small ones like Sweden and Belgium, have grown too complex, too fast to manage?

How can we prevent mass future shock, selectively adjusting the tempos of change, raising or lowering levels of stimulation, when governments—including those with the best intentions—seem unable even to point change in the right direction?

Thus a leading American urbanologist writes with unconcealed disgust: "At a cost of more than three **billion dollars,** the Urban Renewal Agency has succeeded in materially reducing the supply of low cost housing in American cities." Similar debacles could be cited in a dozen fields. Why do welfare programs today often cripple rather than help their clients? Why do college students, supposedly a pampered elite, riot and rebel? Why do expressways add to traffic congestion rather than reduce it? In short, why do so many well-intentioned liberal programs turn rancid so rapidly, producing side effects that cancel out their central effects? No wonder Raymond Fletcher, a frustrated Member of Parliament in Britain, recently complained: "Society's gone random!"

If random means a literal absence of pattern, he is, of course, overstating the case. But if random means that the outcomes of social policy have become erratic and hard to predict, he is right on target. Here, then, is the political meaning of future shock. For just as individual future shock results from an inability to keep pace with the rate of change, governments, too, suffer from a kind of collective future shock—a breakdown of their decisional processes.

With chilling clarity, Sir Geoffrey Vickers, the eminent British social scientist, has identified the issue: "The rate of change increases at an accelerating speed, without a corresponding acceleration in the rate at which further responses can be made; and this brings us nearer the threshold beyond which control is lost."

THE DEATH OF TECHNOCRACY

What we are witnessing is the beginning of the final breakup of industrialism and, with it, the collapse of technocratic planning. By technocratic planning, I do not mean only the centralized national planning that has, until recently, characterized the USSR, but also the less formal, more dispersed attempts at systematic change management that occur in all the high technology nations, regardless of their political persuasion. Michael Harrington, the socialist critic, arguing that we have rejected planning, has termed ours the "accidental century." Yet, as Galbraith demonstrates, even within the context of a capitalist economy, the great corporations go to enormous lengths to rationalize production and distribution, to plan their future as best they can. Governments, too, are deep into the planning business. The Keynesian manipulation of post-war economies may be inadequate, but it is not a matter of accident. In France, *Le Plan* has become a regular feature of national life. In Sweden, Italy, Germany and Japan, governments actively intervene in the economic sector to protect certain industries, to capitalize others, and to accelerate growth. In the United States and Britain, even local governments come equipped with what are at least *called* planning departments.

Why, therefore, despite all these efforts, should the system be spinning out of control? The problem is not simply that we plan too little; we also plan too poorly. Part of the trouble can be traced to the very premises implicit in our planning.

First, technocratic planning, itself a product of industrialism, reflects the values of that fast-vanishing era. In both its capitalist and communist variants, industrialism was a system focused on the maximization of material welfare. Thus, for the technocrat, in Detroit as well as Kiev, economic advance is the primary aim; technology the primary tool. The fact that in one case the advance redounds to private advantage and in the other, theoretically, to the public good, does not alter the core assumptions common to both. Technocratic planning is *econocentric*.

Second, technocratic planning reflects the time-bias of industrialism. Struggling to free itself from the stifling past-orientation of previous societies, industrialism focused heavily on the present. This meant, in practice, that its planning dealt with futures near at hand. The idea of a five-year plan struck the world as insanely futuristic when it was first put forward by the Soviets in the 1920's. Even today, except in the most advanced organizations on both sides of the ideological curtain, one- or two-year forecasts are regarded as "long-range planning." A handful of corporations and government agencies, as we shall see, have begun to concern themselves with horizons ten, twenty, even fifty years in the future. The majority, however, remain blindly biased toward next Monday. Technocratic planning is *short-range*.

Third, reflecting the bureaucratic organization of industrialism, technocratic planning was premised on hierarchy. The world was divided into manager and worker, planner and plannee, with decisions made by one for the other. This system, adequate while change unfolds at an industrial tempo, breaks down as the pace reaches super-industrial speeds. The increasingly unstable environment demands more and more non-programmed decisions down below; the need for instant feedback blurs the distinction between line and staff; and hierarchy totters. Planners are too remote, too ignorant of local conditions, too slow in responding to change. As suspicion spreads that top-down controls are unworkable, plannees begin clamoring for the right to participate in the decision-making. Planners, however, resist. For like the bureaucratic system it mirrors, technocratic planning is essentially *undemocratic*.

The forces sweeping us toward super-industrialism can no longer be channeled by these bankrupt industrial-era methods. For a time they may continue to work in backward, slowly moving industries or communities. But their misapplication in advanced industries, in universities, in cities—wherever change is swift—cannot but intensify the instability, leading to wilder and wilder swings and lurches. Moreover, as the evidences of failure pile up, dangerous political, cultural and psychological currents are set loose.

One response to the loss of control, for example, is a revulsion against intelligence. Science first gave man a sense of mastery over his environment, and hence over the future. By making the future seem malleable, instead of immutable, it shattered the opiate religions that preached passivity and mysticism. Today, mounting evidence that society is out of control breeds disillusionment with science. In consequence, we witness a garish revival of mysticism. Suddenly astrology is the rage. Zen, yoga, seances, and witchcraft become popular pastimes. Cults form around the search for Dionysian experience, for non-verbal and supposedly non-linear communication. We are told it is more important to "feel" than to "think," as though there were a contradiction between the two. Existentialist oracles join Catholic mystics, Jungian psychoanalysts, and Hindu gurus in exalting the mystical and emotional against the scientific and rational.

This reversion to pre-scientific attitudes is accompanied, not surprisingly, by a tremendous wave of nostalgia in the society. Antique furniture, posters from a bygone era, games based on the remembrance of yesterday's trivia, the revival of Art Nouveau, the spread of Edwardian styles, the rediscovery of such faded pop-cult celebrities as Humphrey Bogart or W. C. Fields, all mirror a psychological lust for the simpler, less turbulent past. Powerful fad machines spring into action to capitalize on this hunger. The nostalgia business becomes a booming industry.

The failure of technocratic planning and the consequent sense of lost control also feeds the philosophy of "now-ness." Songs and advertisements hail the appearance of the "now generation," and learned psychiatrists, discoursing on the presumed dangers of repression, warn us not to defer our gratifications. Acting out and a search for immediate payoff are encouraged. "We're more oriented to the present," says a teen-age girl to a reporter after the mammoth Woodstock rock music festival. "It's like do what you want to do now. . . . If you stay anywhere very long you get into a planning thing. . . . So you just move on." Spontaneity, the personal equivalent of social planlessness, is elevated into a cardinal psychological virtue.

All this has its political analog in the emergence of a strange coalition of right wingers and New Leftists in support of what can only be termed a "hang loose" approach to the future. Thus we hear increasing calls for anti-planning or non-planning, sometimes euphemized as "organic growth." Among some radicals, this takes on an anarchist coloration. Not only is it regarded as unnecessary or unwise to make long-range plans for the future of the institution or society they wish to overturn, it is sometimes even regarded as poor taste to plan the next hour and a half of a meeting. Planlessness is glorified.

Arguing that planning imposes values on the future, the anti-planners overlook the fact that non-planning does so, too—often with far worse consequence. Angered by the narrow, econocentric character of technocratic planning, they condemn systems analysis, cost benefit accounting, and similar methods, ignoring the fact that, used differently, these very tools might be converted into powerful techniques for humanizing the future.

When critics charge that technocratic planning is anti-human, in the sense that it neglects social, cultural and psychological values in its headlong rush to maximize economic gain, they are usually right. When they charge that it is shortsighted and undemocratic, they are usually right. When they charge it is inept, they are usually right.

But when they plunge backward into irrationality, anti-scientific attitudes, a kind of sick nostalgia, and an exaltation of now-ness, they are not only wrong, but dangerous. Just as, in the main, their alternatives to industrialism call for a return to pre-industrial institutions, their alternative to technocracy is not post-, but pre-technocracy.

Nothing could be more dangerously maladaptive. Whatever the theoretical arguments may be, brute forces are loose in the world. Whether we wish to prevent future shock or control population, to check pollution or defuse the arms race, we cannot permit decisions of earth-jolting importance to be taken heedlessly, witlessly, planlessly. To hang loose is to commit collective suicide.

We need not a reversion to the irrationalisms of the past, not a passive acceptance of change, not despair or nihilism. We need, instead, a strong new strategy. For reasons that will become clear, I term this strategy "social futurism." I am convinced that, armed with this strategy, we can arrive at a new level of competence in the management of change. We can invent a form of planning more humane, more far-sighted, and more democratic than any so far in use. In short, we can transcend technocracy.

THE HUMANIZATION OF THE PLANNER

Technocrats suffer from econo-think. Except during war and dire emergency, they start from the premise that even non-economic problems can be solved with economic remedies.

Social futurism challenges this root assumption of both Marxist and Keynesian managers. In its historical time and place, industrial society's single-minded pursuit of material progress served the human race well. As we hurtle toward super-industrialism, however, a new ethos emerges in which other goals begin to gain parity with, and even supplant, those of economic welfare. In personal terms, self-fulfillment, social responsibility, aesthetic achievement, hedonistic individualism, and an array of other goals vie with and often overshadow the raw drive for material success. Affluence serves as a base from which men begin to strive for varied post-economic ends.

At the same time, in societies arrowing toward super-industrialism, economic variables—wages, balance of payments, productivity—grow increasingly sensitive to changes in the non-economic environment. Economic problems are plentiful, but a whole range of issues that are only secondarily economic break into prominence. Racism, the battle between the generations, crime, cultural autonomy, violence—all these have economic dimensions; yet none can be effectively treated by econo-centric measures alone.

The move from manufacturing to service production, the psychologization of both goods and services, and ultimately the shift toward experiential production all tie the economic sector much more tightly to non-economic forces. Consumer preferences turn over in accordance with rapid life style changes, so that the coming and going of subcults is mirrored in economic turmoil. Super-industrial production requires workers skilled in symbol manipulation, so that what goes on in their heads becomes much more important than in the past, and much more dependent upon cultural factors.

There is even evidence that the financial system is becoming more responsive to social and psychological pressures. It is only in an affluent society on its way to super-industrialism that one witnesses the invention of new investment vehicles, such as mutual funds, that are consciously motivated or constrained by non-economic considerations. The Vanderbilt Mutual Fund and the Provident Fund refuse to invest in liquor or tobacco shares. The giant Mates Fund spurns the stock of any company engaged in munitions production, while the tiny Vantage 10/90 Fund invests part of its assets in industries working to alleviate food and population problems in developing nations. There are funds that invest only, or primarily, in racially integrated housing. The Ford Foundation and the Presbyterian Church both invest part of their size-able portfolios in companies selected not for economic payout alone, but for their potential contribution to solving urban problems. Such developments, still small in number, accurately signal the direction of change.

In the meantime, major American corporations with fixed investments in urban centers, are being sucked, often despite themselves, into the roaring vortex of social change. Hundreds of companies are now involved in providing jobs for hard-core unemployed, in organizing literacy and job-training programs, and in scores of other unfamiliar activities. So important have these new involvements grown that the largest corporation in the world, the American Telephone and Telegraph Company, recently set up a Department of Environmental Affairs. A pioneering venture, this agency has been assigned a range of tasks that include worrying about air and water pollution, improving the aesthetic appearance of the company's trucks and equipment, and fostering experimental preschool learning programs in urban ghettos. None of this necessarily implies that big companies are growing altruistic; it merely underscores the increasing intimacy of the links between the economic sector and powerful cultural, psychological and social forces.

While these forces batter at our doors, however, most technocratic planners and managers behave as though nothing had happened. They continue to act as though the economic sector were hermetically sealed off from social and psychocultural influences. Indeed, econocentric premises are buried so deeply and held so widely in both the capitalist and communist nations, that they distort the very information systems essential for the management of change.

For example, all modern nations maintain elaborate machinery for measuring economic performance. We know virtually day by day the directions of change with respect to productivity, prices, investment, and similar factors. Through a set of "economic indicators" we gauge the overall health of the economy, the speed at which it is changing, and the overall directions of change. Without these measures, our control of the economy would be far less effective.

By contrast, we have no such measures, no set of comparable "social indicators" to tell us whether the society, as distinct from the economy, is also healthy. We have no measures of the "quality of life." We have no systematic indices to tell us whether men are more or less alienated from one another; whether education is more effective; whether art, music and literature are flourishing; whether civility, generosity or kindness are increasing. "Gross National Product is our Holy Grail," writes Stewart Udall, former United States Secretary of the Interior, ". . . but we have no environmental index, no census statistics to measure whether the country is more livable from year to year."

On the surface, this would seem a purely technical matter—something for statisticians to debate. Yet it has the most serious political significance, for lacking such measures it becomes difficult to connect up national or local policies with appropriate long-term social goals. The absence of such indices perpetuates vulgar technocracy.

Little known to the public, a polite, but increasingly bitter battle over this issue has begun in Washington. Technocratic planners and economists see in the social indicators idea a threat to their entrenched position at the ear of the political policy maker. In contrast, the need for social indicators has been eloquently argued by such prominent social scientists as Bertram M. Gross of Wayne State University, Eleanor Sheldon and Wilbert Moore of the Russell Sage Foundation, Daniel Bell and Raymond Bauer of Harvard. We are witnessing, says Gross, a "widespread rebellion against what has been called the 'economic philistinism' of the United States government's present statistical establishment."

This revolt has attracted vigorous support from a small group of politicians and government officials who recognize our desperate need for a post-technocratic social intelligence system. These include Daniel P. Moynihan, a key White House adviser; Senators Walter Mondale of Minnesota and Fred Harris of Oklahoma; and several former Cabinet officers. In the near future, we can expect the same revolt to break out in other world capitals as well, once again drawing a line between technocrats and post-technocrats.

The danger of future shock, itself, however, points to the need for new social measures not yet even mentioned in the fast-burgeoning literature on social indicators. We urgently need, for example, techniques for measuring the level of transience in different communities, different population groups, and in individual experience. It is possible, in principle, to design a "transience index" that could disclose the rate at which we are making and breaking relationships with the things, places, people, organizations and informational structures that comprise our environment.

Such an index would reveal, among other things, the fantastic differences in the experiences of different groups in the society—the static and tedious quality of life for very large numbers of people, the frenetic turnover in the lives of others. Government policies that attempt to deal with both kinds of people in the same way are doomed to meet angry resistance from one or the other—or both.

Similarly, we need indices of novelty in the environment. How often do communities, organizations, or individuals have to cope with first-time situations? How many of the articles in the home of the average working-class family are actually "new" in function or appearance; how many are traditional? What level of novelty—in terms of things, people or any other significant dimension—is required for stimulation without over-stimulation? How much more novelty can children absorb than their parents—if it is true that they can absorb more? In what way is aging related to lower novelty tolerances, and how do such differences correlate with the political and intergenerational conflict now tearing the techno-societies apart? By studying and measuring the invasion of newness, we can begin, perhaps to control the influx of change into our social structures and personal lives.

And what about choice and overchoice? Can we construct measures of the degree of significant choice in human lives? Can any government that pretends to be democratic not concern itself with such an issue? For all the rhetoric about freedom of choice, no government agency in the world can claim to have made any attempt to measure it. The assumption simply is that more income or affluence means more choice and that more choice, in turn, means freedom. Is it not time to examine these basic assumptions of our political systems? Post-technocratic planning must deal with precisely such issues, if we are to prevent future shock and build a humane super-industrial society.

A sensitive system of indicators geared to measuring the achievement of social and cultural goals, and integrated with economic indicators, is part of the technical equipment that any society needs before it can successfully reach the next stage of eco-technological development. It is an absolute precondition for post-technocratic planning and change management.

This humanization of planning, moreover, must be reflected in our political structures as well. To connect the superindustrial social intelligence system with the decisional centers of society, we must institutionalize a concern for the quality of life. Thus Bertram Gross and others in the social indicators movement have proposed the creation of a Council of Social Advisers to the President. Such a Council, as they see it, would be modeled after the already existing Council of Economic Advisers and would perform parallel functions in the social field. The new agency would monitor key social indicators precisely the way the CEA keeps its eye on economic indices, and interpret changes to the President. It would issue an annual report on the quality of life, clearly spelling out our social progress (or lack of it) in terms of specified goals. This report would thus supplement and balance the annual economic report prepared by the CEA. By providing reliable, useful data about our social condition, the Council of Social Advisers would begin to influence planning generally, making it more sensitive to social costs and benefits, less coldly technocratic and econocentric.*

The establishment of such councils, not merely at the federal level but at state and municipal levels as well, would not solve all our problems; it would not eliminate conflict; it would not guarantee that social indicators are exploited properly. In brief, it would not eliminate politics from political life. But it would lend recognition—and political force— to the idea that the aims of progress reach beyond economics. The designation of agencies to watch over the indicators of change in the

---

* Proponents differ as to whether the Council of Social Advisers ought to be organizationally independent or become a part of a larger Council of Economic *and* Social Advisers. All sides agree, however, on the need for integrating economic and social intelligence.

quality of life would carry us a long way toward that humanization of the planner which is the essential first stage of the strategy of social futurism.

TIME HORIZONS

Technocrats suffer from myopia. Their instinct is to think about immediate returns, immediate consequences. They are premature members of the now generation.

If a region needs electricity, they reach for a power plant. The fact that such a plant might sharply alter labor patterns, that within a decade it might throw men out of work, force large-scale retraining of workers, and swell the social welfare costs of a nearby city—such considerations are too remote in time to concern them. The fact that the plant could trigger devastating ecological consequences a generation later simply does not register in their time frame.

In a world of accelerant change, next year is nearer to us than next month was in a more leisurely era. This radically altered fact of life must be internalized by decision-makers in industry, government and elsewhere. Their time horizons must be extended.

To plan for a more distant future does not mean to tie oneself to dogmatic programs. Plans can be tentative, fluid, subject to continual revision. Yet flexibility need not mean shortsightedness. To transcend technocracy, our social time horizons must reach decades, even generations, into the future. This requires more than a lengthening of our formal plans. It means an infusion of the entire society, from top to bottom, with a new socially aware future-consciousness.

One of the healthiest phenomena of recent years has been the sudden proliferation of organizations devoted to the study of the future. This recent development is, in itself, a homeostatic response of the society to the speed-up of change. Within a few years we have seen the creation of future-oriented think tanks like the Institute for the Future; the formation of academic study groups like the Commission on the Year 2000 and the Harvard Program on Technology and Society; the appearance of futurist journals in England, France, Italy, Germany and the United States; the spread of university courses in forecasting and related subjects; the convocation of international futurist meetings in Oslo, Berlin and Kyoto; the coalescence of groups like Futuribles, Europe 2000, Mankind 2000, the World Future Society.

Futurist centers are to be found in West Berlin, in Prague, in London, in Moscow, Rome and Washington, in Caracas, even in the remote jungles of Brazil at Belém and Belo Horizonte. Unlike conventional technocratic planners whose horizons usually extend no further than a few years into tomorrow, these groups concern themselves with change fifteen, twenty-five, even fifty years in the future.

Every society faces not merely a succession of *probable* futures, but an array of *possible* futures, and a conflict over *preferable* futures. The management of change is the effort to convert certain possibles into probables, in pursuit of agreed-on preferables. Determining the probable calls for a science of futurism. Delineating the possible calls for an art of futurism. Defining the preferable calls for a politics of futurism.

The worldwide futurist movement today does not yet differentiate clearly among these functions. Its heavy emphasis is on the assessment of probabilities. Thus in many of these centers, economists, sociologists, mathematicians, biologists, physicists, operations researchers and others invent and apply methods for forecasting future probabilities. At what date could aquaculture feed half the world's population? What are the odds that electric cars will supplant gas-driven automobiles in the next fifteen years? How likely is a Sino-Soviet détente by 1980? What changes are most probable in leisure patterns, urban government, race relations?

Stressing the interconnectedness of disparate events and trends, scientific futurists are also devoting increasing attention to the social consequences of technology. The Institute for the Future is, among other things, investigating the probable social and cultural effects of advanced communications technology. The group at Harvard is concerned with social problems likely to arise from bio-medical advances. Futurists in Brazil examine the probable outcomes of various economic development policies.

The rationale for studying probable futures is compelling. It is impossible for an individual to live through a single working day without making thousands of assumptions about the probable future. The commuter who calls to say, "I'll be home at six" bases his prediction on assumptions about the probability that the train will run on time. When mother sends Johnny to school, she tacitly assumes the school will be there when he arrives. Just as a pilot cannot steer a ship without projecting its course, we cannot steer our personal lives without continually making such assumptions, consciously or otherwise.

Societies, too, construct an architecture of premises about tomorrow. Decision-makers in industry, government, politics, and other sectors of society could not function without them. In periods of turbulent change, however, these socially-shaped images of the probable future become less accurate. The breakdown of control in society today is directly linked to our inadequate images of probable futures.

Of course, no one can "know" the future in any absolute sense. We can only systematize and deepen our assumptions and attempt to assign probabilities to them. Even this is difficult. Attempts to forecast the future inevitably alter it. Similarly, once a forecast is disseminated, the act of dissemination (as distinct from investigation) also produces a perturbation. Forecasts tend to become self-fulfilling or self-defeating. As the time horizon is extended into the more distant future, we are forced to rely on informed hunch and guesswork. Moreover, certain unique events—assassinations, for example—are, for all intents and purposes, unpredictable at present (although we can forecast classes of such events).

Despite all this, it is time to erase, once and for all, the popular myth that the future is "unknowable." The difficulties ought to chasten and challenge, not paralyze. William F. Ogburn, one of the world's great students of social change, once wrote: "We should admit into our thinking the idea of approximations, that is, that there are varying degrees of accuracy and inaccuracy of estimate." A rough idea of what lies ahead is better than none, he went on, and for many purposes extreme accuracy is wholly unnecessary.

We are not, therefore, as helpless in dealing with future probabilities as most people assume. The British social scientist Donald G. MacRae correctly asserts that "modern sociologists can in fact make a large number of comparatively short-term and limited predictions with a good deal of assurance." Apart from the standard methods of social science, however, we are experimenting with potentially powerful new tools for probing the future. These range from complex ways of extrapolating existing trends, to the construction of highly intricate models, games and simulations, the preparation of detailed speculative scenarios, the systematic study of history for relevant analogies, morphological research, relevance analysis, contextual mapping and the like. In a comprehensive investigation of technological forecasting, Dr. Erich Jantsch, formerly a consultant to the OECD and a research associate at MIT, has identified scores of distinct new techniques either in use or in the experimental stage.

The Institute for the Future in Middletown, Connecticut, a prototype of the futurist think tank, is a leader in the design of new forecasting tools. One of these is Delphi—a method largely developed by Dr. Olaf Helmer, the mathematician-philosopher who is one of the founders of the IFF. Delphi attempts to deal with very distant futures by making systematic use of the "intuitive" guesstimates of large numbers of experts. The work on Delphi has led to a further innovation which has special importance in the attempt to prevent future shock by regulating the pace of change. Pioneered by Theodore J. Gordon of the IFF, and called Cross Impact Matrix Analysis, it traces the effect of one innovation on another, making possible, for the first time, anticipatory analysis of complex chains of social, technological and other occurrences—and the rates at which they are likely to occur.

We are, in short, witnessing a perfectly extraordinary thrust toward more scientific appraisal of future probabilities, a ferment likely, in itself, to have a powerful impact on the future. It would be foolish to oversell the ability of science, as yet, to forecast complex events accurately. Yet the danger today is not that we will overestimate our ability; the real danger is that we will under-utilize it. For even when our still-primitive attempts at scientific forecasting turn out to be grossly in error, the very effort helps us identify key variables in change, it helps clarify goals, and it forces more careful evaluation of policy alternatives. In these ways, if no others, probing the future pays off in the present.

Anticipating *probable* futures, however, is only part of what needs doing if we are to shift the planner's time horizon and infuse the entire

society with a greater sense of tomorrow. For we must also vastly widen
our conception of possible futures. To the rigorous discipline of science,
we must add the flaming imagination of art.

Today as never before we need a multiplicity of visions, dreams and
prophecies—images of potential tomorrows. Before we can rationally
decide which alternative pathways to choose, which cultural styles to
pursue, we must first ascertain which are possible. Conjecture, speculation and the visionary view thus become as coldly practical a necessity
as feet-on-the-floor "realism" was in an earlier time.

This is why some of the world's biggest and most tough-minded corporations, once the living embodiment of presentism, today hire intuitive futurists, science fiction writers and visionaries as consultants. A
gigantic European chemical company employs a futurist who combines
a scientific background with training as a theologian. An American communications empire engages a future-minded social critic. A glass manu-
facturer searches for a science fiction writer to imagine the possible
corporate forms of the future. Companies turn to these "blue-skyers" and
"wild birds" not for scientific forecasts of probabilities, but for mind-
stretching speculation about possibilities.

Corporations must not remain the only agencies with access to such
services. Local government, schools, voluntary associations and others
also need to examine their potential futures imaginatively. One way to
help them do so would be to establish in each community "imaginetic
centers" devoted to technically assisted brainstorming. These would be
places where people noted for creative imagination, rather than technical expertise, are brought together to examine present crises, to anticipate future crises, and to speculate freely, even playfully, about possible
futures.

What, for example, are the possible futures of urban transportation?
Traffic is a problem involving space. How might the city of tomorrow
cope with the movement of men and objects through space? To speculate about this question, an imaginetic center might enlist artists,
sculptors, dancers, furniture designers, parking lot attendants, and a
variety of other people who, in one way or another, manipulate space
imaginatively. Such people, assembled under the right circumstances,
would inevitably come up with ideas of which the technocratic city
planners, the highway engineers and transit authorities have never
dreamed.

Musicians, people who live near airports, jack-hammer men and
subway conductors might well imagine new ways to organize, mask or
suppress noise. Groups of young people might be invited to ransack
their minds for previously unexamined approaches to urban sanitation,
crowding, ethnic conflict, care of the aged, or a thousand other present
and future problems.

In any such effort, the overwhelming majority of ideas put forward
will, of course, be absurd, funny or technically impossible. Yet the essence of creativity is a willingness to play the fool, to toy with the absurd, only later submitting the stream of ideas to harsh critical judg-

ment. The application of the imagination to the future thus requires an environment in which it is safe to err, in which novel juxtapositions of ideas can be freely expressed before being critically sifted. We need sanctuaries for social imagination.

While all sorts of creative people ought to participate in conjecture about possible futures, they should have immediate access—in person or via telecommunications—to technical specialists, from acoustical engineers to zoologists, who could indicate when a suggestion is technically impossible (bearing in mind that even impossibility is often temporary).

Scientific expertise, however, might also play a generative, rather than merely a damping role in the imaginetic process. Skilled specialists can construct models to help imagineers examine all possible permutations of a given set of relationships. Such models are representations of real life conditions. In the words of Christoph Bertram of the Institute for Strategic Studies in London, their purpose is "not so much to predict the future, but, by examining alternative futures, to show the choices open."

An appropriate model, for example, could help a group of imagineers visualize the impact on a city if its educational expenditures were to fluctuate—how this would affect, let us say, the transport system, the theaters, the occupational structure and health of the community. Conversely, it could show how changes in these other factors might affect education.

The rushing stream of wild, unorthodox, eccentric or merely colorful ideas generated in these sanctuaries of social imagination must, after they have been expressed, be subjected to merciless screening. Only a tiny fraction of them will survive this filtering process. These few, however, could be of the utmost importance in calling attention to new possibilities that might otherwise escape notice. As we move from poverty toward affluence, politics changes from what mathematicians call a zero sum game into a non-zero sum game. In the first, if one player wins another must lose. In the second, all players can win. Finding non-zero sum solutions to our social problems requires all the imagination we can muster. A system for generating imaginative policy ideas could help us take maximum advantage of the non-zero opportunities ahead.

While imaginetic centers concentrate on partial images of tomorrow, defining possible futures for a single industry, an organization, a city or its sub-systems, however, we also need sweeping, visionary ideas about the society as a whole. Multiplying our images of possible futures is important; but these images need to be organized, crystallized into structured form. In the past, utopian literature did this for us. It played a practical, crucial role in ordering men's dreams about alternative futures. Today we suffer for lack of utopian ideas around which to organize competing images of possible futures.

Most traditional utopias picture simple and static societies—i.e., societies that have nothing in common with super-industrialism. B. F. Skinner's *Walden Two*, the model for several existing experimental communes, depicts a pre-industrial way of life—small, close to the earth, built on farming and handcraft. Even those two brilliant anti-utopias, *Brave New World* and *1984*, now seem oversimple. Both describe societies based on high technology and low complexity: the machines are sophisticated but the social and cultural relationships are fixed and deliberately simplified.

Today we need powerful new utopian and anti-utopian concepts that look forward to super-industrialism, rather than backward to simpler societies. These concepts, however, can no longer be produced in the old way. First, no book, by itself, is adequate to describe a super-industrial future in emotionally compelling terms. Each conception of a super-industrial utopia or anti-utopia needs to be embodied in many forms—films, plays, novels and works of art—rather than a single work of fiction. Second, it may now be too difficult for any individual writer, no matter how gifted, to describe a convincingly complex future. We need, therefore a revolution in the production of utopias: collaborative utopianism. We need to construct "utopia factories."

One way might be to assemble a small group of top social scientists —an economist, a sociologist, an anthropologist, and so on—asking them to work together, even live together, long enough to hammer out among themselves a set of well-defined values on which they believe a truly super-industrial utopian society might be based.

Each member of the team might then attempt to describe in nonfiction form a sector of an imagined society built on these values. What would its family structure be like? Its economy, laws, religion, sexual practices, youth culture, music, art, its sense of time, its degree of differentiation, its psychological problems? By working together and ironing out inconsistencies, where possible, a comprehensive and adequately complex picture might be drawn of a seamless, temporary form of super-industrialism.

At this point, with the completion of detailed analysis, the project would move to the fiction stage. Novelists, film-makers, science fiction writers and others, working closely with psychologists, could prepare creative works about the lives of individual characters in the imagined society.

Meanwhile, other groups could be at work on counter-utopias. While Utopia A might stress materialist, success-oriented values, Utopia B might base itself on sensual, hedonistic values, C on the primacy of aesthetic values, D on individualism, E on collectivism, and so forth. Ultimately, a stream of books, plays, films and television programs would flow from this collaboration between art, social science and futurism, thereby educating large numbers of people about the costs and benefits of the various proposed utopias.

Finally, if social imagination is in short supply, we are even more lacking in people willing to subject utopian ideas to systematic test. More and more young people, in their dissatisfaction with industrialism, are experimenting with their own lives, forming utopian communities, trying new social arrangements, from group marriage to living-learning communes. Today, as in the past, the weight of established society comes down hard on the visionary who attempts to practice, as well as merely preach. Rather than ostracizing utopians, we should take advantage of their willingness to experiment, encouraging them with money and tolerance, if not respect.

Most of today's "intentional communities" or utopian colonies, however, reveal a powerful preference for the past. These may be of value to the individuals in them, but the society as a whole would be better served by utopian experiments based on super- rather than pre-industrial forms. Instead of a communal farm, why not a computer software company whose program writers live and work communally? Why not an education technology company whose members pool their money and merge their families? Instead of raising radishes or crafting sandals, why not an oceanographic research installation organized along utopian lines? Why not a group medical practice that takes advantage of the latest medical technology but whose members accept modest pay and pool their profits to run a completely new-style medical school? Why not recruit living groups to try out the proposals of the utopia factories?

In short, we can use utopianism as a tool rather than an escape, if we base our experiments on the technology and society of tomorrow rather than that of the past. And once done, why not the most rigorous, scientific analysis of the results? The findings could be priceless, were they to save us from mistakes or lead us toward more workable organizational forms for industry, education, family life or politics.

Such imaginative explorations of possible futures would deepen and enrich our scientific study of probable futures. They would lay a basis for the radical forward extension of the society's time horizon. They would help us apply social imagination to the future of futurism itself.

Indeed, with these as a background, we must consciously begin to multiply the scientific future-sensing organs of society. Scientific futurist institutes must be spotted like nodes in a loose network throughout the entire governmental structure in the techno-societies, so that in every department, local or national, some staff devotes itself systematically to scanning the probable long-term future in its assigned field. Futurists should be attached to every political party, university, corporation, professional association, trade union and student organization.

We need to train thousands of young people in the perspectives and techniques of scientific futurism, inviting them to share in the exciting venture of mapping probable futures. We also need national agencies to provide technical assistance to local communities in creating their own futurist groups. And we need a similar center, perhaps jointly funded by American and European foundations, to help incipient futurist centers in Asia, Africa, and Latin America.

We are in a race between rising levels of uncertainty produced by the acceleration of change, and the need for reasonably accurate images of what at any instant is the most probable future. The generation of reliable images of the most probable future thus becomes a matter of the highest national, indeed, international urgency.

As the globe is itself dotted with future-sensors, we might consider creating a great international institute, a world futures data bank. Such an institute, staffed with top caliber men and women from all the sciences and social sciences, would take as its purpose the collection and systematic integration of predictive reports generated by scholars and imaginative thinkers in all the intellectual disciplines all over the world.

Of course, those working in such an institute would know that they could never create a single, static diagram of the future. Instead, the product of their effort would be a constantly changing geography of the future, a continually re-created overarching image based on the best predictive work available. The men and women engaged in this work would know that nothing is certain; they would know that they must work with inadequate data; they would appreciate the difficulties inherent in exploring the uncharted territories of tomorrow. But man already knows more about the future than he has ever tried to formulate and integrate in any systematic and scientific way. Attempts to bring this knowledge together would constitute one of the crowning intellectual efforts in history—and one of the most worthwhile.

Only when decision-makers are armed with better forecasts of future events, when by successive approximation we increase the accuracy of forecast, will our attempts to manage change improve perceptibly. For reasonably accurate assumptions about the future are a precondition for understanding the potential consequences of our own actions. And without such understanding, the management of change is impossible.

If the humanization of the planner is the first stage in the strategy of social futurism, therefore, the forward extension of our time horizon is the second. To transcend technocracy, we need not only to reach beyond our economic philistinism, but to open our minds to more distant futures, both probable and possible.

ANTICIPATORY DEMOCRACY

In the end, however, social futurism must cut even deeper. For technocrats suffer from more than econo-think and myopia; they suffer, too, from the virus of elitism. To capture control of change, we shall, therefore, require a final, even more radical breakaway from technocratic tradition: we shall need a revolution in the very way we formulate our social goals.

Rising novelty renders irrelevant the traditional goals of our chief institutions—state, church, corporation, army and university. Acceleration produces a faster turnover of goals, a greater transience of purpose. Diversity or fragmentation leads to a relentless multiplication of goals. Caught in this churning, goal-cluttered environment, we stagger, future shocked, from crisis to crisis, pursuing a welter of conflicting and self-cancelling purposes.

Nowhere is this more starkly evident than in our pathetic attempts to govern our cities. New Yorkers, within a short span, have suffered a nightmarish succession of near disasters: a water shortage, a subway strike, racial violence in the schools, a student insurrection at Columbia University, a garbage strike, a housing shortage, a fuel oil strike, a breakdown of telephone service, a teacher walkout, a power blackout, to name just a few. In its City Hall, as in a thousand city halls all over the high-technology nations, technocrats dash, firebucket in fist, from one conflagration to another, without the least semblance of a coherent plan or policy for the urban future.

This is not to say no one is planning. On the contrary, in this seething social brew, technocratic plans, sub-plans and counter-plans pour forth. They call for new highways, new roads, new power plants, new schools. They promise better hospitals, housing, mental health centers, welfare programs. But the plans cancel, contradict and reinforce one another by accident. Few are logically related to one another, and none to any overall image of the preferred city of the future. No vision—utopian or otherwise—energizes our efforts. No rationally integrated goals bring order to the chaos. And at the national and international levels, the absence of coherent policy is equally marked and doubly dangerous.

It is not simply that we do not know which goals to pursue, as a city or as a nation. The trouble lies deeper. For accelerating change has made obsolete the methods by which we arrive at social goals. The technocrats do not yet understand this, and, reacting to the goals crisis in knee-jerk fashion, they reach for the tried and true methods of the past.

Thus, intermittently, a change-dazed government will try to define its goals publicly. Instinctively, it establishes a commission. In 1960 President Eisenhower pressed into service, among others, a general, a judge, a couple of industrialists, a few college presidents, and a labor leader to "develop a broad outline of coordinated national policies and programs" and to "set up a series of goals in various areas of national activity." In due course, a red-white-and-blue paperback appeared with the commission's report, *Goals for Americans*. Neither the commission nor its goals had the slightest impact on the public or on policy. The juggernaut of change continued to roll through America untouched, as it were, by managerial intelligence.

A far more significant effort to tidy up governmental priorities was initiated by President Johnson, with his attempt to apply PPBS (Planning-Programming-Budgeting-System) throughout the federal establishment. PPBS is a method for tying programs much more closely and rationally to organizational goals. Thus, for example, by applying it, the Department of Health, Education and Welfare can assess the costs and benefits of alternative programs to accomplish specified goals. But who specifies these larger, more important goals? The introduction of PPBS and the systems approach is a major governmental achievement. It is of paramount importance in managing large organizational efforts. But it leaves entirely untouched the profoundly political question of how the overall goals of a government or a society are to be chosen in the first place.

President Nixon, still snarled in the goals crisis, tried a third tack. "It is time," he declared, "we addressed ourselves, consciously and systematically, to the question of what kind of a nation we want to be . . ." He thereupon put his finger on the quintessential question. But once more the method chosen for answering it proved to be inadequate. "I have today ordered the establishment, within the White House, of a National Goals Research Staff," the President announced, "This will be a small, highly technical staff, made up of experts in the collection . . . and processing of data relating to social needs, and in the projection of social trends."

Such a staff, located within shouting distance of the Presidency, could be extremely useful in compiling goal proposals, in reconciling (at least on paper) conflicts between agencies, in suggesting new priorities. Staffed with excellent social scientists and futurists, it could earn its keep if it did nothing but force high officials to question their primary goals.

Yet even this step, like the two before it, bears the unmistakable imprint of the technocratic mentality. For it, too, evades the politically charged core of the issue. How are preferable futures to be defined? And by whom? Who is to set goals for the future?

Behind all such efforts runs the notion that national (and, by extension, local) goals for the future of society ought to be formulated at the top. This technocratic premise perfectly mirrors the old bureaucratic forms of organization in which line and staff were separated, in which rigid, undemocratic hierarchies distinguished leader from led, manager from managed, planner from plannee.

Yet the real, as distinct from the glibly verbalized, goals of any society on the path to super-industrialism are already too complex, too transient and too dependent for their achievement upon the willing participation of the governed, to be perceived and defined so easily. We cannot hope to harness the runaway forces of change by assembling a kaffee klatsch of elders to set goals for us or by turning the task over to a "highly technical staff." A revolutionary new approach to goal-setting is needed.

Nor is this approach likely to come from those who play-act at revolution. One radical group, seeing all problems as a manifestation of the "maximization of profits," displays, in all innocence, an econocentricism as narrow as that of the technocrats. Another hopes to plunge us willy-nilly back into the pre-industrial past. Still another sees revolution exclusively in subjective and psychological terms. None of these groups is capable of advancing us toward post-technocratic forms of change management.

By calling attention to the growing ineptitudes of the technocrats and by explicitly challenging not merely the means, but the very goals of industrial society, today's young radicals do us all a great service. But they no more know how to cope with the goals crisis than the technocrats they scorn. Exactly like Messrs. Eisenhower, Johnson and Nixon, they have been noticeably unable to present any positive image of a future worth fighting for.

Thus Todd Gitlin, a young American radical and former president of the Students for a Democratic Society, notes that while "an orientation toward the future has been the hallmark of every revolutionary—and, for that matter, liberal—movement of the last century and a half," the New Left suffers from "a disbelief in the future." After citing all the ostensible reasons why it has so far not put forward a coherent vision of the future, he succinctly confesses: "We find ourselves incapable of formulating the future."

Other New Left theorists fuzz over the problem, urging their followers to incorporate the future in the present by, in effect, living the life styles of tomorrow today. So far, this has led to a pathetic charade—"free societies," cooperatives, pre-industrial communes, few of which have anything to do with the future, and most of which reveal, instead, only a passionate penchant for the past.

The irony is compounded when we consider that some (though hardly all) of today's young radicals also share with the technocrats a streak of virulent elitism. While decrying bureaucracy and demanding "participatory democracy" they, themselves, frequently attempt to manipulate the very groups of workers, blacks or students on whose behalf they demand participation.

The working masses in the high-technology societies are totally indifferent to calls for a political revolution aimed at exchanging one form of property ownership for another. For most people, the rise in affluence has meant a better, not a worse, existence, and they look upon their much despised "suburban middle class lives" as fulfillment rather than deprivation.

Faced with this stubborn reality, undemocratic elements in the New Left leap to the Marcusian conclusion that the masses are too bourgeoisified, too corrupted and addled by Madison Avenue to know what is good for them. And so, a revolutionary elite must establish a more humane and democratic future even if it means stuffing it down the throats of those who are too stupid to know their own interests. In short, the goals of society have to be set by an elite. Technocrat and anti-technocrat often turn out to be elitist brothers under the skin.

Yet systems of goal formulation based on elitist premises are simply no longer "efficient." In the struggle to capture control of the forces of change, they are increasingly counter-productive. For under super-industrialism, democracy becomes not a political luxury, but a primal necessity.

Democratic political forms arose in the West not because a few geniuses willed them into being or because man showed an "unquenchable instinct for freedom." They arose because the historical pressure toward social differentiation and toward faster paced systems demanded sensitive social feedback. In complex, differentiated societies, vast amounts of information must flow at even faster speeds between the formal organizations and subcultures that make up the whole, and between the layers and substructures within these.

Political democracy, by incorporating larger and larger numbers in social decision-making, facilitates feedback. And it is precisely this feed-back that is essential to control. To assume control over accelerant change, we shall need still more advanced—and more democratic—feed-back mechanisms.

The technocrat, however, still thinking in top-down terms, frequently makes plans without arranging for adequate and instantaneous feed-back from the field, so that he seldom knows how well his plans are working. When he does arrange for feedback, what he usually asks for and gets is heavily economic, inadequately social, psychological or cul-tural. Worse yet, he makes these plans without sufficiently taking into account the fast-changing needs and wishes of those whose participa-tion is needed to make them a success. He assumes the right to set social goals by himself or he accepts them blindly from some higher authority.

He fails to recognize that the faster pace of change demands—and creates—a new kind of information system in society: a loop, rather than a ladder. Information must pulse through this loop at accelerating speeds, with the output of one group becoming the input for many others, so that no group, however politically potent it may seem, can independently set goals for the whole.

As the number of social components multiplies, and change jolts and destabilizes the entire system, the power of subgroups to wreak havoc on the whole is tremendously amplified. There is, in the words of W. Ross Ashby, a brilliant cyberneticist, a mathematically provable law to the effect that "when a whole system is composed of a number of sub-systems, the one that tends to dominate is the one that is *least* stable."

Another way of stating this is that, as the number of social com-ponents grows and change makes the whole system less stable, it be-comes less and less possible to ignore the demands of political minori-ties—hippies, blacks, lower-middle-class Wallacites, school teachers, or the proverbial little old ladies in tennis shoes. In a slower-moving, in-dustrial context, America could turn its back on the needs of its black minority; in the new, fast-paced cybernetic society, this minority can, by sabotage, strike, or a thousand other means, disrupt the entire system. As interdependency grows, smaller and smaller groups within society achieve greater and greater power for critical disruption. Moreover, as the rate of change speeds up, the length of time in which they can be ignored shrinks to near nothingness. Hence: "Freedom now!"

This suggests that the best way to deal with angry or recalcitrant minorities is to open the system further, bringing them into it as full partners, permitting them to participate in social goal-setting, rather than attempting to ostracize or isolate them. A Red China locked out of the United Nations and the larger international community is far more likely to destabilize the world than one laced into the system. Young people forced into prolonged adolescence and deprived of the right to partake in social decision-making will grow more and more unstable until they threaten the overall system. In short, in politics, in industry, in education, goals set without the participation of those affected will be increasingly hard to execute. The continuation of top-down technocratic goal-setting procedures will lead to greater and greater social instability, less and less control over the forces of change; an ever greater danger of cataclysmic, man-destroying upheaval.

To master change, we shall therefore need both a clarification of important long-range social goals *and* a democratization of the way in which we arrive at them. And this means nothing less than the next political revolution in the techno-societies—a breathtaking affirmation of popular democracy.

The time has come for a democratic reassessment of the directions of change, a reassessment made not by the politicians or the sociologists or the clergy or the elitist revolutionaries, not by technicians or college presidents, but by the people themselves. We need, quite literally, to "go to the people" with a question that is almost never asked of them: "What kind of a world do you want ten, twenty, or thirty years from now?" We need to initiate, in short, a continuing plebiscite on the future.

The moment is right for the formation in each of the high-technology nations of a movement for total self-review, a public self-examination aimed at broadening and defining in social, as well as merely economic, terms, the goals of "progress." On the edge of a new millennium, on the brink of a new stage of human development, we are racing blindly into the future. But where do we *want* to go?

What would happen if we actually tried to answer this question?

Imagine the historic drama, the power and evolutionary impact, if each of the high-technology nations literally set aside the next five years as a period of intense national self-appraisal; if at the end of five years it were to come forward with its own tentative agenda for the future, a program embracing not merely economic targets but, equally important, broad sets of social goals—if each nation, in effect, stated to the world what it wished to accomplish for its people and mankind in general during the remaining quarter century of the millennium.

Let us convene in each nation, in each city, in each neighborhood, democratic constituent assemblies charged with social stock-taking, charged with defining and assigning priorities to specific social goals for the remainder of the century.

Such "social future assemblies" might represent not merely geographical localities, but social units—industry, labor, the churches, the intellectual community, the arts, women, ethnic and religious groups, students—with organized representation for the unorganized as well. There are no sure-fire techniques for guaranteeing equal representation for all, or for eliciting the wishes of the poor, the inarticulate or the isolated. Yet once we recognize the need to include them, we shall find the ways. Indeed, the problem of participating in the definition of the future is not merely a problem of the poor, the inarticulate and the isolated. Highly paid executives, wealthy professionals, extremely articulate intellectuals and students—all at one time or another feel cut off from the power to influence the directions and pace of change. Wiring them into the system, making them a part of the guidance machinery of the society, is the most critical political task of the coming generation. Imagine the effect if at one level or another a place were provided where all those who will live in the future might voice their wishes about it. Imagine, in short, a massive, global exercise in anticipatory democracy.

Social future assemblies need not—and, given the rate of transience —cannot be anchored, permanent institutions. Instead, they might take the form of ad hoc groupings, perhaps called into being at regular intervals with different representatives participating each time. Today citizens are expected to serve on juries when needed. They give a few days or a few weeks of their time for this service, recognizing that the jury system is one of the guarantees of democracy, that, even though service may be inconvenient, someone must do the job. Social future assemblies could be organized along similar lines, with a constant stream of new participants brought together for short periods to serve as society's "consultants on the future."

Such grass roots organisms for expressing the will of large numbers of hitherto unconsulted people could become, in effect, the town halls of the future, in which millions help shape their own distant destinies.

To some, this appeal for a form of neo-populism will no doubt seem naive. Yet nothing is more naive than the notion that we can continue politically to run the society the way we do at present. To some, it will appear impractical. Yet nothing is more impractical than the attempt to impose a humane future from above. What was naive under industrialism may be realistic under super-industrialism; what was practical may be absurd.

The encouraging fact is that we now have the potential for achieving tremendous breakthroughs in democratic decision-making if we make imaginative use of the new technologies, both "hard" and "soft," that bear on the problem. Thus, advanced telecommunications mean that participants in a social future assembly need not literally meet in a single room, but might simply be hooked into a communications net that straddles the globe. A meeting of scientists to discuss research goals for the future, or goals for environmental quality, could draw participants from many countries at once. An assembly of steelworkers, unionists and executives, convened to discuss goals for automation and for the improvement of work itself, could link up participants from many mills, offices and warehouses, no matter how scattered or remote.

A meeting of the cultural community in New York or Paris—artists and gallery-goers, writers and readers, dramatists and audiences—to discuss appropriate long-range goals for the cultural development of the city could be shown, through the use of video recordings and other techniques, actual samples of the kinds of artistic production under discussion, architectural designs for new facilities, samples of new artistic media made available by technological advance, etc. What kind of cultural life should a great city of the future enjoy? What resources would be needed to realize a given set of goals?

All social future assemblies, in order to answer such questions, could and should be backed with technical staff to provide data on the social and economic costs of various goals, and to show the costs and benefits of proposed trade-offs, so that participants would be in a position to make reasonably informed choices, as it were, among alternative futures. In this way, each assembly might arrive, in the end, not merely in vaguely expressed, disjointed hopes, but at coherent statements of priorities for tomorrow—posed in terms that could be compared with the goal statements of other groups.

Nor need these social future assemblies be glorified "talkfests." We are fast developing games and simulation exercises whose chief beauty is that they help players clarify their own values. At the University of Illinois, in Project Plato, Charles Osgood is experimenting with computers and teaching machines that would involve large sectors of the public in planning imaginary, preferable futures through gaming.

At Cornell University, José Villegas, a professor in the Department of Design and Environmental Analysis, has begun constructing with the aid of black and white students a variety of "ghetto games" which reveal to the players the consequences of various proposed courses of action and thus help them clarify goals. *Ghetto 1984* showed what would happen if the recommendations made by the Kerner riot commission—the U. S. National Advisory Commission on Civil Disorder—were actually to be adopted. It showed how the sequence in which these recommendations were enacted would affect their ultimate impact on the ghetto. It helped players, both black and white, to identify their shared goals as well as their unresolved conflicts. In games like *Peru 2000* and *Squatter City 2000,* players design communities for the future.

In *Lower East Side,* a game Villegas hopes actually to play in the Manhattan community that bears that name, players would not be students, but real-life residents of the community—poverty workers, middle-class whites, Puerto Rican small businessmen or youth, unemployed blacks, police, landlords and city officials.

In the spring of 1969, 50,000 high school students in Boston, in Philadelphia and in Syracuse, New York, participated in a televised game involving a simulated war in the Congo in 1975. While televised teams simulated the cabinets of Russia, Red China, and the United States, and struggled with the problems of diplomacy and policy planning, students and teachers watched, discussed, and offered advice via telephone to the central players.

Similar games, involving not tens, but hundreds of thousands, even millions of people, could be devised to help us formulate goals for the future. While televised players act out the role of high government officials attempting to deal with a crisis—an ecological disaster, for example—meetings of trade unions, women's clubs, church groups, student organizations and other constituencies might be held at which large numbers could view the program, reach collective judgments about the choices to be made, and forward those judgments to the primary players. Special switchboards and computers could pick up the advice or tabulate the yes-no votes and pass them on to the "decision-makers." Vast numbers of people could also participate from their own homes, thus opening the process to unorganized, otherwise non-participating millions. By imaginatively constructing such games, it becomes not only possible but practical to elicit futural goals from previously unconsulted masses.

Such techniques, still primitive today, will become fantastically more sophisticated in the years immediately ahead, providing us with a systematic way to collect and reconcile conflicting images of the preferable future, even from people unskilled in academic debate or parliamentary procedure.

It would be pollyanna-like to expect such town halls of the future to be tidy or harmonious affairs, or that they would be organized in the same way everywhere. In some places, social future assemblies might be called into being by community organizations, planning councils or government agencies. Elsewhere, they might be sponsored by trade unions, youth groups, or individual, future-oriented political leaders. In other places, churches, foundations or voluntary organizations might initiate the call. And in still other places, they might arise not from a formal convention call, but as a spontaneous response to crisis.

It would similarly be a mistake to think of the goals drawn up by these assemblies as constituting permanent, Platonic ideals, floating somewhere in a metaphysical never-never land. Rather, they must be seen as temporary direction-indicators, broad objectives good for a limited time only, and intended as advisory to the elected political representatives of the community or nation.

Nevertheless, such future-oriented, future-forming events could have enormous political impact. Indeed, they could turn out to be the salvation of the entire system of representative politics—a system now in dire crisis.

The mass of voters today are so far removed from contact with their elected representatives, the issues dealt with are so technical, that even well-educated middle-class citizens feel hopelessly excluded from the goal-setting process. Because of the generalized acceleration of life, so much happens so fast between elections, that the politician grows increasingly less accountable to "the folks back home." What's more, these folks back home keep changing. In theory, the voter unhappy with the performance of his representative can vote against him the next time around. In practice, millions find even this impossible. Mass mobility removes them from the district, sometimes disenfranchising them altogether. Newcomers flood into the district. More and more, the politician finds himself addressing new faces. He may never be called to account for his performance—or for promises made to the last set of constituents.

Still more damaging to democracy is the time-bias of politics. The politician's time horizon usually extends no further than the next election. Congresses, diets, parliaments, city councils—legislative bodies in general—lack the time, the resources, or the organizational forms needed to think seriously about the long-term future. As for the citizen, the last thing he is ever consulted about is the larger, more distant goals of his community, state or nation.

The voter may be polled about specific issues, never about the general shape of the preferable future. Indeed, nowhere in politics is there an institution through which an ordinary man can express his ideas about what the distant future ought to look, feel or taste like. He is never asked to think about this, and on the rare occasions when he does, there is no organized way for him to feed his ideas into the arena of politics. Cut off from the future, he becomes a political eunuch.

We are, for these and other reasons, rushing toward a fateful breakdown of the entire system of political representation. If legislatures are to survive at all, they will need new links with their constituencies, new ties with tomorrow. Social future assemblies could provide the means for reconnecting the legislator with his mass base, the present with the future.

Conducted at frequent and regular intervals, such assemblies could provide a more sensitive measure of popular will than any now available to us. The very act of calling such assemblies would attract into the flow of political life millions who now ignore it. By confronting men and women with the future, by asking them to think deeply about their own private destinies as well as our accelerating public trajectories, it would pose profound ethical issues.

. . .